A World of Change

Britain in the Early Modern Age
1450–1700

Topic books which may be used alongside this book (further details are given on page 218):

A City at War: Oxford 1642–46, Rosemary and Tony Kelly
Elizabeth and Akbar: Portraits of Power, Annabel Wigner
To the New World: The Founding of Pennsylvania, Roger Whiting
Scolding Tongues: The Persecution of 'Witches', Michael Harrison
Bare Ruined Choirs: The Fate of a Welsh Abbey, Robert Morris
Children in Tudor England, Tony Kelly
The Cromwell Family, John Cooper and Susan Morris
Exploring Other Civilisations, Richard Tames

A World of Change

Britain in the Early Modern Age
1450–1700

Rosemary Kelly
Head of History, Headington School, Oxford

Stanley Thornes (Publishers) Ltd

First published in 1987 by:
Stanley Thornes (Publishers) Ltd
Old Station Drive
Leckhampton
CHELTENHAM GL53 0DN
England

British Library Cataloguing in Publication Data

Kelly, Rosemary
    A world of change: Britain in the early
    modern age 1450-1700.
    1. Great Britain — History — Wars of
    the Roses, 1455-1485   2. Great Britain —
    History — Tudors, 1485-1603   3. Great
    Britain — History — Stuarts, 1603-1714
    I. Title
    941   DA300

    ISBN 0-85950-249-X

Typeset by Afal, Cardiff in Optima 10$\frac{1}{2}$/12$\frac{1}{2}$, 9$\frac{1}{2}$/11$\frac{1}{2}$ and Helvetica 10/11
Printed and bound in Great Britain at The Bath Press, Avon

Contents

Acknowledgements   xii

Introduction   1

How to use this book   3

1 **Ordinary people — ordinary lives**   5
Lighting and heating ● Measuring time ● Work in the countryside
● People in towns ● An 'extraordinary abundance' of wool
● London in 1500

2 **The Four Sorts**   23
Marriage and the family ● Schools ● Diet and disease
●Doctors and cures ● Attitudes and beliefs

3 **New ideas and new worlds**   38
The shape you choose ● Painting moves forward ● Europe
discovers the world ● An invention which changed the world
● Change in the Church

4 **The Renaissance Prince**   60
Crown under threat ● Challenges to power ● Power-building
again: The first Tudor ● James IV of Scotland ● The Renaissance
Prince in person ● Success as a Renaissance Prince

5 **Crown and Church**   83
The King's 'Great Matter' ● New men and a new plan
● The end of the monasteries ● The Bible in English ● Opposition
● Wives ● The Protestant Court of Edward VI ● Catholic Queen
●The middle way ● The Northern Kingdom ● Traitors or martyrs?
● The Enterprise of England ● The parish church

6 **Crown and people**   117
Royal favour ● Money problems ● The Court of Elizabeth I
●The Queen and her Parliaments ● Sovereigns of Ireland and
Wales ● The problem of poverty

7 **Power problems**   137
The first two Stuart kings ● Trouble with Parliament
●Steps to war

8   **The world turned upside down**   156
    Experiences of war ● God made them as 'stubble to our
    swords' ● Britain without a king ● The Lord Protector

9   **The King comes to his own again**   180
    Whigs and Tories ● Catholic King ● Choosing another ruler

10 **The widening world**   197
    Wider horizons: Trade and colonies ● The great ocean of truth
    ● A united kingdom? ● Strangers in Britain ● London by 1700
    ●Living in 1700

    Links: Topic books and *A World of Change*   218

    Index   219

Detail from July in the calendar at the beginning of 'Les Très Riches Heures du Duc de Berry', c. 1520

'The procession of Queen Elizabeth I', attributed to Robert Peake the Elder, c. 1600

'The Numbering of the People at Bethlehem', by Pieter Bruegel

Acknowledgements

The author and publishers are grateful to the following for permission to reproduce material.

Ashmolean Museum, pages 23, 66, 104, 117, 130, 133, 158; James Austin, page 51; BBC Hulton Picture Library, pages 6, 30, 78, 104, 109, 165, 177; Board of Trustees of the Royal Armouries (Crown ©), page 122; Bridgeman Art Library/ Private Collection, page 179; British Library, pages 9, 11, 62, 64, 89, 136, 149, 159, 163, 176; British Museum, pages 49, 106, 141, 154, 189, 191, 192; Biblioteca Nacional, Madrid, page 58; Bibliothèque Nationale, Paris, page (vii); Cambridge University Press, page 45 (Key); Canon David Owen, page 50; Chapter of the College of Arms, page 76; Castle Museum, York, page 161; *Country Life*, page 108; Dean of Exeter Cathedral, page 8; Dean and Chapter of Hereford Cathedral, pages 43, 45, 48; Dean and Chapter of Westminster, pages 68, 71, 73, 74; Dean and Canons of Windsor, page 63; Directors of the Lamport Hall Preservation Trust, page 139; Fotomas Index, pages 20, 38, 53, 56, 79, 92, 94, 110, 123, 129, 150, 152, 163, 171, 179, 191, 193; Freer Gallery of Art, Smithsonian Institution, Washington DC, page 203; Gill and Macmillan Ltd, page 32; Guildhall Library, City of London, pages 132, 190; His Grace the Archbishop of Canterbury and the Trustees of Lambeth Palace Library, pages 65, 148; The Hutchinson Library, page 201; Mansell Collection, page 9, 16, 17, 27, 35, 36, 40, 101, 135, 147, 172, 181, 184, 185, 188, 197, 206, 210; Marquess of Tavistock, and the Trustees of the Bedford Estates, page 126; Mary Evans Picture Library, pages 15, 28, 33, 34, 35, 42, 84, 174, 175, 186; Musées Royaux des Beaux-Arts de Belgique, Brussels, pages (x)–(xi) and 6; Museum of London, pages 21, 22, 28, 168, 200, 211, 213; National Gallery, pages 25, 41, 140, 170, 180; National Galleries of Scotland, page 105; National Maritime Museum, pages 46, 111, 112; National Portrait Gallery, pages 61, 64, 69, 73, 78, 83, 86, 87, 96, 97, 99, 100, 103, 107, 109, 118, 127, 128, 129, 137, 138, 142, 147, 150, 151, 156, 161, 162, 172, 177, 182, 183, 187, 188, 194, 197, 198; National Trust, page 134; Oeffentliche Kunstsammlung, Kupferstichkabinett (Print Room) Basel, page 55; Public Record Office, pages 18 and 164; Photosource, page 52; Royal Mint, page 85; Science Museum, pages 38, 44, 205; Sudeley Castle, Glos, page 116; Uffizi Gallery, Firenze, pages 41, 120; Sir Ralph Verney, page 160; Victoria & Albert Museum, pages 50, 95, 126, 136, 211; Wayland Picture Library, page 37; Weidenfeld and Nicolson Ltd, page 178, 208; Wellcome Institute Library, page 34.

The following are reproduced by gracious permission of Her Majesty the Queen: pages 54, 87, 93, 95, 98, 107, 121, 123, 138, 143, 155, 171, 181, 182.

The cover picture is *The Feast at Bermondsey* by J Hoefnagel, reproduced with the permission of the Marquess of Salisbury and John R Freeman & Company. The pictures on pages (viii)–(ix) and 162 are in private collections.

Every effort has been made to contact copyright holders, and we apologise if any have been missed.

Introduction

The people in the pictures at the front of this book lived in the **Early Modern Age**. Early Modern Age is just a name for the time between about 1450 and 1700 which historians find useful, just as they describe earlier ages as Prehistoric Times, the Ancient World and the Middle Ages.

The ordinary men and women in the picture on page (vii) are working hard on a hot summer day, shearing sheep and cutting hay. It made no difference to them whether they were born before or after 1450 (the picture in fact was painted a little before). During the Early Modern Age, the work they had to do to survive, their problems and difficulties, as well as the ways they enjoyed themselves, all remained more or less the same.

On the cover of the book, people who are neither very rich nor very poor are enjoying themselves at a wedding in Bermondsey. This is now a district in the heart of London; you can see how different it was in 1570, when this picture was probably painted.

The picture on pages (viii)–(ix) shows Queen Elizabeth I surrounded by her courtiers; it was painted in 1600, and shows this famous monarch of the Early Modern Age at her grandest. Obviously the men and women in this picture lived very different lives from the workers in the hayfields. In this book, we shall find out about these kinds of people and others too.

We shall be looking mainly at **Britain**; and 'Britain' too was a confusing name in the Early Modern Age. The people were not united and knew little about one another; they lived without television, radio, and newspapers, which tell us so much today. People did not travel widely either. Scholars visited different universities; merchants journeyed on business; craftsmen such as clockmakers and masons went where their skills were needed; pedlars sold their wares; and the very poor looked for work, or the chance to beg or steal, wherever they could. But many people never went further than their local village or town. An English person might never visit London at all, and Wales, Ireland and Scotland seemed remote and unknown.

The Welsh had their own language and their poets and musicians. Though officially they were under English rule, they were a proud and separate people. So were the Irish, and the Church in Ireland had been strong since the days of St Patrick (c390-460), and his later followers, who played an important part in spreading Christianity in the rest of the British Isles. The people were poor, and deeply loyal to their clan chieftains. English kings were only 'Lords of Ireland'; they controlled the area around Dublin, but not much else.

The people of Scotland had never forgotten that Robert the Bruce and his army had prevented an English conquest in 1314. Visitors agreed that dislike of the English was one of the few things which united the Scots. They were more loyal to their clans than their king, and there was a great difference between the 'wild Scots' of the Highlands and the 'household Scots' of the Lowlands. In the bare and rugged Highlands it was hard to scrape a living from the soil; in the Lowlands of the south the land was more fertile, and there were more towns. Kings of Scotland needed to be firm rulers. They often relied on the 'Auld Alliance' — friendship with England's long-standing enemy, France, first formally arranged in 1295 during the struggle for independence. But neither Scots nor English kings could prevent the border between the two countries being a wild and lawless area where there was cattle-thieving, pillage, plundering and murder on both sides.

Wales, Ireland and Scotland were poor compared to England, because they were further from profitable European trade routes, and the land was less fertile.

However, the English could never ignore their three 'back doors' which any enemy might creep through. A 'United Kingdom' began to seem an attractive idea to some of them — but the Welsh, Irish and Scots were not very ready to agree.

In this book, you can find out about the exciting 'World of Change' in which the different peoples of Britain lived in the Early Modern Age — and how far those changes affected their everyday lives.

Author's Acknowledgement

A textbook of this nature owes a great debt to numbers of distinguished historians. I should, however, like to acknowledge the following in particular:

L A Clarkson, *Death, Disease and Famine in Pre-Industrial England* (Macmillian, 1975)
A Fraser, *The Weaker Vessel* (Weidenfeld and Nicolson, 1984)
P Fryer, *Staying Power: The History of Black People in Britain* (Pluto Press, 1984)
M Prior, *Women in Society, 1500–1800* (Methuen, 1985)
C Wilson, *England's Apprenticeship, 1603–1763* (Longman, 1965)
J Youings, *Sixteenth Century England* (Pelican Social History of Britain, 1984).

I am also very grateful to Annabel Wigner for invaluable help on the Mughal Emperors, Akbar and Jahangir, and their contacts with Europeans; to Robert Morris for enlightenment on Wales in the Early Modern Age; and to Professor J D Hargreaves of Aberdeen University for help with the slave trade.

This book is dedicated to Tony, Alison, Sarah, Bill and Martin, who have helped in many different ways.

Rosemary Kelly
Oxford, 1987

How to use this book

History is about the past.

When we try to find out about the past, we have to do several things.

We must understand *what happened*, and how the facts link together.

We must test the *evidence* for these facts.

We must use our *imagination*, so that we realise what it was like to live in times very different from our own.

In this book, we try to do these three things; and every so often there are questions to help you. There are also 'flashback' page references like this: ←78 to link up what you already know with new facts and ideas.

Evidence of different kinds helps us to discover the past

Written evidence includes diaries, letters and eye-witness accounts. These can tell us much about people's feelings and attitudes, though they may only give one side of the story. Official documents and government records show us how the actions of rulers and their advisers affected the lives of everyone else.

Even propaganda produced to win people over to one particular view-point help us to understand the attitudes of the time, and sometimes provide us with opposing views.

Pictures tell us more than just what people looked like, and what they wore. Portraits of important people often tell us about the impression they wanted to make, and that in turn can indicate what kind of people they were.

Cartoons and little pictures on pedlars' ballad sheets tell us about poorer people who could never have afforded to have a portrait painted.

Places give clues about the events which happened there. If you can visit any of the places mentioned in this book, it will help to bring their story to life. Photographs and maps play an important part here too.

With these ways of looking at the past, we can make the exciting leap into the colourful, changing world of the Early Modern Age.

1 Ordinary people — ordinary lives

History is not just about rich and famous people — kings, queens, archbishops, nobles and country gentlemen. They were of course important, and there is plenty about them in this book. They were also a very small group. There were many more ordinary people, and their lives were important too.

So what was it like to be an ordinary, rather poor, person at the beginning of the Early Modern Age? The picture on pages (x)–(xi) was painted by Pieter Bruegel (pronounced Broygel), an artist who lived in The Netherlands (modern Holland and Belgium) in the middle of the sixteenth century. Artists at that time nearly always painted important people who could afford to pay for their pictures; but Bruegel was unusual, because he painted ordinary people doing everyday, often humble tasks. His pictures tell us a great deal about them; and their lives were much the same, whether they lived in England or the Netherlands, and whether it was the mid-fifteenth century or a hundred years later.

The picture shows the well-known beginning of the Christmas story: Mary and Joseph are arriving at a crowded Bethlehem; in the painting, everyone is being counted at the local inn. But Bruegel's Bethlehem is just like a village of his own time, in the depths of a cold winter. The people in the front are being counted, but almost everyone else is busy getting on with the work they have to do before darkness falls.

You can find out a good deal about their work by looking closely at the picture.

1 What kinds of things do you think are being loaded on to the carts in the foreground?

2 What do you think is in those heavy sacks being carried across the lake in the distance?

3 What other kinds of work can you see going on?

There are some children enjoying the ice and snow, but most people in the picture are working very hard. A pig is being killed in front of the inn; the innkeeper is probably quite prosperous, and owns the chickens as well. But almost all the others are unlikely to be able to afford a good dinner with meat as a main course, however cold and hungry they may be feeling.

Imagine what it would be like to be transported back more than five hundred years, and to live in a house like this, as so many men and women did.

Think what this house would have been like:

1 What building materials would be used for the walls and roof?

2 What would the floor be like?

3 Draw a picture to show what the inside of the house was like. You can assume that there was only one room, and that there was just the one window and door you can see. Decide what furniture there might be. There were no cupboards then; chests were used for storage. Everything would have been made by the occupants or the local carpenter. Remember that all food stores and livestock would be indoors in winter time.

4 It is a reasonable guess that the old woman working outside lives in the house. What do you think she is doing?

5 Make a list of the disadvantages of living in this house.

A rushlight usually had a special stand for the grease-soaked reed. What advantages would such a stand give? How does this picture help us to understand the phrase which is often used for extravagance: 'burning the candle at both ends'? How has the meaning of this phrase changed in our times?

Life was certainly very different at the beginning of the Early Modern Age. It is worth thinking about some other simple things we now take for granted, but which men and women then would not have known in the same way.

Lighting and heating

Sometimes we have to do without electric light (or we choose to do so), and we use wax candles; we find the flickering light attractive, but quite difficult to see by. In the Early Modern Age, only rich people could afford candles made of wax. Candles made of tallow (mostly animal fat) were more common, but even these were quite expensive. Tallow could cost four times as much as lean meat, which itself was a luxury for most people. The reason was that it was very difficult to fatten cattle in those days. You can work out why if you look at Bruegel's picture again, and think about the problems of keeping animals healthy and well fed in winter.

Ordinary people therefore usually used simple rushlights — a rush or a reed soaked in any waste fat they might have. They were smoky, and smelt unpleasant, and were a great deal less efficient than candles. They were usually lit with a tinder box, and it was not easy to learn the knack of producing a spark from one of these. Your wrist also needed to be quite strong.

Even in the daytime, houses were dark. In the fifteenth century, only the very rich could afford glass, and quite prosperous people made do with very thin layers of horn or oiled linen stretched over their windows.

Neither of these materials let in much light. It was also difficult to make them fit properly; so houses had few windows, to avoid letting in the cold and the rain. In fact, windows were seldom built on the sunny south side of a house. This may have been because diseases like the plague were thought to come from that direction.

A fire was essential for cooking and to provide heat, and that gave a little light too. People tried never to let their fires go out, and as you can see in Bruegel's picture, they had to work hard to gather fuel. At night, fires would be covered with turf; in times of trouble, this had to be done at a certain time, after which everyone had to stay indoors. This was a curfew, a word which probably comes from 'couvre-feu' — French for 'cover the fire'.

So people did not sit around much on dark, cold evenings. They went to bed soon after sunset, and got up as soon as it was light. The dark was frightening. There were no cheerful lights in the village street, and who knew what dangerous beasts and evil spirits might lurk in the woods beyond?

Measuring time

We take it for granted that we are always able to look at a watch or a clock to tell the time. But in the late fifteenth century, ordinary people would not have had either in their homes. They might see a clock if they went to the local town, either in the market place or on the church tower, but it might not have looked like one we would recognise; and they would probably not have bothered to look at it. People did not need to 'tell the time' as we do. They worked when it was daylight, and went to bed when it was dark, and they just used phrases like 'at dawn', 'about noon', or 'at sunset'. The bell at the local monastery, which tolled regularly for the monks' services, also helped them to keep track of the time.

When the owner of Cotehele House in Cornwall built a new chapel, sometime between 1485 and 1489, he installed a clock. It is worked by a system of heavy weights balanced against each other, and has never been altered, even when the pendulum was introduced into clocks, providing a more accurate movement. So we can see it exactly as it was when it was built. It is interesting that, like many clocks of the time, it has no face. It is really just a mechanism for two bells: one struck the hours, the other the time for church services. When many people still could not read and write, that was all they needed from a clock, even in a large, busy and prosperous household like Cotehele.

The Exeter clock

You can still see this clock in Exeter Cathedral today. It is thought to be the gift of Peter Courtenay, who was Bishop of Exeter from 1478 to 1487. The main clock face shows the earth in the centre. The moon revolves around it, and turns on its own axis, to show how it waxes and wanes through thirty days.

The sun, which is decorated with the lily shape of the fleur-de-lis, revolves round both of them. It points to the hour on the outer circle, and the age of the moon on the inner one.

The upper dial, which shows the minutes, was added much later, in 1760.

The Latin words at the bottom mean: 'They [the hours] perish and are reckoned to our account'.

1 List some differences between this clock and a modern one.

2 What is the approximate date of the clock?

3 What clues does this clock give about people's ideas of the earth and the universe at this time?

4 We would not find much use for a clock which did not give the minutes as well as the hours. What kind of changes might have taken place in people's ordinary lives by 1760, that would make them feel they needed a minute hand?

5 Clocks were not the only way of telling the time at the beginning of the Early Modern Age. What other ways of telling the time were there?

These ways of telling the time worked well for the people who lived then, though by modern standards they were not very accurate.

Calendars varied too. The Church began its year on Lady Day, 25 March, as the spring flowers were beginning to show, and the days were becoming a little warmer. It is not surprising that this seemed a good time to start a new year. Lawyers, however, preferred the date the western world now uses — 1 January.

So, just by thinking about light, heat and measuring time, we can begin to understand some of the differences between the Early Modern Age and our own. Now we need to find out more about how people lived.

Work in the countryside

Most people in the Western world today live in or near a town. In the Early Modern Age, nine out of every ten lived and worked in the countryside. In many English villages, the land was still used in the way it had been for centuries: there were three big open fields surrounding the village, divided into strips, and shared out amongst the villagers. Each field in turn was left fallow — or empty — so that the soil did not become exhausted. There was also a stretch of common land; whatever animals the people could afford to own were grazed there. People lived on what they could produce themselves, what we now call 'subsistence farming'.

Work had changed little too. Look at the pictures below, of villagers ploughing. The one at the top left was painted in the margin of a book of psalms, about 1340. The big one on the right comes from a book of farming advice published in 1523. The smaller one, below left, is early seventeenth century.

1 Roughly how many years are there between the earliest and the latest picture?

2 What animals are being used in each picture to pull the plough?

3 What were the jobs of the people shown in each picture?

4 What is the main difference between the early plough and the two later ones? How much of an improvement do you think it was?

5 What other jobs as well as ploughing are being done in the seventeenth-century picture?

Enclosures

One change was already happening in some areas of England at the beginning of the Early Modern Age. The big fields with strips were being replaced by smaller square fields, enclosed by hedges. This was usually done by rich people, on whose land ordinary villagers lived and worked. Sheep farming was more profitable than corn-growing. For every plough, six men were needed to do all the necessary jobs through the year; but a flock of sheep kept in an enclosed field rarely needed more than one shepherd. There were good profits to be made from wool, too, as you can find out later in this chapter. Sometimes, this change did not affect local people too much; but in many places, especially in the Midlands, villagers lost their land and their livelihood, and were forced to leave to search for work elsewhere. Then a whole village might disappear, to be replaced by fields full of sheep.

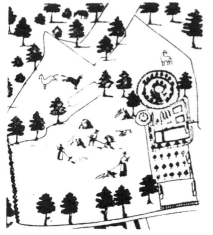

Haymaking

In 1512, a sheep farmer called John Spencer was given permission by the King to enclose his lands in 'Olthorp'. A government inquiry of 1517 found:

> he converted lands from their original cultivation and use into pasture for sheep and other animals whereby . . . four persons rendered idle . . . (who) . . . up to then had been living and working there to their great loss were *driven into vagrancy* [they became wandering beggars].

Only a few people lost everything because of John Spencer's enclosure — but it meant great hardship for them. Meanwhile, Spencer became a knight and High Sheriff of Northamptonshire — and the Spencer family still own a beautiful house at Althorp today.

A shepherd

How many people?

In modern Britain we have no difficulty in knowing how many people there are because every birth and death is recorded, and a census is taken every ten years. In the Early Modern Age, there were few records like that, and those that exist are very incomplete. Yet historians think that the population was growing steadily, both in Britain and Europe. Here are some facts they use: work out why they show that there were more people than there had been in the later Middle Ages.

Prices were rising.

Wages did not go up.

There was a great deal of poverty and unemployment.

There was much buying and selling of land, and rents went up.

There could be other reasons too, as well as a rising population, which helped to cause these things; perhaps you can think of some of them. In Chapter 6, we shall see some of the effects all this had on the people of the Early Modern Age.

Threshing with a flail

People in towns

There were fewer towns in Early Modern England than there are now, and they were smaller. They were exciting lively places, crowded with people and often very confusing to strangers from outside. Many towns still had walls and gates, and were centred round a main crossroads or square, where the market would probably be. People lived in towns in order to carry out their trade safely and profitably. A town had to be easy for other traders to reach; and if it was well organised, pleasant, as clean as possible, free from disease and other dangers, then it was prosperous and often grew bigger. Shrewsbury was like many towns of the time.

This sixteenth-century picture of Shrewsbury gives us a good idea of a town in the Early Modern Age.

It was well protected: the great curve of the River Severn provided a natural defence, reinforced by walls and fortified gateways. Why is the position of the castle especially important? The walls were old by this time, and needed to be kept in good repair. But there are signs that people were feeling more secure — a few houses lie beyond the city walls.

It was easy to reach: the two bridges bring the main roads into the centre of the town. Quite large ships can obviously reach the town by river, and it was usually easier and cheaper to transport goods by water. Can you see how one ship is being moved along?

Houses were closely packed together. Travel was not easy, and people lived where they worked, and where they could easily buy and sell. Most obviously still preferred to live within the security of the walls. However, even in that small space, there are plenty of gardens. It was a good insurance against hard times if even a little food could be grown, and herbs were widely used both for food and medicine.

Streets were so narrow that it was often possible to reach out and touch the house opposite. People of the same trade usually lived in the same street, and names like Milk Street and Butcher Row in modern Shrewsbury tell us where some of these trades were.

Houses in Butcher Row

Churches are easy to see in the city. There were more than we might think necessary for its size. Wealthy citizens were always ready to add improvements like stained glass windows, and beautifully decorated chapels where prayers could be said for their souls.

Here is some evidence on conditions in towns:

Rules and regulations made in York

<table>
<tr><td>1517</td><td>No manner of person . . . shall cast any manner of filth . . . of gougs or dogs . . . against Greyfriars Wall but . . . behind the new jetty.</td></tr>
<tr><td>1524</td><td>No man dwelling on the water bank of the Ouse shall cast any manner of filth . . . nor dung into the said water of the Ouse.</td></tr>
<tr><td>1527</td><td>Every Alderman . . . of this City shall hang a lantern with a light therein burning over their . . . door every night from five of the clock unto nine of the clock on pain (of a fine).</td></tr>
<tr><td>1526</td><td>Three cornchapmen to see to the . . . Town Walls, to be kept clean . . . without scrub growing in the same . . . and to repair as much of the said walls now fallen.</td></tr>
<tr><td>1520</td><td>No man . . . dwelling within this City . . . shall suffer their children to go with clappers upon Shrove Tuesday and Good Friday . . . only the parish clerk shall go with the said clappers.</td></tr>
<tr><td>1530</td><td>All strange beggars now being within this City to the common nuisance shall avoid this City within twenty four hours . . . on pain of scourging of their bodies.</td></tr>
</table>

Margin notes:

This may mean hogs. Animals were allowed to wander in city streets.

one of the chief citizens chosen to help the Mayor

corn salesman
weeds

allow
noisy rattles used to summon people to church

leave

These were some plague precautions in York in 1552:

In infected houses, doors and windows had to be closed for six weeks.

One person only had to bring in food and drink.

No cloth, yarns or bedding was to be removed from the building.

Four persons had to bury corpses, and sweep and clean the houses.

At night the houses had to have a light outside.

Some accusations in Nottingham law courts

1496   Elizabeth Stafford, housewife, exposed for sale . . . meat and pies unwholesome and corrupt for human food.

Joan Hunt spinster is a common receiver of servants . . . and they there keep disorderly conduct and make outcries so that her neighbours cannot sleep in their beds.

John Clitherow . . . weaver . . . is a common listener at windows and houses of his neighbours to sow strife and discord amongst his neighbours.

■ From the regulations in York, and accusations in Nottingham, make a list of problems likely to arise in towns in the Early Modern Age.

Trades and occupations

Life in towns depended on the trades and occupations there, and they were carefully organised. Records such as lists of taxpayers, and of leading citizens attending the appointment of a new mayor, tell us what they were. These are the numbers of the twelve most important kinds of tradesmen in three very different towns in the early sixteenth century:

Northampton		York		Norwich	
Shoemakers	50	Merchants	118	Worsted weavers	160
Bakers	21	Tailors	87	Mercers	71
Tailors	20	Cordwainers	61	Tailors	71
Weavers	20	Fishers	47	Shoemakers	42
Tanners	15	Butchers	43	Grocers	37
Mercers	15	Bakers	41	Shearmen	31
Butchers	14	Tanners	41	Carpenters	30
Glovers	13	Weavers	39	Masons	23
Fullers	12	Haberdashers	37	Rafmen	23
Dyers	9	Tapiters	37	Butchers	21
Drapers	9	Millers	35	Smiths	18
Millers	9	Carpenters	32	Barbers	16

Cordwainers: makers of fine leather goods. **Tapiters:** makers of tapestry and wall hangings. **Mercers:** dealers in luxury textiles, e.g. silk. **Rafmen:** probably chandlers, who sold candles, soap, oil and paint. **Fullers** operated the bleaching process in clothmaking. **Shearmen** smoothed the surface of woollen cloth to produce worsted. **Drapers** bought and sold cloth. York **merchants** were probably involved mainly in the cloth trade.

1 Write down the main trade in each town, and make sure you understand the meaning of any unusual ones. (Use a dictionary if necessary.)

2 Even if this list included all the trades in each town, why would it still not be an accurate way of judging population figures? Which is likely to be the smallest town of the three?

3 Make lists of trades dealing in *food, clothing, building, luxury goods*. Under *luxury goods*, you may need to repeat trades already listed under *food, clothing* and *building*.

4 How many modern surnames can you find in this list?

Trade and Industry in England, 1500

Main exports
Cloth — by far the biggest export
Wool
Tin
Lead
Fish

Main imports
From the Mediterranean and Flanders:
Wine
Raisins
Dyestuffs — woad, indigo
Alum — chemical used in cloth production
Soaps
Hides
Paper
Glass
Armour for tournaments

From the Baltic, via Flanders:
Pitch
Tar
Canvas

Main trade along the coasts
Coal
Fish
Salt
Timber

Main industries
Tin mining
Lead mining
Coal mining
Copper mining
Iron working
Shipbuilding
Leather working
Wool and cloth

The butchers of Northampton

These are some rules made by the butchers of Northampton in 1535:

trade

> Twelve men of the same *craft* had to see that the meat that 'they kill . . . be good, and able to be man's meat.

prepare

> No man of the said craft *dress* . . . old sheep instead of lamb to the deceit of the King's people.

> No man . . . cast no manner of offal as lights, lungs, horns and other annoyable things behind the stalls nor on the pavements.

> No man wilfully slay swine . . . openly.

> No pocky sheep . . . to be sold.

> No man of the said craft shall call another of his fellowship knave in anger nor other unkind word.

> No flesh to be cast in the river.

> No one shall sell before 4 o'clock in the morning . . . and no longer than 9 o'clock in the summer, and 8 o'clock in the winter . . . and no selling on Sunday.'

stall

> A butcher must not 'call buyers from his neighbour's *board* to his board'.

1 Which of these rules are made to see that butchers are efficient, and do not cheat their customers or one another?

2 Which rules are made to keep the town clean and pleasant?

3 Butchers and tanners often worked in the same part of the town. Why were these trades connected? In York this was called 'The Shambles'. What does this word mean now?

4 What other trades in Northampton are connected with tanners?

Guilds

The butchers of Northampton, like everyone who worked in a trade in a town, belonged to an organisation called a guild. This guaranteed the quality of goods; looked after members of the guild and their families in times of sickness or trouble; and when a member died, paid for prayers to be said for his (sometimes her) soul. Guilds helped to run the affairs of the town, and provided entertainment on feast days. Their most important task was to train their members in their particular skill, and the story of a citizen of Shrewsbury at the beginning of the Early Modern Age shows how this was done.

Degory Watur was born into quite a poor family in Shrewsbury. His father was a journeyman (a worker paid by the day — *journée* in French) in the most powerful guild in the town, the Drapers. This guild bought woollen cloth from Wales, packed it in bales, and sold some in the town, but sent most of it to London and Bristol for export.

When Degory was about nine, he became an apprentice to a Master Draper. This meant that he went to live in his master's house, and received food, clothes and training. In return, he had to work very hard; not surprisingly, apprentices did the boring routine jobs. If the master was a good one, they also learnt a great deal about their trade. This lasted for seven years, then Degory became a journeyman like his father.

Degory must have been ambitious and able, because by the time he was twenty-two he had made the difficult step up to being a Master Draper. If he had belonged to a guild which made a product — for instance the Bakers — he would have had to produce his 'masterpiece', the best loaf of bread he could make. As he was a Draper, he had to buy his own shop. He also had to pay the guild £20 — a lot of money when a day's wages was about five old pennies. Even then, the guild could refuse to accept him, if they felt there were too many drapers already. However, Degory overcame all these obstacles: he soon became a leading citizen, much involved in the affairs of the town. He also founded an almshouse, where thirteen poor citizens could live out their last years in peace and comfort. At the end of a long life, when he was ninety, a local rival tried to take over the almshouse. Although he was blind as well as very old, Degory wrote to Edward IV for help, and the rival was ordered out. The Master Draper died in 1478 when he was 97, leaving money for his almshouse, as well as for his own family and friends.

Apprentices

Many apprentices did not live and work in their home town. A register kept in Bristol between 1532 and 1542 shows that many were a long way from home:

400 were from Bristol, but —

100 came from Ireland,
174 came from Wales,
185 came from Gloucestershire,
147 came from Somerset,
75 came from Shropshire,
72 came from Worcestershire,
41 came from Lancashire and the Lake District,
8 came from Devon and Dorset.

1 On squared paper, show these statistics as a block graph, using one square to represent ten apprentices.

2 Why do you think so many came from places as far away as Ireland and the Lake District?

The happiness of an apprentice depended on his employer. The picture of a shoemaker's shop on the next page shows that everyone lived and worked close together. The Master and his wife played an important part in the life of an apprentice; so did the other apprentices, and the journeymen. It could be a cheerful friendly life — or it could be the opposite.

In this barber's shop, the master cuts the hair of an important-looking customer, and the apprentice does the hair washing. Barbers also pulled out teeth and performed other minor operations. Bandages hang from the ceiling. Work out the uses of some of the other pieces of equipment in the picture.

A shoemaker's shop

Indenture of a baker's apprentice

John Harbord was about nine years old when his parents 'bound him apprentice' to a baker. This is part of the indenture, or legal agreement, that they made with William Tebbe, the baker.

> John Harbord does bind himself prentice to William Tebbe . . . Mayor of Leicester to the Baker's craft for the term of seven years, and the eighth year journeyman, . . . to be kept as a prentice should be, that is, meat and drink, *hose* and shoes, . . . and his craft to be taught him . . .

stockings

> The said John does bind himself . . . to be a true servant for those years and that he shall steal none of his master's goods, . . . and he shall use no gaming, nor shall he make no promise of *wedlock* except his master give him leave, nor shall he buy nor sell except it be for his master's profit, and he shall keep his master's counsel in all manner of things that is lawful. In witness thereof of William Tebbe, Thomas Kattelyn, bailiff, John Wester, Thomas Bette, justices of the peace . . . with others more.

marriage

1 What advantages did John get from this agreement?

2 What might he find to be disadvantages when he got older?

3 Why did William Tebbe make John promise 'to keep his master's counsel'?

4 Using this agreement, and the story of Degory Watur, make a chart to show the stages of training provided by guilds, from apprentice to master. Decide which craft or trade you are going to show.

Naturally apprentices liked to go out and enjoy themselves when they had the chance. They played a very violent form of football, with hardly any rules, usually in the narrow crowded streets near their shop. So it was not surprising there was often trouble, and the apprentices got the blame. In London in 1479, the Mayor forbade 'all labourers, servants, and apprentices from playing tennis, or football, or to use cards or dice' but they were given permission to practice archery — presumably outside the city walls! London apprentices were also often in the thick of any trouble with foreigners, which was another common problem in the busy capital, always full of visiting businessmen and diplomats.

As towns grew — and many did as the population increased — Master Guildsmen became more anxious to limit their numbers and prevent competition. So, during the sixteenth century, it became much more difficult for apprentices and journeymen to rise any higher. Many became frustrated, and more ready to cause trouble. Perhaps Degory Watur would not have done so well if he had been born a hundred years later.

←10

Women in guilds

Although most guilds were run by men, they depended greatly on their wives to run the large households on which their business and prosperity were based. Women also often ran a business on their own. The most usual opportunity arose if a widow inherited her husband's business. Alice Chester of Bristol continued her husband's trade importing iron from Spain. She did so well that she gave the city a loading crane for the docks and a fine carved wooden screen for one of the city churches.

The silkwomen of London ran their own guild. They bought raw silk, spun it into different kinds of silk thread, and then wove it into beautiful fabrics, or made ribbon, laces, tassels and fringes. They trained their own apprentices; as was usual, they got on well with some, and had problems with others. One silkwoman got on so well with her apprentice that she left her a pair of sheets and 'a girdle of green silk garnished with silver', when she died. These silkwomen were mostly the wives of prosperous masters in other guilds; one married twice, first to a goldsmith, and then to an alderman (see page 12). They must have been both efficient and very busy, for as well as running their own guilds, they had to organise the large household working on their husband's trade.

Alice Chester's crane in Bristol was probably like this one at Bruges, which was the first of its type. How is the power provided to lift the heavy casks of wine?

■ Imagine you are a London silkwoman in the late fifteenth century. Decide what trade your husband follows (the previous pages will help), and describe a typical day in your life. Remember you will have a good deal to do with his apprentices as well as your own.

An 'extraordinary abundance' of wool

'They have an enormous number of sheep which yield them quantities of wool of the best quality.' So wrote an Italian reporting to his native city of Venice on England and the English, around 1500. He emphasised the 'extraordinary abundance' of English wool which was famous throughout Europe, and had been the basis of the country's prosperity for a long time. The Lord Chancellor, when he presides over the House of Lords today, still sits on a bulky woolsack, rather than a grand throne, as a reminder of what used to be England's most important export.

Wool came mainly from three areas: the Cotswolds, East Anglia, and Yorkshire. We know a great deal about the organisation of the Cotswold wool trade in the late fifteenth century from letters written by the Celys, a family of wool merchants who had a house in London and lands in Essex. They would go to the Cotswolds and make a deal with a woolman to buy wool and 'fells' (fleeces). A professional packer then sorted and packed the wool into 'sarplers' (big bales which were sent to London by pack-horse). There, after weighing in the presence of both buyer and seller, a price was agreed. Then the wool was shipped across the Channel to Calais, where the next stage took place, in a big market called the Staple. Another Italian visitor to England described this stage:

> From Britain they import a vast quantity of wool which is later conveyed to Italy, or into France, or anywhere else by land . . . If merchants want to buy English wool, and do not want to go to the island themselves, they have to buy it at Calais.

The Celys were Merchants of the Staple, and it was at Calais they made their profits. One member of the family was always there, and sometimes also travelled to other wool markets like Bruges (see map on page 19). In November 1479, Richard Cely, the head of the family, wrote to his son George at Calais. George was sometimes rather unreliable, especially over money, and his father was often severe with him; but this letter shows how fond he was of his son, as well as showing how the family worked:

> I greet you well, desiring for to hear of your recovering, for I understand . . . you were sore sick at Bruges, whereof your mother and both your brothers . . . were sore and heavy for you. I trust to God you be recovered and well mended. The comfort of your letter caused me to buy 60 sacks of Cotswold wool, the which is in pile at Northleach. John Cely hath gathered and bought for me in the Cotswolds 37 sacks.

Richard Cely goes on to tell his son to buy canvas for sarplers, then says:

> I am advised to pack the wool after Christmas . . . I trust you shall be at the packing of the said wool in the Cotswolds. I will ship no wool before March . . . I write no more at this time, but Jesu keep you. Written at London, 6th day of November in haste.

This is the address on one of the Cely letters. It says: 'To my right worshipful masters Richard and George Cely, Merchants of the Staple at Calais, at London in Mark Lane.' They added their merchants' mark, which was put on all the bales of wool they sold.

1 Richard Cely had a brother, John. Richard and his wife Agnes had two other sons, Robert and Richard; George was the youngest. Draw a small family tree. How many of the family are mentioned in the letter?

2 When is George most likely to travel to England? Where will he have to go for the packing?

3 Assuming that Richard had only just bought the wool when he wrote, how long will it be before it is on sale at Calais?

4 Make your own copy of the map on the next page, and draw in the journeys the Cely family had to make to sell these 97 sacks of wool.

5 Write George's answer to his father. It does not exist, so you can use your imagination and common sense to decide how he might have replied.

By the beginning of the Early Modern Age, many merchants had found they made more profit by selling wool that had already been made up into cloth; so much more cloth was being exported than raw wool. The cloth trade employed a great many expert craftsmen: spinners, weavers, fullers, ←13 tenters, shearmen, and dyers. Some lived in towns, others in the country. When times were good, wage-earners all over England did well; when cloth did not sell, they suffered.

The guild of Merchant Adventurers in London organised the export of English cloth to Antwerp, where it was sold all over Europe. Because cloth was the biggest export, they were the most powerful guild at the beginning of the Early Modern Age, though whether their name was a truthful one is another matter. All they did was to ship cloth across the short and well-known sea passage to Antwerp, where there were sure to be merchants waiting to buy. Having sold their cloth, they bought luxuries to sell at home — silks, spices, and dyestuffs. None of this could really be called 'adventurous', but it certainly brought in good profits.

■ Complete your map showing the Celys' trading journeys. Add the following:

a) The trade route for imports and exports used by the Merchant Adventurers.

b) The route used for bales of wool shipped from Southampton and Bristol (by guilds like Degory Watur's Drapers) south to Florence and other Italian cities.

c) The imports coming into London, Bristol, and Southampton from the Mediterranean.

d) The imports coming into Lynn from the Baltic.

Look at the lists of imports and exports on page 13, to remind yourself of the goods involved. Make labels, small drawings, and a key to your map.

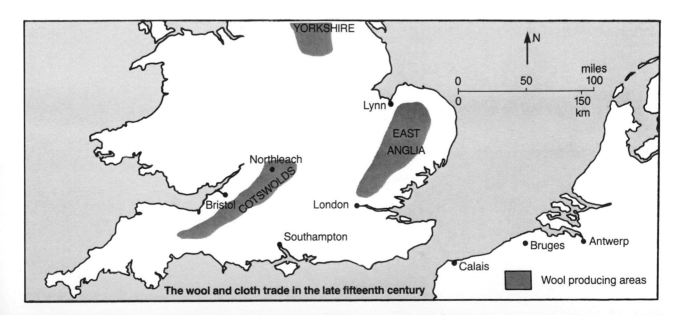

The wool and cloth trade in the late fifteenth century

London

London was by far the biggest city in the whole of Britain, with a population of about 60,000 by 1500, and it was growing fast. Like any city, great wealth existed beside bitter poverty in its crowded streets — and it certainly was crowded. A street was usually only wide enough for two carts to pass, and any lane was barely more than a metre wide. It is not difficult to guess which trades already mentioned in this chapter operated in Stinking Lane. Visitors did not usually go there, and were happy to stay in Cheapside — a wide main road where the luxury trades could be found. One Italian visitor counted 52 goldsmiths there — 'all the shops of Milan, Rome, and Venice could not show so much'. This was probably an exaggeration, but it shows he was impressed.

Another Italian however, wrote this about the same time:

> All the streets are so badly paved that they get wet at the slightest quantity of water, and this happens frequently owing to the large numbers of cattle carrying water, as well on account of the rain of which there is a great deal in this island. Then a vast amount of evil smelling mud is formed.

■ Look up the word *conduit* in the dictionary. There were many of these in London streets, supplied by wooden water pipes. Where else would a Londoner get water? Write down some obvious differences from water supplies today.

This Italian visitor was impressed by London's position on the Thames, and especially the strong high tide, 'which stops the river's current and forces it back upstream . . . every day during six hours' and allowed quite large ships to dock close to London Bridge. (He would have been used to the non-tidal Mediterranean.) He also thought highly of:

> the handsome walls . . . within these stands a strongly defended castle on the banks of the river where the King and his Queen sometimes have their residence . . . There are also other great buildings, and especially a beautiful and convenient bridge over the Thames, of many marble arches, which has on it many shops built of stone, and mansions and even a church of considerable size. Nowhere have I seen a finer or more richly built bridge.

Why was London the capital?

What gave the city of London such an advantage that it was the obvious capital?

All the following reasons helped:

> The Thames estuary lies opposite the prosperous Netherlands and the main European trade routes. Because of the tide, quite big merchant ships could reach the capital.

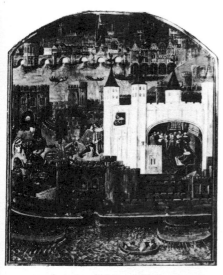

London Bridge with its narrow arches, and buildings on it
This view is from the Tower.

There had been a bridge since Roman times when it was discovered that here the river had a hard gravel bed, which made a good foundation. No other bridges spanned the Thames until much further inland.

Look at the maps on pages 19 and below and work out how the river, bridge and roads helped communications to all parts of Britain and Europe.

The artist who drew this view of London in 1510 was not interested in making an accurate picture. Yet in the very small space, he has managed to give a vivid idea of the capital. You can see much of what the Italian visitor describes, and more. Find London Bridge, the Tower ('the strongly defended castle'), Old St Paul's (one of the most famous churches in the kingdom), the walls, one of the gateways (When you have located the other landmarks, can you see why it must be Ludgate? Use the map below.), the river (used more than the muddy roads as the main thoroughfare) and the countryside just outside the walls.

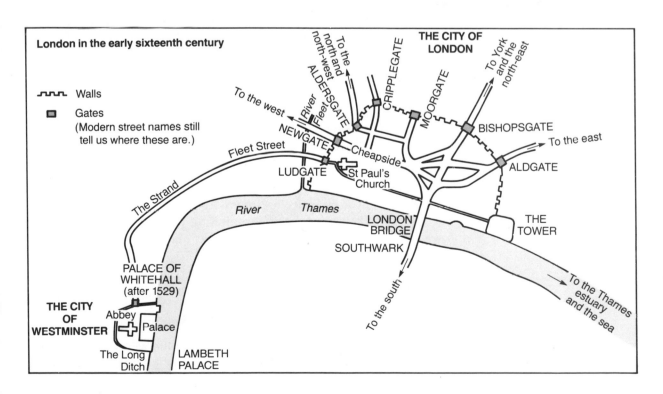

London in the early sixteenth century

ᴖᴖᴖ Walls

▣ Gates
(Modern street names still tell us where these are.)

THE CITY OF LONDON

To the north and north-west
To the west
To York and the north-east
To the east
ALDERSGATE
CRIPPLEGATE
MOORGATE
BISHOPSGATE
River Fleet
NEWGATE
Cheapside
LUDGATE
St Paul's Church
ALDGATE
Fleet Street
The Strand
River Thames
LONDON BRIDGE
SOUTHWARK
THE TOWER
To the Thames estuary and the sea
To the south
PALACE OF WHITEHALL (after 1529)
THE CITY OF WESTMINSTER
Abbey Palace
The Long Ditch
LAMBETH PALACE

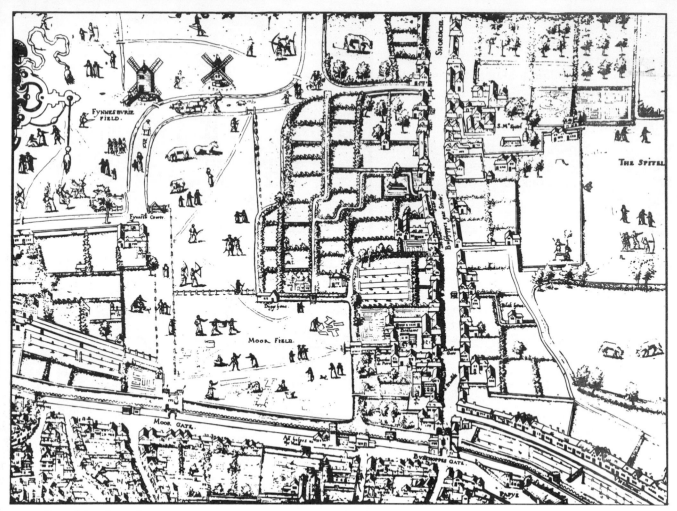

Part of the city walls

A great deal went on just outside the city walls. Washing was laid out to dry, apprentices practised their archery. Use the map on page 21 to find which part of the city wall this shows.

Because it was convenient to trade from London, merchants and their guilds became rich and powerful. They often lent or gave money to the King, and in return won many privileges, and complete control of the affairs of their city.

London was only a mile or so from the King's most important palace at Westminster, which was really a separate city itself. It was there that the King spent much of his time, the main law courts were held, the taxes brought in, and Parliament sat when the King chose to summon it. There too was the great abbey church where kings and queens were crowned, married and buried.

If you go through these reasons you will see that they all, in one way or another, ensured that London had

GOOD COMMUNICATIONS — SECURITY — WEALTH — IMPORTANCE

It was the centre of the kingdom's affairs. For anyone who wanted to go up in the world, London was the place to be. And so it continued to grow.

2 The Four Sorts

William Harrison, a clergyman in the reign of Elizabeth I, wrote a description of the people of England in his time; it was also true of people living a hundred years before his time, and continued to be true long after:

> We in England divide our people commonly into four sorts, as gentlemen, citizens or burgesses, yeomen, and . . . labourers.

The most important of the *First Sort* were the nobles with titles — dukes, earls, viscounts, barons. They owned a great deal of land, and dominated the area where their lands were. They had several great houses, often fortified, with many servants or retainers; some of these were armed, and they wore their lord's livery — a special kind of uniform. Nobles wore fine clothes: velvets and silks, often embroidered with gold and silver thread, furs, and soft leather. They owned fine horses, and enjoyed hunting and jousting. They attended the King's court; most were in his council, to give advice, and when Parliament was summoned, they sat in the House of Lords. If they were accused of a crime, they could only be tried by their equals; if they were condemned to death, they were allowed a swift execution by the axe, rather than the horrors of hanging, drawing and quartering, which common criminals suffered.

It is not difficult to see that the nobles were powerful people. They were 'next the King', Harrison says. And the lives of all the other 'sorts' depended on them.

'Gentlemen' also counted as the first sort, and were nearly as powerful. As far as they could, they lived like the nobles. A man was a gentlemen if he owned a big house and some land; if he could afford to wear rich and fashionable clothes; if he employed servants (for a gentleman did not work with his hands); if he sent his sons to school. The King depended on the First Sort to help him rule the country, even though there were only a small number of them, perhaps 5 per cent of the population:

Clothes were one of the best ways to tell to which 'sort' a person belonged. Which 'sorts' do you think are shown in these pictures, produced in the time of William Harrison?

> Citizens and burgesses have place next to gentlemen, who be those that are free within cities, and *are of some likely substance* to bear office in the same.

had enough money

This *Second Sort* were townspeople, merchants and master craftsmen like Degory Watur.

←14

The *Third Sort* were the yeomen, 'freemen born English'. Hugh Latimer, who rose to be a bishop, was the son of a yeoman. In a sermon to the King, he spoke of his father:

My father was a yeoman, and had no lands of his own, only he had a farm *of £3 or £4 a year* . . . and he tilled so much as kept by half a dozen men.

this was the rent he paid

He had walk for a hundred sheep, and my mother milked 30 *kine* . . . He kept me to school, else I had not been able to preach before the King's Majesty now. He *married my sister with £5*; so that he brought them (his children) up in godliness and fear of God. He kept hospitality for poor neighbours, and he gave . . . to the poor.

cows

he provided a dowry: see opposite page

Harrison then describes the *Fourth Sort:*

The Fourth and last sort of people in England are day labourers, poor *husbandmen* . . . and all *artificers* such as tailors, shoemakers, carpenters.

farmworkers; wage earners

The Fourth Sort, in town or country, were the large majority of the population — and most of them lived in the country.

■ Look at the picture on the cover of this book. The artist shows people of different 'sorts' at a wedding. How many different 'sorts' can you see?

Going up in the world

For people living in the twentieth century, it is difficult to understand that everyone accepted these divisions in society, and everyone believed it was right. It did not always mean however that people stayed in the 'sort' into which they were born. Those with drive and ability could rise in the world, and a man could fall, too, into a lower 'sort'.

One family who bettered themselves in the fifteenth century were the Pastons of Norfolk. We know a great deal more about them than other similar families, because many of the letters they wrote to each other have survived; these letters tell us much about their lives.

The rise of the Pastons began with Clement Paston. A neighbour described him as:

A good plain husbandman and lived on the land he had in Paston, and kept thereon a plough all times of the year . . . and he rode to the mill on bare horseback with his corn under him, and brought home *meal* . . . and drove his cart with corn to sell as a good husbandman should . . . Other *livelode* nor manors had he none . . . The said Clement had a son William, which he sent to school . . . and after that he learned the law; and there he begat much good . . . and afterwards made a justice . . . and a right cunning man in the law. And he purchased much land in Paston.

flour

way of earning a living

Going to school, then becoming a lawyer, set William on the upward path. Two other things helped him as well. He made a good marriage, which brought him more land; and he had an important friend locally, Sir John Fastolf. When Sir John died, he left William land, including Caister Castle. But the family also had problems. The two important nobles in the area were not always friendly; one of them, the Duke of Norfolk, actually besieged Caister for a time. But by the end of the century, the Pastons were one of the leading families in Norfolk. The head of the family, John, was sheriff of the county, and a friend of one of the King's leading councillors, the Earl of Oxford. The Pastons had travelled from the Fourth Sort to the First.

■ Make a list of the things which helped the Pastons to become a rich land-owning family. Put them in the order which you think most important, giving a reason why each helped.

In the first chapter, we dealt mainly with ordinary people, though we saw too, how some of the prosperous made their living. Now we shall look at some things which affected the lives of all four 'sorts', though often in different ways.

Marriage and the family

Marriage was an important step in people's lives, just as it is now. But marriages were very different, especially for women, who did not expect to lead independent lives as they can now. This first big step was arranged for them, by the two sets of parents. Women had to bring a dowry, or payment, with them; and whether the family was rich or poor, the two families would bargain hard before anything was settled.

A prosperous merchant and his wife by the Flemish artist, Jan Van Eyck

This picture was probably painted to celebrate their marriage. The detail is so carefully painted that the artist has even shown his own reflection in the mirror.

25

The cunning lawyer William Paston gained four manors by his marriage to his wife Agnes; but even an ordinary husbandman would hope to gain at least some cattle, or a few extra strips of ploughland, when he married. This could be a problem for a girl. If she was one of several daughters in a poor family, there might be no dowry for her. If she could not stay at home, she had few other choices. She might go into a convent as a nun, which suited some, but not all; or she might become a servant. Even a high-born unmarried woman usually became a sort of poor relation in the home of one of her married sisters.

So a girl seemed to have little choice of husband, though the stories of some of Shakespeare's plays show that people did expect love to come into it. In February 1477, Margery Brews wrote a Valentine to John Paston, whom she was hoping to marry. In it, she says there is only one thing she wants:

> a conclusion of the matter between my father and you . . . and if the matter take to no effect, then I should be much more sorry and full of heaviness.

She goes on to say that her father will pay no more than £100 and 50 marks, and that if John will be content with that, 'I would be the merriest maid on earth . . . good, true and loving Valentine'; for her father was worried that if he paid more, 'her sisters would fare the worse'. Finally, in spite of these problems, the families came to an agreement, and Margery and John were married a few months later, in the summer of 1477.

Another Margery in the Paston family managed to marry the man she loved in spite of bitter opposition from her parents. Unknown to them, she betrothed herself to Richard Calle, the bailiff. He looked after part of the family's lands, and was definitely not a good enough match for a Paston girl. In those days a formal promise to marry was binding. So when the betrothal was discovered, the storm broke, and the lovers were in trouble.

'This is a painful life we lead, I suppose they think we be not betrothed together,' wrote Richard to his Margery, and he begs her to stand up for herself, even if she had earlier denied their betrothal for fear:

> Though I tell them the truth they will not believe me as well as they will you, and therefore good lady, at the reverence of God, be plain to them and tell the truth.

Finally, the lovers won the support of the Bishop of Norwich, and the family grudgingly allowed them to marry. Perhaps the Pastons forgave the couple; Richard continued to work for them, and when Margery's mother died, she left £20 to their eldest child. Margery and Richard won through, but there must have been many who did not. However, arranged marriages often worked out happily, as the couple got to know each other. Margery's mother, Margaret, had no choice when she married John Paston; perhaps that is why she opposed her daughter's choice so bitterly. But the letters she wrote to her 'right worshipful husband' show the marriage worked well.

Once a woman was married, she was legally in the power of her husband; but in a prosperous family like the Pastons, Margaret had plenty of responsibility. She had to run a large household, and managed everything from lawsuits to local riots, when her husband was away from home.

If a woman was widowed, she might become independent. She could carry on her husband's business like the townswomen we saw in Chapter 1, or she could sometimes arrange another marriage herself, and, if she was rich, become even more prosperous.

But there is no doubt that it was a matter of luck as well as character. On the whole, women's lives were very limited. They had few opportunities; and needed a great deal of drive and energy if they wanted to be active outside the home. And inside it, they worked very hard indeed, whether in the town or the country. Work in the fields had to be fitted in with everything they did indoors. (Look at the picture of haymaking on page 10.)

A woman churning butter

Work in the dairy was one of women's many everyday tasks in the house.

Parents and children

> Reverence to thy parents dear, so duty doth thee bind
> Such children as virtue delight, be gentle, meek and kind
> Against thy parents multiply no words, but be demure

This is part of a sixteenth-century verse giving advice to children on how to behave towards their parents. The language may be old-fashioned, but the message is clear: obey your parents without question, and be seen and not heard. Children were strictly brought up, and whipping was a common punishment. One of the Italian visitors to London in about 1500 thought the English attitude to their children was very strange:

> The *want* of affection in the English is strongly shown towards their children — for after having kept them at home till they arrive at the age of 7 or 9 years at utmost, they put them out, both males and females, to hard service in the houses of other people, binding them generally for another 7 to 9 years. And these are called apprentices.

lack

He goes on to say that the rich do the same, sending their children to other rich households:

> They said they did it in order that their children might learn better manners . . . I believe they do it because they like to enjoy all their comforts themselves.

1 We know very little about this writer and his visit. For instance, he may not have travelled much outside London, and we do not know whom he met. If you were this visitor, what sort of people would you choose to meet, and what questions would you ask, in order to find out about the lives of English children in 1500?

2 What facts do you already know which support part of what this writer says? Do you think he may be right about the way English children were treated in general?

←14

A fifteenth-century schoolmaster — with his rod poised — and his pupils

It is difficult for us to discover what it was really like for children in the Early Modern Age, because we do not know much about their feelings. It is clear that compared with modern children their lives were hard, and people often expected them to behave like miniature adults. As for poorer children, they had to keep up with the adults too. They had to help on the farm or in the shop, and as soon as they were old enough, they worked for the whole day. They rarely went to school, unless they had a father like Hugh Latimer's or William Paston's.

Schools

There were more schools as the Early Modern Age progressed. Eton College had been founded in 1440 to provide free education, but boys had to pay for their keep. It soon became a school for the well-to-do. William, one of the Paston boys, went there in the 1470s, and this was a sign that the family had gone up in the world. In many towns grammar schools were started, like the one in Stratford-upon-Avon, which William Shakespeare attended. They were correctly named; the boys learnt a great deal of Latin and sometimes Greek grammar, and hours were very long.

Children learnt to read from a 'horn book' — a piece of wood protected by a layer of transparent horn. A cross reminded them of their religious duties, and the alphabet and the Lord's Prayer had to be learnt by heart.

A fifteenth-century grammar book

This had sentences in English and Latin, which had to be learnt by heart. Here are some of them:

> I shall begin my grammar on Monday.
> Would God we might go to play.
> I have no leisure to con [learn] my Latin.
> I have blotted my book.
> The children be staring about in the master's absence.
> Lend me the copy of thy Latin and I shall give it to thee again by and by.
> Thou stinkest.
> Wipe thy nose.
> My head is full of lice.

■ Whoever wrote these sentences was thinking of the things schoolchildren say when they think the teacher is not listening. Write a modern version of these sentences, that you might hear in your school.

Reading and writing

Children were usually taught to read and write at home before they went to school. First the alphabet was learnt; the next step was to learn the Lord's Prayer, or part of a chapter of the Bible. Once reading was mastered, then there was the task of learning to write. There were no pencils or coloured crayons. A quill pen made from a feather had to be used straight away, and the child had to learn to sharpen the end with a special knife — a penknife. There were punishments for ink blots. To make things more complicated, there were different kinds of writing for different jobs. When a man became a lawyer, for instance, he would have to learn a new 'hand'.

1 Make lists in two columns to show the differences in learning to read and write in the sixteenth and in the twentieth century. You may have to rely on your own memory for the twentieth century — think about the books and equipment you used.

2 Why did more people learn to read than to write in the Early Modern Age?

3 Describe and illustrate a scene in which a young child is being taught to read, and an older one (probably male) is trying to learn to write.

In spite of all the difficulties, more people learnt to read and even to write in the Early Modern Age. This was a very important change, which had begun to happen as the Early Modern Age dawned. For centuries before that, churchmen had been the only educated people; because of their skills they usually held the most important jobs in the kingdom. They still did, but others were now learning the same skills, and opportunities were widening.

Diet and disease

Both rich and poor have to eat, and both may become ill. Diet and disease are often linked, though there are of course other causes of disease as well.

Bread and pot-herbs

For ordinary people, the most usual meal was bread floating in a watery soup made of whatever vegetables were available. These were called pot-herbs and could be beans, peas, onions, herbs and plants from the hedgerows and woods, including nettles. They seldom ate meat; they might have 'white meat' (milk, butter, cheese and eggs) if they kept livestock or could buy from those who did. They drank ale which they brewed themselves; tea and coffee were still unknown. Their main food was a coarse grey bread, made from the rye or barley which they grew. Only the rich ate fine white loaves made from wheat flour. Most people depended on the corn harvest to live. When harvests were bad, famine was a real danger.

Probably one harvest in four or five was poor, and food was scarce the following winter. When that happened, the problem did not end when the warm weather returned. The next harvest depended on seed left from the crop grown the year before. In the depths of a cold winter, when everyone was hungry, the temptation to grind next year's seed into flour to make bread must have been very strong.

Evidence for bad harvests

Records of harvest yields were not kept as they are now. However, it is likely that there were, for instance, poor harvests from 1549 to 1556, for the following reasons:

1. Grain prices rose sharply everywhere. In 1549, they were 84 per cent higher than 1548. By 1556, they were 240 per cent higher.

2. The Government forbade the export of corn from 1546 to 1550, though why they did not continue to do so is not clear. Who would normally profit from such exports?

3. In 1556, the City Council of Worcester spent £133 buying rye 'for the relief of the poor within our city'.

4. Bakers often became unpopular. A baker in Norwich in 1551 was in trouble because of a violent argument in his shop about 'the great prices of grain and *victual* (food), the fall and loss of money'.

1 Explain in your own words why prices rise when there are shortages, and why this is linked with the rise in population (page 10).

2 Look at the lists of tradesmen on page 13 and decide which, as well as bakers, might become unpopular in times of shortage.

■ 'The Witch of Famine maketh men eat slovenly.' Thomas Dekker, a sixteenth-century writer, wrote this. What does 'slovenly' mean? Using the sentence as a headline, design an illustrated pamphlet giving advice on diet, and what to do in times of famine. How do you think people might have survived, if they lived near a forest, or by the sea?

In 1558, the Earl of Shrewsbury's household (probably about 150 people) ate in Christmas week:

3 quarters (38 kg) of wheat
441 gallons (1764 litres) of beer
12 sheep
10 capons (large chickens)
26 hens
6 geese
7 cygnets
1 turkey
118 rabbits
7 pigs

Food shortages lowered resistance to infection, and made it more likely that people would fall ill. Most people in the Early Modern Age were probably ill for about half the year. It does not take much imagination to realise the effect that must have had on everyone's lives.

Roast swan, oysters and sweet meats

It was of course different for the rich. Even in bad years, they probably did not go short of food. However, they seem to have been ill just as much as the poor, though probably for different reasons. It may have been because they ate too much of the wrong kind of food. The Italian writer of 1500 said of the rich:

> They delight in banquets and a variety of meat . . . with excessive abundance. They eat very frequently, at times more than is suitable, and are particularly fond of young swans, rabbits, deer, and sea birds. They often eat mutton and beef. They have all kinds of fish in plenty and great quantities of oysters.

A late sixteenth-century description of a banquet talks of:

A waxy, fatty, substance found in the intestines of sperm whales, with a strong scent. Now used in perfume.

> pies of carp's tongues, their pheasants drenched with *ambergris*, the carcase of three fat *wethers* [sheep] bruised for gravy to make sauce for a single peacock.

Between courses, people ate sweetmeats made of sugared pastry, often in fantastic designs.

1 Using the information above, and this picture, design an illustrated menu for a sixteenth-century banquet.

2 Plan a day's healthy diet according to modern ideas (without too much fat or sugar, and with enough fibre). List the ways in which a rich person's diet in the Early Modern Age was not healthy. Are there any reasons to think a poor person's diet was healthier?

A banquet being prepared in a great house

You can find out a great deal from this picture about what it was like to work in a sixteenth-century kitchen. How many live animals and birds can you see?

Plague and pestilence

Diet and food shortage had a good deal to do with disease, but there were many other reasons for illness. Both rich and poor lived in what we should consider very dirty conditions. People did not wash themselves or their clothes very often, and they took smells for granted. Towns, as we have seen, had problems in keeping streets and rivers free from filth; houses both in town and country were equally dirty. The Dutch scholar, Erasmus, who visited several well-to-do English friends in 1518, said:

> The floors are generally . . . covered with rushes that are now and then removed, but not so as to disturb the foundation, which sometimes remains for about twenty years, nursing a collection of spittle, vomits, excrements of dogs and humans, spilt beer and fishbones and other filth I need not mention.

Everyone in the Early Modern Age was in danger from many killer diseases. *Influenza*, or 'the ague', was much more dangerous then. The 'English sweat' was a very dangerous type as a late fifteenth-century chronicle shows:

> In the same year (1485) . . . a new kind of disease swept the whole country . . . A sudden deadly sweating attacked the body and at the same time head and stomach were in pain from the violence of the fever . . . scarce one in a hundred escaped death.

This dreaded disease mysteriously disappeared after a bad outbreak in 1551, when 'there were some dancing at court at nine o'clock that were dead by eleven'. But in 1557 a similar epidemic raged 'through the realm' and 'so many husbandmen . . . died, and were . . . sick, . . . in some places corn stood and shed on the ground for lack of workmen'.

Plague was a word used by people in the Early Modern Age for any serious epidemic, but it very often meant the terrible bubonic plague. Glands in the neck, armpits and groin swelled into black abscesses; there was a high fever, and the victim usually died within a few days. Everyone knew it was very catching; we still use the old phrase 'avoiding someone like the plague'. But no one in the Early Modern Age realised the cause of infection, which was the bacteria spread by the rat flea. In the dirty conditions in which everyone lived, rats thrived, especially the bolder black rat which preferred towns. Plague was a disease of rats. When the rat flea, which lived on black rats, fed on their infected blood, the bacteria blocked its oesophagus (food pipe) and it became very hungry. At the same time the sick rat usually died, so the starving flea looked elsewhere for food — and humans were usually the nearest. These infected fleas could survive for about six weeks in warm temperatures, in clothing, straw, thatch and plaster. So in warm summer weather, and in towns, where houses were mainly built of these materials, plague spread like wildfire. Fleas could travel too, in bales of cloth, grain or flour, so country people, living in similar houses, did not escape either.

Plague remedies

All kinds of treatments were tried, both to avoid and cure the plague.

Medicine One popular remedy, believed to be Edward IV's special potion, was used long after his reign.

> A potion of herbs including a handful of rue, marigolds, and sorrel, simmered and strained, and if it be bitter, put thereto a little sugar-candy, and this may be drunk oft-time; and if it be drunken before any purple (swelling) appear by the Grace of God there shall be no peril of death.

Prevention People believed, not surprisingly, that plague was carried through the air. So many remedies tried to deal with that.

Sometimes people carried bunches of herbs. In one London epidemic, the price of rosemary went up from 12 pence to 6 shillings. (An average daily wage was 5 pence.)

In the serious London epidemic of 1563, about a quarter of the city's population died. Householders were ordered to light bonfires in the streets 'to consume the corrupt airs'. Searchers — usually old women — carrying white sticks were sent to check on reports of people with plague. If they found the disease, a cross was painted on the door of the house and it was shut up for forty days. Each night, the corpses of those who had died were buried in plague pits on the outskirts of the city, six feet deep so that dogs would not dig them up.

At the same time, Queen Elizabeth I left London for Windsor. She ordered a gallows to be put up in the market place there to hang anyone coming from the capital. Any Windsor citizen who had already received goods from London before the Queen arrived was turned out of his or her house and told to go elsewhere.

Epidemics of plague occurred frequently in the Early Modern Age. This picture was on the cover of a pamphlet printed in London in a bad epidemic in 1625. Out of the cloud at the top, God's judgement descends like lightning on the doomed city. The citizens who stay die: you can find several in the picture. Others try to leave, saying 'We fly'. But what does the skeleton 'Death' say to them? In any case, soldiers with drawn swords bar their escape, telling them to 'Keep out', so that the disease will not spread. It is easy to understand how frightened people must have been of diseases like the plague. Pictures like this cannot have been much comfort.

1 Make a list of the real causes of bubonic plague. Use what you already know about living conditions, especially in towns (pages 11, 12, 20, 31), and trade movement (pages 13, 19) which might carry the epidemic.

2 Write an illustrated pamphlet dated 1563, giving advice to London citizens on how to deal with the plague epidemic. You might make it more comforting than the one on this page.

The Spotted Fever was probably typhus, and so was 'camp fever', which often killed more soldiers in garrison towns and camps than battles ever did. Rats spread this disease too, because they carried infected lice, which also infected humans. Rich and poor people wore layers of heavy clothes which were seldom washed, and typhus epidemics usually happened in winter when people huddled together for warmth — and caught each other's lice.

Griping in the guts was the name used for dysentery, and other gastric infections, all caused by dirty conditions.

Smallpox was on the increase in the sixteenth century. Elizabeth I caught it; she survived and may have escaped the terrible scarring it often caused, but many victims were not so lucky.

There were many other killer diseases. Some, like measles and scarlet fever, were far more dangerous than they are now. However, leprosy was dying out. Lepers had long been treated as outcasts. As leprosy was infectious they carried a bell, so that everyone could hear them coming, and avoid them. They were forced to keep away from towns and this treatment was effective, though cruel. By the sixteenth century, a former lazar (leper) house in St Giles, Holborn, had provided shelter for ordinary poor people for more than a century.

Mothers and children

Mothers, babies, and young children were specially at risk from all kinds of infection. Children were particularly likely to catch chest infections. Even rich people lived in cold draughty houses, and the poor were much worse off. Look at this scene of a mother being cared for just after the birth of her baby, with the kitchen in the background, and the family celebrating around her. How many things can you see which put her and her baby at risk? Probably half the children born in each family died before they were five, and mothers often died during, or after, childbirth.

Doctors and cures

Bishop Hugh Latimer, the son of a ploughman, never forgot what it was like to be poor. He said, 'Physic (medicine) is a remedy only for rich folks and not for poor: the poor man is not able to wage (pay) the physician'.

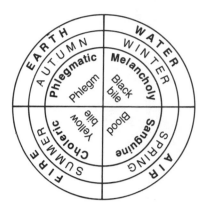

However, being able to pay for a doctor did not often help a sick person, for the doctors did not understand the causes of disease. No one knew about bacteria or viruses, or the way in which the human body works. It was difficult to find out, too, because for centuries people believed dissection (cutting up) of the body was wrong. Even the skilful Arab doctors, who were in many ways more advanced than the Europeans, believed it was wrong to dissect a human body.

Doctors in the West based their medical treatment on the beliefs of the Ancient Greeks, who thought the human body was made up of four 'humours' or characteristics: sanguine, choleric, melancholy, and phlegmatic.

Copy the diagram giving each section a suitable colour. Look up the names of the four humours in the dictionary, and then add to your diagram four illustrations to show how a sanguine, choleric, melancholy, and phlegmatic person looks and behaves. As you do this, try to understand why people without modern medical knowledge would find these ideas sensible.

In a sick person, it was believed, these humours became unbalanced. There was too much of one of the liquids, so many cures depended on 'purging'; that meant getting rid of the excess, which was causing the disease. This was done in two ways:

Blood-letting (shown in the picture on the left) was done either by 'cupping' (drawing off blood), or by using leeches (worms which sucked blood). Doctors used blood-letting for all sorts of ills, including wounds, when blood had already been lost.

Purges were herbal potions, like Edward IV's remedy for plague; they caused diarrhoea and vomiting. In a very sick patient, this must often have hindered rather than helped a cure.

Astrology was also used. The best places to bleed a patient were linked to the signs of the zodiac. All sorts of other kinds of superstition were common; for instance, scrofula, or the King's Evil, (a form of tuberculosis of the glands) was treated by the touch of the reigning monarch — if the patient had the opportunity for such exalted treatment. Most English monarchs held ceremonies to 'touch for the King's Evil'. Since a patient's attitude to illness plays an important part in recovery, we should not be too superior about the effect of such cures.

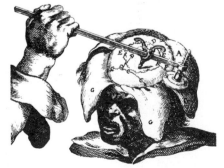

Surgery must have been a horrifying experience before anaesthetics were discovered; and infection very often set in afterwards. The picture on the left shows 'trepanning' — drilling a hole in the skull, used to try to relieve headaches, or to cure mental illness.

There were three different kinds of doctors in the Early Modern Age:

Physicians (see the picture on the right) For centuries, these had been churchmen; but in 1518 the Royal College of Physicians was founded, and a separate profession began. Good physicians knew Latin, Greek, some Arabic, Logic, Rhetoric, Geometry, Astronomy and Philosophy. They were the top of the medical profession, and very expensive.

Apothecaries (Potycaries) (see the picture below) were originally grocers, who sold herbs and spices. They still usually kept a shop and belonged to a guild. As well as providing purges and potions, they would treat patients, and diagnose disease.

Surgeons were usually barbers as well, and were the lowest rank in the profession. They too had their own guild and a shop. Sometimes, as in the picture below, surgeons were soldiers. He is removing an arrow-head from a very calm patient. As the battle still goes on in the background, he will soon have more work. Surgeons needed 'a good eye, and a steadfast hand ... (to) be wise, gentle, sober and not drunken'.

There were very few hospitals, and these were in London and the larger towns. Most sick people were therefore looked after at home, and women in both rich and poor houses were often skilled in nursing. In fact, good nursing was probably more effective than doctors' cures, since the body's natural powers of recovery had more chance to operate.

1 Make a list of the different jobs done by doctors and others in modern hospitals, health centres and chemists' shops. Which of them are closest to the three groups above?

2 Why are surgeons certainly not the lowest rank of doctor today?

3 People *did* recover from illness and injury in the Early Modern Age. The population was increasing, and some people lived to a great age (Degory Watur to 97; Elizabeth I to 70). Make a list of things which may have helped them to avoid or recover from disease.

Attitudes and beliefs

Life was hard for most people in the Early Modern Age — much harder in many ways than it is now. But it would be a mistake to think that everyone was gloomy and depressed. After all, they could not know how different life would be five hundred years later. We have been making some comparisons with our lives now, but it is also important to understand how people looked at life then. One big difference is that we know a great deal about what is going on in the rest of the world through television, radio and the press. For most people in the Early Modern Age, knowledge of the outside world was much more limited, so they did not know what they might be missing.

The skeleton, Death, snatches a young child from his terrified parents. The child looks surprisingly plump; nevertheless, what has the artist done to show that this was a very poor family?

Death was present in everyday life in a way that it is not nowadays, for there were few hospitals, and the child death rate was much higher. What else in the picture is a reminder that time is running out? Why did artists often put these reminders in their pictures?

So far we have not mentioned the Church, although it was the centre of people's lives in all kinds of ways, as we shall see later. For the moment, it is enough to remember that no one was likely to go out of doors without seeing a church. Count how many churches you can see in the pictures of Shrewsbury and London on pages 11, 21 and 22. In a village, in about 1500, the church was still often the only stone building apart from the nearest gentleman's house. It was the only place apart from the alehouse where the villagers met together when they were not working, and the only place too, where they would see pictures and bright colours.

The church's year followed the seasons, and therefore the work of the villagers. The great Christian festivals took place at times when long ago people celebrated the old pagan feasts. The word Easter comes from 'Eostre', the ancient celebration at seed-time, when the world seemed to spring back to life after the winter. The crops were blessed at Rogationtide, as they began to grow, and when the harvest was gathered in there were 'church ales', feasts in the churchyard, or nearby, to celebrate. Wells, which provided essential water supplies, were 'dressed' or decorated.

'Touching wood' originally meant touching the cross on which Christ was crucified; many churches all over Europe claimed to have a piece of the true cross. Relics of saints' bones, straw from Christ's manger, and angels' feathers could hardly have been genuine, but they played a part in making people feel they could control the dangers around them. Officially, the Church was against magic, but in an age when so many ordinary people could not read, it was hard to make a distinction between belief and magic.

Witches and cunning men (wizards) were sometimes feared as an evil influence, but they could help people too, and often used the Church in their own way. A Suffolk witch in 1499 told her clients to give their horses holy bread from the church, so that no one would steal them.

So both religion and magic were important parts of people's lives at the beginning of the Early Modern Age, and continued to be so. It is worth thinking about how much superstition still plays a part in our modern lives.

Bad witches and cunning men were believed to meet the Devil in person, as this picture shows. They were also supposed to have a 'familiar' — a cat, a toad, a mouse or even a fly — which was their link with the Devil. They had a Devil's mark on them too, which could be a wart or a mole. It was not very difficult to find such 'evidence' to prove an unpopular old woman or man was in league with the Devil.

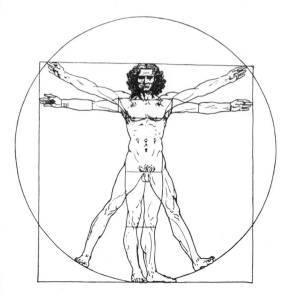

A drawing of the human figure by Leonardo da Vinci, 1492

Leonardo da Vinci (1452–1519), artist, inventor, scholar, was one of the greatest figures of the Renaissance. He was born near Florence, and spent part of his working life there.

3 New ideas and new worlds

The shape you choose

Thus spake the Lord . . . you will determine your nature according to your own free will to which I have entrusted you. I have put you into the world so that from there you can better see all that is in the world . . . you can carve yourself into the shape you choose.

This is how a fifteenth-century Italian writer imagined that God spoke to Adam, the first man. Educated men and women were beginning to see life as an exciting voyage of discovery about themselves and the world around them. It was an Italian too who called this voyage of discovery 'The Renaissance'.

The word means 'rebirth'. It is used now to describe the great surge of new ideas, and new ways of looking at the world, which began to happen in Europe as the Early Modern Age dawned. In the Middle Ages, people looked to the Church as the guardian of all knowledge which 'carved the shape of man'. It still remained an important part of people's lives, but scholars also looked further back to the Ancient Greeks and Romans, who seemed to have the key to great new discoveries. The study of their writings and works of art was like a great adventure; learning Greek was as new, exciting and fashionable as computer learning is now. This 'New Learning' helped to bring great changes; above all, the feeling that people were individuals who carved themselves into the shape they chose.

Europe was becoming a world of change. In this chapter we shall look at some of those changes; we can then see how they affected Britain.

Italy, the magnet

In Britain, and the rest of Europe, people looked to Italy as the centre of the New Learning. If educated people travelled, Italy drew them; if traders wanted luxury goods, they went to Italy. The map on the next page shows why. It is also important to understand that in the Early Modern Age, Italy was not a united country. The Pope ruled the land round Rome; cities such as Venice, Milan, and Florence were independent states.

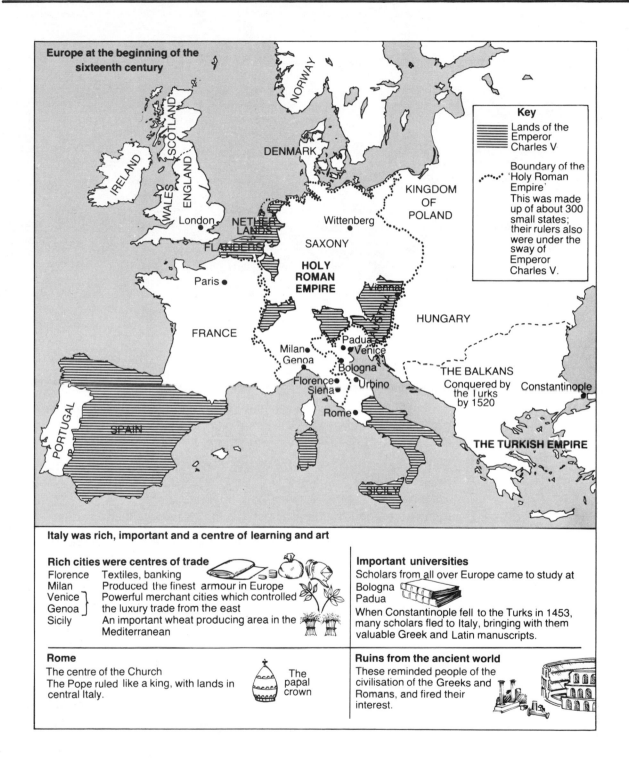

Europe at the beginning of the sixteenth century

Key
- Lands of the Emperor Charles V
- Boundary of the 'Holy Roman Empire'. This was made up of about 300 small states; their rulers also were under the sway of Emperor Charles V.

THE BALKANS
Conquered by the Turks by 1520

THE TURKISH EMPIRE

Italy was rich, important and a centre of learning and art

Rich cities were centres of trade

Florence	Textiles, banking
Milan	Produced the finest armour in Europe
Venice	Powerful merchant cities which controlled
Genoa	the luxury trade from the east
Sicily	An important wheat producing area in the Mediterranean

Important universities

Scholars from all over Europe came to study at
Bologna
Padua
When Constantinople fell to the Turks in 1453, many scholars fled to Italy, bringing with them valuable Greek and Latin manuscripts.

Rome

The centre of the Church
The Pope ruled like a king, with lands in central Italy.

The papal crown

Ruins from the ancient world

These reminded people of the civilisation of the Greeks and Romans, and fired their interest.

A view of fifteenth-century Florence

Florence in the fifteenth century was one of the most famous and beautiful of the powerful Italian cities. It was larger than London, with a population of about 100,000. In this picture, find: the Cathedral (*Duomo* in Italian) with its great dome; the River Arno with its three bridges (One of these still survives today, and has luxury shops on it as it did then.); the fortified walls and gates to defend the city.

Many citizens built towers on their houses for defence, as rivalry between powerful families and their supporters often led to outbreaks of violence in the streets. But houses were built of stone, streets were well paved; and there were public baths. Florence was a cleaner city than London.

The River Arno linked Florence to her port of Pisa, which she had recently conquered. The city's riches came mainly from trade in luxury fabrics: damasks, brocades and velvets. Rich merchants lent money on which they charged interest, and so Florence became a centre of banking too.

Wealthy families acted as patrons to scholars and artists, providing them with work and a living — so Florence became a centre of learning and the arts.

The English came to Florence mainly to trade English wool and cloth for luxury goods. There was often a well-paid job to be had fighting for the city in its constant wars with neighbours; mercenary soldiers from all over Europe were employed. Almost a century before, Sir John Hawkwood became such a successful commander in Florence's army that there is a memorial portrait of him in the Duomo.

Painting moves forward

In Renaissance Italy, artists began to find different ways to paint the world around them. The two paintings on this page try to show something of these changes; this is a huge and exciting subject to explore further. Both paintings are of the same subject, the Virgin Mary and the Christ child. Religious pictures had always been popular (partly because artists often worked for churchmen) and this did not change, though artists also began to paint more varied subjects, such as landscapes and portraits — and often brought them into their religious pictures too.

On the right is the *Rucellai Madonna* painted by Duccio, in about 1258 — the very early dawn of the Renaissance. The Virgin's robe is deep ultramarine blue, which was the most expensive paint, and therefore used by artists to honour Christ's mother. The folds of material are edged in gold. Duccio is not interested in making Mary or her baby look like solid, living people. The picture is a richly coloured, flat pattern of flowing lines. (Look at the curving border of Mary's cloak). The mother and baby are distant and remote. The picture was painted to go above the altar of a great church — for people to gaze at in wonder and awe.

By the fifteenth century, artists had become interested in creating the effect of space and distance in a picture.

Three of the great artists of the 'High Renaissance' were Raphael (1483—1520), Michelangelo (1475—1564), and Leonardo da Vinci (1452—1519); see page 38. In Leonardo's *Virgin of the Rocks*, painted about 1506, he skilfully uses light and shade to take you far into his picture. The Virgin still wears blue, and her halo is gold. The folds of her robe, and her out-stretched hands, reach to the Christ child and the young John the Baptist, as well as the angel watching over them. The figures are solid and realistic; they touch and look at each other. Christ is a chubby baby, yet there is something wise and special about him. Leonardo has used his knowledge of rock formations to create a distant and mysterious landscape background.

■ Find out how fifteenth- and sixteenth-century artists created space in their pictures. In the National Gallery, London, pictures by Masaccio, Uccello and Piero della Francesco are useful. (The *Virgin of the Rocks* is there too.) Collect Christmas cards and postcards of the Virgin and Child, to make a class picture gallery, putting them in the right date order. Find fifteenth-century examples of other subjects too, to add to the display.

Europe discovers the world

The goal

Trade was not limited only to Europe. For Europeans, the East was fascinating and mysterious, and its luxuries were highly prized. Spices such as pepper, ginger, mace and cinnamon were in great demand. Strongly flavoured food was popular (remember the ambergris, page 30). There was a good reason for this. Meat was often tainted, or salted or dried, which made it tough and tasteless. Fine silks and cottons, and delicately coloured porcelain were quite unlike anything produced in Europe. Though not much gold seemed to come out of the East, everyone was sure it was there; and by the end of the fifteenth century there was not enough gold left in Europe to satisfy the demand for high value coins, and beautiful objects to grace rich people's houses.

So trade with the East was very profitable, because it dealt in rare and expensive goods. The two great Italian trading ports of Venice and Genoa were rich and powerful because they made great profits from bringing these goods into Europe, from centres in the Eastern Mediterranean and the Black Sea. There, the Italians traded with Arab merchants whose camel trains had travelled the long overland routes from India and China.

Other Europeans wanted a share in this trade, but they did not want to risk a quarrel with Venice and Genoa. There was also a threat to the old trade routes. The Moslem Turks were advancing westwards and threatening Christian Europe. The overland routes lay through Turkish territory, and Turkish galleys were causing trouble in the Eastern Mediterranean. How long would the old routes stay open?

The solution lay in a new route to the East, which would have to go through unknown seas. The new route, people believed, would bring untold riches to the explorers. Also, heathen souls could be won for Christ. The Church looked kindly on the search; after all, was there not the legend of a mighty Christian kingdom in Africa, full of riches, and ruled over by a priest-King, Prester John? And Christ's disciple Thomas might have reached India, so Christians might be there as well to welcome European explorers.

Cinnamon (on the left) and cloves, two of the highly prized spices from the East

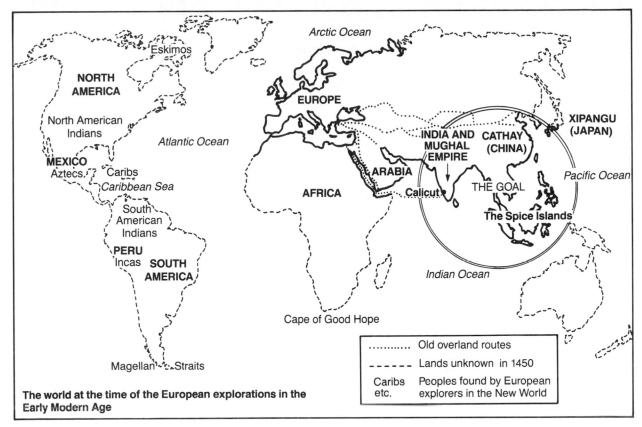

The world at the time of the European explorations in the Early Modern Age

....	Old overland routes
- - - - -	Lands unknown in 1450
Caribs etc.	Peoples found by European explorers in the New World

Facts and myths

So what was the East like, and how could it be reached? Europeans had plenty of ideas about Cathay (China). The thirteenth-century traveller, Marco Polo, had actually been there, and had written about its fabulous riches; and they knew of an equally strange and fabulous area, India, or the Indies, although they had little idea *where* it was. They were sure about the luxury goods they would find there, including perhaps a mountain of gold; and about the strange and probably dangerous monsters they would meet, as this picture shows. The journey would be full of unknown dangers too. Perhaps in the hottest climates, the seas boiled; or were solid with weeds which could trap a ship for ever. And monsters were not only on land. Most educated people were fairly sure the world was like a round ball — the Ancient Greeks had realised it long ago — but that did not make the journey seem safer.

It is not difficult in our age of space exploration to understand how Europeans felt about these frightening, unknown dangers, and why they were prepared to take such risks all the same. But it is easy to forget another puzzle about this great change which was about to begin in the mid-fifteenth century. Why was it the Europeans who set out on these journeys of exploration? Why did the skilful and civilised peoples of the East not discover the West?

The monster below, apparently found in Asia and called a 'sciapod', is an illustration in a European book of travellers' tales written in the fourteenth century.

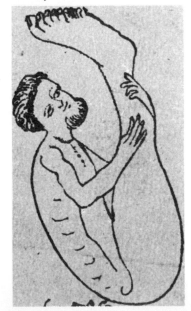

The answer is fairly simple. People in the East, especially the Chinese and Arabs, who had met Europeans, were not impressed. They found the Europeans dirty and uncouth, and did not believe what they were told about the civilisation of the West. While Europeans wanted to buy luxuries from the East, there was nothing which the Easterners wanted which they did not already obtain through trade. Also, their beliefs and culture discouraged adventurous travel. For Hindus in India, there were penalties for those who crossed the seas; and a century later in 1636, the Japanese were forbidden to travel abroad on pain of death. The ships used in the East were not suited to long sea voyages, and this may have had an influence; but people usually overcome such practical difficulties, if they really want to do so. The Europeans did exactly that.

Tools for the journey: Problems and some solutions

Finding the way Once a ship sailed out into an unknown sea, familiar landmarks disappeared. So, for centuries European sailors never ventured far out of sight of land. In the open sea, it was vitally important to be able to navigate; maps, as we understand them, did not exist. Sailors used 'dead reckoning'. That meant a compass told them the direction in which they were going, and a logline enabled them to make a rough calculation of their speed. A logline was a piece of wood with a rope attached. On the rope were knots at regular intervals. When the piece of wood was thrown overboard, the rope unwound as the ship sailed on. By counting the knots, they could roughly calculate their speed. 'Knots' are still used today at sea to mean nautical miles per hour. As a further check, a cross-staff or quadrant was used to measure the position of the Pole and other stars, in relation to the horizon.

Ships The explorers used ships called *caravels*, which probably looked like the one on this page. The big square sails caught the wind well, so the ship could travel at a fair speed. The triangular lateen sail at the back made it easy to 'tack' (in a zig-zag direction) when sailing into the wind. Caravels were very small compared to modern ships but they were deep enough in the water not to capsize easily. They were also large enough to take the crew needed to deal with the complicated rigging, the necessary stores, and guns, which could be fired through 'ports' (holes) cut into the high sides.

A healthy crew this was a problem which the early explorers did not solve, though some were luckier than others. Crews had to face a good deal. Conditions below decks were cramped, dark, and dirty; often the sleeping space was not more than a metre high. Rats and lice flourished. In bad weather, water seeped in through the ship's planks, and there was no escape to the open deck. And in bad weather too the work was hardest and most dangerous — think of climbing the rigging to adjust the sails in a violent storm. In fine weather there could be a different problem. When the wind dropped, and there was nothing to do or see in a flat,

A model which shows what Columbus's caravel, the 'Santa Maria', may have looked like

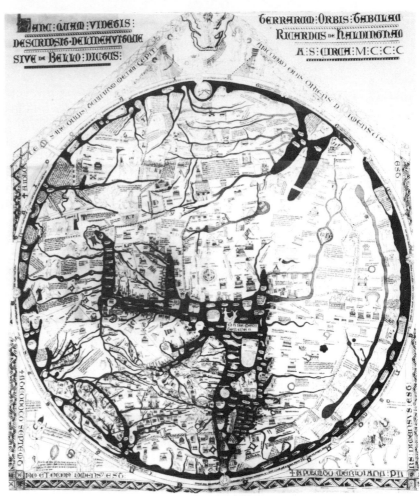

Maps as we know them did not exist. This thirteenth-century one, still in Hereford Cathedral, is very different from a modern one, as the key shows. Jerusalem was put in the centre. How much is imaginary? What do you think of the artist's ideas of Europe?

calm sea, the crew soon became bored. Fire was a constant risk in wooden ships with seams which were painted with tar to keep them watertight. (You can probably think of other inflammable materials on board.) Diet became worse as the journey went on.

Hot food was cooked on a fire in a box of sand, when weather permitted. Water stored in barrels soon went foul, and wine turned sour. Food did not survive much better: the hard 'ship's biscuits', everyone's staple diet, were soon full of weevils. In unknown seas, bordering lands full of possibly hostile people, it was difficult and dangerous to re-stock with food and water.

This is what the explorer Magellan took with him when he set out with 280 men:

9,700 kg of biscuits
258 kg of salt beef
238 dozen dried fish
200 barrels of sardines
508 kg of cheese
770 kg of fish
216 kg of oil

Also sacks of beans, peas, lentils, flour, honey, onions, figs and salt, as well as 2310 kg of gunpowder.

■ Make a list of dangers and diseases facing sailors. What disease were they also likely to get because of their diet?

←31

The cost of the voyage An explorer had to find a good deal of money before he could set out. He needed several ships, and stores and equipment; the crew also had to be paid enough to persuade them to risk the journey. Of course the explorer hoped he would find untold riches, far greater than the cost of the voyage; but he had to convince a powerful patron that the risk was worth taking.

Spices, gold and Christians

The story of the discovery of the rest of the world by Europeans is a long and fascinating one, and there is a great deal to find out about it. The following paragraphs tell of some of the best-known discoveries and milestones in exploration; each voyage provided a piece of the jigsaw which finally fitted together, and gave us the knowledge we have today of the world we live in.

The story began in two European countries with an Atlantic coastline — Portugal and Spain. They found two different pieces of the jigsaw.

The route round Africa

Encouraged and trained by Prince Henry the Navigator, Portuguese explorers began to inch their way southwards along the coast of Africa. They were trying to find the way round to the East that they were sure must be there. The vast size of the African continent explains why it took them so long to find they were right. Finally, *Bartholomew Diaz* reached what came to be called the Cape of Good Hope in 1487. *Vasco Da Gama* in 1497 completed the journey, and with help from Arab sailors, reached Calicut in India. The Portuguese now controlled this route to the East.

Sailors in Arab dhows had been crossing the Indian Ocean for seven centuries before the Portuguese arrived. They used the monsoon winds to travel from Arabia to the east coast of Africa, and to India.

The route westwards

If the world was round, the quickest route could lie to the West. In 1492 *Christopher Columbus* persuaded Queen Isabella of Spain to pay for his expedition. He landed on what he called the 'West Indies', since he was sure he had reached the goal and that Cathay was nearby. In fact, he found the islands of the Caribbean, though his name has stuck. Although he never realised it, his voyages opened up a 'New World' for Spain, and later for other Europeans. The Spanish conquest of the ancient Aztec and Inca civilisations of Mexico and Peru followed, as explorers realised they had discovered a new continent rich in gold.

The Pope's line

In 1494, the Pope, in order to prevent war, drew an imaginary line on the world map that Spain and Portugal were beginning to piece together. It ran from the North to the South Pole through what we now call Brazil, and divided 'the World' between them.

It took no account of other European countries who might enter the race. For the peoples of the East, it made no sense at all. Most of them had never heard of the Pope, or his line. It did however influence the way in which European languages spread. In what South American country is Portuguese spoken?

The round world

Ferdinand Magellan set sail from Spain in 1519 to prove the world was round. The voyage took three months to reach the southern tip of the New World; then 38 days in the dangerous 'Magellan Straits'; and three months in the empty reaches of the Pacific until he reached the Spice Islands. There Magellan was killed in a fight. One ship, the Victoria, completed the journey round the world in 1082 days.

North-west or North-east?

England and the Netherlands came late into the race, and tried to find northerly routes to the East to avoid the hostility of Portugal and Spain. *John* and *Sebastian Cabot*, for England, sailed in 1497 and 1509 to the northern coasts of North America, and reached 'New Found Land'.

Martin Frobisher in 1576, and *Henry Hudson* (1610) were two of several English explorers who also tried to find this North-west Passage to the East through the icebergs and pack ice of these northern seas. They failed; but their voyages helped to open up what became Canada to Europeans.

Hugh Willoughby and *Richard Chancellor* (1553—4) tried to find a way to the East through the cold seas north of Norway and Russia. Willoughby died trapped in the ice; Chancellor made his way to the coast of Russia, and opened up trade in Moscow.

Latecomers to the East

No one found a North-west or a North-east Passage. But both the British and the Dutch finally challenged Spain and Portugal, and set up their own trade in the New World and the East. France too entered the contest. The last chapter in this book will tell you something of that.

After the great discoveries, Europe was never the same place again. Countries with an Atlantic coastline, such as Britain, were no longer on the edge of the world. Now they were the best placed of the European nations to gain from the explorations. In time, trade began to change. Luxuries such as sugar and cotton became more common; new goods, such as tea, coffee, tobacco and potatoes appeared. For Europe, there were many new opportunities. For the peoples of the East and the New World, it was rather different.

An invention which changed the world

Seven hundred years before the Early Modern Age, the Chinese invented printing. First they used blocks of wood or stone with writing carved on them; they inked the blocks and pressed them on to paper. Later people used these blocks to make the first playing cards, which reached Europe in the late fourteenth century. Playing cards today still have a medieval look to them, because we use the pictures designed by those first European block printers.

If you have done block-printing with potatoes or lino-cuts, you will understand that this is a clumsy way to print a whole book. The Chinese solved this problem by inventing movable letters; these could be fitted into a frame, and altered when necessary. Until quite recently, mechanised printing presses still worked on this basic principle.

Hand-written books were so valuable that they were kept chained to the shelves, as they are in this library in Hereford Cathedral.

However, this invention was slow to reach Europe. Beautiful books were produced there, painstakingly written and illuminated (coloured) by hand by patient monks. The books were usually written on vellum. A book of 200 pages needed the skins of a hundred sheep, which then had to be stretched and polished to make a smooth, shiny surface. So books were both expensive and rare.

Europeans had learnt, probably from Arab traders, about other Chinese inventions like the compass and gunpowder, and adopted them. Marco Polo saw printed paper money on his travels in China. Yet it took a long time for Europeans to see how important and useful printing was.

1 Why did the following two facts probably delay the spread of printing in Europe?

a) Arabs did not approve of printing, because they believed their holy book, the Qu'ran (Koran), should be written as beautifully as possible by hand.

b) Anyone who decided to start a printing press needed 'capital' — money to buy machinery and paper, and to pay workers' wages. They had to be sure they could make a living from printing.

2 Why did the following two facts help to overcome the problem of capital?

a) By the mid-fifteenth century, another much earlier Chinese invention had reached Europe: the skill of making paper cheaply from bark, vegetable fibres and rags. Paper mills began to do good business.

b) More people were learning to read and write, so more books were needed.

In Mainz, in Germany, around 1450, a goldsmith called Gutenberg set up the first European printing press. He had experimented for a long time to find a suitable metal to make the movable type; probably he used the traditional design of a wine-press to enable the type in its frame to be pressed hard on the page. Other businessmen quickly followed him. William Caxton, a successful London mercer who had travelled much in the Netherlands and Germany, learnt his skills from these printers; he set up the first English printing press, in Westminster, in 1476. James IV of Scotland gave two Edinburgh citizens permission to set up a press there in 1508.

William Caxton's trade mark

The spread of printing

These places, and the date beside them, show where early printing presses were set up:

Mainz, about 1450; Cologne, 1464; Basel, 1466; Rome, 1467; Venice, 1469; Paris, Utrecht, Nuremberg, 1470; Milan, Naples, Florence, 1471; Augsberg, 1472; Lyons, Valencia, Budapest, 1473; Cracow, Bruges 1474; Lübeck, Breslau, 1475; Westminster, Rostock, 1476; Edinburgh, 1508.

In 1500, 20 million printed books probably existed. By 1600, it was probably 200 million. In the modern world, the printed word is everywhere.

1 In an atlas, find the modern countries where most of these places are. In which two countries were most of the early presses? Can you think of reasons for this?

2 How did Gutenberg and Caxton make their living before they became printers? Why did the first printers need to be fairly rich men?

3 How many times, and for what reasons, have you read printed words today? What difference would it make to your life if you lived in a world without printing, with only a few rare and expensive books available?

4 Write down as many reasons as you can why the invention of printing was so important.

An early printing press

Find in this picture: workers checking the metal type; a man covering the type with ink (it is now ready in its frame to go into the press); a man removing a page from the frame; piles of blank paper waiting to be used, and pages which have now been printed.

Change in the Church

1515 was an important year in the quiet little town of Louth in Lincolnshire. For fourteen years the citizens had watched a new steeple being built on their parish church. It had cost them £305 — perhaps £100,000 in modern money. Now at last it was almost finished. It soared into the sky, nearly 100 metres high, and they were delighted with it. Finally, the weathercock was put in place, right at the top:

> There being Will Ayleby, the parish priest, with many of his brother priests there present, hallowing the said weathercock, and the stone it stands upon . . . and then the said priests singing . . . with organs; and then the churchwardens ring all the bells, and caused all the people there to have bread and ale, and all to the loving of God, our Lady, and all saints.

The new steeple meant a great deal to the people of Louth. The parish church was part of everyone's lives; and it was not just in Louth that local people took trouble and spent money to beautify a building they cared about. That building was part of one world-wide Church, with its centre in Rome. Anything which happened to that Church, whether in Britain or the rest of 'Christendom', made a difference to ordinary people as well as to popes, bishops, kings, queens and nobles.

The beautiful steeple, which the citizens of Louth built in the sixteenth century, still stands today.

The Last Judgment

A painting in the parish church of Chaldon, Surrey

When people went to church, they very often saw a picture like this. The 'Last Judgment' was at the heart of the Church's teaching. An angel weighs the souls of the dead. Those who have lived good lives begin to climb the ladder to endless joy in Heaven, where Christ awaits them. But the Devil grabs the sinners and they descend to terrible tortures in Hell. The damned are there for ever; but more ordinary sinners have to endure a time in Purgatory, a place like Hell, where they must suffer and be cleansed of the sins they have committed. The Church offered hope for sinners in Purgatory. If they repented of their sins in this life, they would spend a shorter time there, and then would go to Heaven. After they were dead, the prayers of those on earth could help them too. So anyone who could afford it, left money to pay a priest to say prayers for them, and sometimes built a church or chapel especially for that purpose. Few people forgot the terrible prospect of Hell.

Problems in the Church

There are always problems when an organisation becomes rich and powerful. Over the centuries, this had happened to the Church. At the beginning of the Early Modern Age, many people were seriously worried.

The Pope, the head of the whole Church, lived in splendour in Rome. People looked on him as God's representative on earth. This had gradually given him a great deal of worldly power. He ruled like a king over rich lands in Italy, going to war, and making deals with other rulers.

This is a description of Pope Alexander VI (1492—1503). He belonged to the ambitious and unpopular Borgia family, and helped to build up their power in central Italy. So he was a man who made enemies:

> He was a man of the utmost power, and of great judgement and spirit . . . But there was in him . . . all vices of flesh and spirit . . . There was in him no religion . . . no care for justice, since in his day, Rome was like a den of thieves and murderers; his ambition was boundless.

Another account, *not* written by an eye-witness, describes his death:

> Seven devils were in the room . . . and when he was dead, his blood began to boil, and his mouth began to foam . . . his corpse swelled to such a size that it lost the very shape of a human body.

Not all pictures in church were frightening. Many, like the one above of St Christopher, who protected travellers, comforted and consoled. All the pictures provided colour and interest for people who, unlike us, hardly ever saw pictures except in church.

1 Some people admired this Pope. What can you find in the first account which shows that the writer cannot help admiring him a little?

2 Why do you think the second account was written? What does it tell you about Alexander's reputation?

Popes, like other people, were a mixture of good and bad; but it is true that at this time they seemed to have forgotten that the Son of God whom they worshipped had lived on earth as a carpenter; and had taught that it was peacemakers and the poor who were especially blessed.

Pope Julius II (1503—13)

The artist Raphael admired this Pope, and painted him as an old man, thinking back, perhaps, over his life. Others did not think as well of him. The scholar Erasmus condemned him for riding off to war in full armour; the artist Michelangelo quarrelled with him over payment for 42 statues the Pope had ordered for his very grand tomb. Some of these are still in Florence today, unfinished, but very impressive.

What is your impression of this Pope?

High-ranking churchmen also had great wealth and power. The most important churchmen were cardinals, many of whom lived in Rome and had the task of electing the Pope; and bishops, who helped the Pope to rule the Church. Such powerful positions could be bought and sold. A three-year-old French boy was made Bishop of Metz, and by the time he was middle-aged, he held eleven other bishoprics and nine abbeys. He could hardly be a good church leader in so many places, but he certainly became a rich man. In contrast, parish priests were often as poor and uneducated as the villagers they served.

St Peter's, Rome

The present church was begun in 1506.

Some educated people were worried too about ways of prayer and worship which seemed to encourage superstition. When many could not read, teaching depended on pictures and statues; often people thought these had magic powers. Services were in Latin, and much that went on in church was not properly understood. The central service, the Mass, when bread and wine was consecrated (made holy), took place at the altar at the east end of the church. This was screened off from the congregation, so it was not easy to see or hear what was going on. The priest wore special clothes (vestments). It is not surprising that ordinary people often found the whole thing rather like a magic spell.

The Bible was in Latin, translated from an earlier and more accurate Greek version; many scholars thought it was full of mistakes which altered the meaning of the words. Only very well-educated people could read it for themselves.

Many churches and monasteries had relics. These were objects said to be connected with Christ or the saints. The ruler of Saxony, in Germany, had 17,000 relics, including what he believed were part of Jesus's cradle, and part of the crown of thorns. People often went on pilgrimages all over Europe to shrines which held relics; they hoped to solve their problems, and gain forgiveness for their sins. The church or monastery which held the shrine became rich from their visitors.

The Church taught that people must earn forgiveness for their sins by doing penance — an action to show they were truly sorry. But Popes also issued *Indulgences.* These were written promises of forgiveness and could be bought. Much of the money from the sale of Indulgences went to Rome. By 1516, it was helping to pay for the rebuilding of the great church of St Peter's. In Germany, John Tetzel, a friar who would have made a good modern salesman, travelled round towns and villages selling Indulgences. He would arrive with great pomp, carrying the papal banner, and was met by all the townspeople. In the church, he would speak to them, promising that anyone who bought an Indulgence would have complete forgiveness of sins, and a shorter time in Purgatory. They could also buy Indulgences for any loved ones who had already died, and help them as well. He had a well-known slogan:

> As soon as gold in the basin rings,
> Right then the soul to Heaven springs.

1 Imagine you are promoting a new brand of soap powder, or a new make of car. Write down the methods you would use to persuade people to buy it. How do they compare with Tetzel's methods?

2 Make a poster to be used by Tetzel, encouraging people to buy Indulgences. Remember to make the most of the horrors they will avoid by buying.

Scholar critics

Desiderius Erasmus (1466?—1536) grew up as an orphan in the Netherlands, in a monastery where he was very unhappy. He was allowed to leave, and became a famous scholar of the New Learning. Erasmus moved between some of the great universities of Europe — Paris, Cambridge and Basle. He was sad about the state of the Church; from his own experience he had a low opinion of monks, and he condemned superstition. Once he said there were enough relics of the 'true' Cross in Europe to build a ship.

This portrait by the German artist, Dürer, shows him standing at his desk, as he always did when he was working. Dürer thought highly of Erasmus, and the Greek writing says 'His writings make a better picture'. This is the first page of his most famous book, a new, accurate Latin translation of the New Testament which clearly showed the mistakes of the old version. In the introduction, Erasmus said he also thought everyone ought to be able to read the Bible in their own tongue — 'I wish that the ploughman might sing (it) . . . at his plough, and the weaver at his shuttle.'

Erasmus also wrote a book called *In Praise of Folly*, which poked fun at the Church, especially the monks he disliked so much. This too became a best-seller.

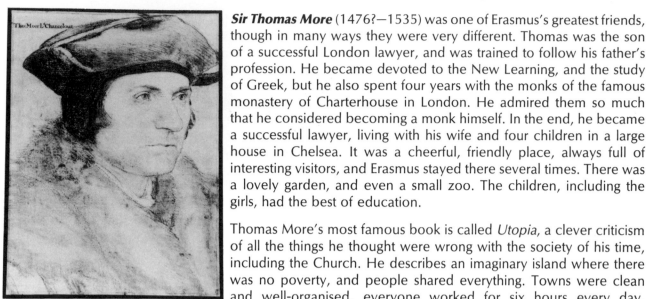

Holbein made several drawings of Sir Thomas More in 1528, before he painted his portrait. In this one, it is easy to see the pinholes which the artist used to transfer the outlines on to the wooden panel on which he would paint the portrait.

Sir Thomas More (1476?—1535) was one of Erasmus's greatest friends, though in many ways they were very different. Thomas was the son of a successful London lawyer, and was trained to follow his father's profession. He became devoted to the New Learning, and the study of Greek, but he also spent four years with the monks of the famous monastery of Charterhouse in London. He admired them so much that he considered becoming a monk himself. In the end, he became a successful lawyer, living with his wife and four children in a large house in Chelsea. It was a cheerful, friendly place, always full of interesting visitors, and Erasmus stayed there several times. There was a lovely garden, and even a small zoo. The children, including the girls, had the best of education.

Thomas More's most famous book is called *Utopia*, a clever criticism of all the things he thought were wrong with the society of his time, including the Church. He describes an imaginary island where there was no poverty, and people shared everything. Towns were clean and well-organised, everyone worked for six hours every day, and then had time for learning and enjoyment. They wore a homespun grey uniform, and shared all the daily tasks — shopping, cooking, caring for children and working on the land. There was no need for money, and silver and gold were just children's playthings. This book did not openly criticise the Church, but it condemned wealth and pomp, and there was plenty of that to be seen amongst churchmen. Thomas dearly wished to see a change for the better, and perhaps that was why he decided to enter the service of Henry VIII in 1518.

The artist Hans Holbein stayed in Thomas More's house in 1528. He did several portraits while he was there, including the drawing of the whole family opposite. Everyone is preparing for family prayers; there are plenty of books in this household, and some of them have just been put down on the floor. Thomas More is seated, wearing his chain of office, next to his elderly father, and his son, John. He is surrounded by the rest of his family: three daughters and two wards. His eldest daughter Margaret kneels in the foreground. On the far right is his second wife Alice, with a tiny monkey (from the zoo perhaps) nestling in her skirts.

This picture was sent to Erasmus as a birthday present. He was delighted with it. 'I should scarcely be able to see you better if I were with you,' he wrote.

Both Erasmus and Thomas More felt that the Church had forgotten many of the teachings of Christ, and needed to reform — to be changed for the better. All their books, which were printed and read by educated people all over Europe, were written to encourage this. But neither ever dreamed of leaving the Church. Two very different men did that, and brought about 'The Reformation', when some people broke away from the Catholic Church to form new churches of their own.

The Reformation: The challenge which split the Church

Martin Luther (1483—1546) was a German monk who taught at the University of Wittenberg. He was an unhappy man, deeply worried by the evil he felt was all around him, and full of fears of Hell. He was also very upset by the wealth and worldliness of the Church, which he had seen when he visited Rome in 1510. Tetzel's sale of Indulgences in Germany was the last straw. On 31 October 1517, Luther nailed a list of 95 Theses, (reasons), why Indulgences were wrong, to the Castle Church door in Wittenberg. The next day was All Saints' Day, when everyone would come to church and see the list. Soon the 95 Theses were printed, and all Germany knew of them. Tetzel belonged to an organisation of friars who challenged Luther to explain himself, and he began to go further. If Indulgences were wrong, what right had the Pope to issue them? Luther began to attack the power of the Pope himself. He had won new confidence too. For many years he had struggled to avoid sin; he had studied widely and had spoken out against empty practices like Indulgences. Now all this seemed to fall into place as he became sure that *faith* based on the Bible was the answer. If people had faith, this alone would transform their lives into something good and holy.

Family portraits were unusual in the early sixteenth century, especially in England. So we are lucky to have Holbein's drawing of Sir Thomas More's family, which is so realistic that it is almost as if we can walk in and join the group ourselves.

D. MARTIN LUTHER.

Luther's new teachings left out all the power and authority of the Church, and the Pope decided he must be condemned. In 1520, a Bull (a special proclamation by the Pope with his personal seal on it) was issued. It began:

> Arise, O Lord, and judge thy case. A wild boar has invaded thy vineyard . . . Arise, all ye saints and the universal church . . . we can no longer suffer the serpent to creep through the field of the Lord.

■ What two creatures is Luther being compared to? Why do you think his enemies chose those two?

The Bull went on to excommunicate Luther — that meant he was cast out from the Church and condemned to Hell.

This did not shake him. When the Bull arrived in Wittenberg, he burnt it in the market place for all to see.

In 1521, the young Emperor of Germany, Charles V, stepped in to support the Church. He summoned a Diet, a meeting of all the princes in Germany, at Worms. The Papal Legate, the Pope's special representative, was there too. Luther was in great danger of being condemned and burnt as a heretic; nevertheless, he went to Worms, and in spite of being very nervous, he made a convincing and rousing declaration:

see page 59

> Unless I am convicted of error by the . . . Scripture . . . my conscience is captive by God's word. I cannot and will not *recant* anything . . . On this I take my stand. I can do no other, God help me.

As Luther left the hall, many felt he was doomed. But he had won support from many Germans, who felt the Pope interfered too much in German affairs, and from some princes, who wanted to be independent of their Emperor. Among them was the Elector of Saxony; Wittenberg was in Saxony. On his way home, Luther was suddenly kidnapped by armed knights, but they turned out to be friendly; they were acting on the Elector's orders to ensure his safety.

So Luther was able to continue to teach and study. He translated the Bible into German so it could be widely read. He wrote hymns and books, and his teachings spread. He stopped being a monk, and married an ex-nun. A new 'Lutheran' Church grew up. Priests were less important and there was no Pope. Teaching was based on the Bible, and services were in German. But although Luther believed conscience was important, he also thought rulers ought to be obeyed. When German peasants took his words to heart and rebelled, he condemned them. Luther was a man of his age; but he had founded a new Church, and those who, like him, 'protested' against what they saw as wrong in the Catholic Church were now called 'Protestants'. Some began to go further than Luther.

John Calvin (1509–64) was a cool, clear-headed thinker, very different from the fiery and emotional Luther. In 1536, he wrote a book called *The Institutes of the Christian Religion* in which he set out his beliefs in a more extreme Protestant Church. Like Luther's works, it was printed and widely read. Calvin was invited to go to Geneva, which had just broken free from its Catholic ruler. There, from 1541, he organised a new Protestant Church which ruled the city. Schools and a university were founded; the sick and poor were cared for; the streets were cleaned. Cheating and over-pricing in shops were forbidden, as well as dancing, theatre-going, bright clothes, swearing, and singing rude songs. Unfaithful husbands and wives were executed, and a boy was beheaded for striking his parents.

In churches, big pulpits were erected, since teaching the Bible through long sermons was the most important part of the service. Pictures and statues were removed, because these caused idolatry (worship of idols). Calvin was just as severe as the Catholic Church on unbelievers. A Spanish reformer, Servetus, went to Geneva to discuss their differences. He was thrown into prison and burned. Any sort of superstition was condemned; about three witches were burned every year. Life was harsh in Geneva, but it had advantages too. Good Calvinists were convinced that God had chosen (elected) them for salvation. They showed this by living as Calvin taught — soberly, without luxury, and plainly dressed. They read the Bible and worked hard: prosperity was also a sign they were 'elect'. Sunday was a special day, set aside for church-going, and Calvinists took a full part in choosing their ministers and running the church, for there were no bishops. They were people with drive and energy. Calvin's teachings spread to places like the Netherlands, where this way of life appealed to the townspeople; to lowland Scotland, where there were fewer towns, but where many people were thrifty and hard-working; and to England, especially to towns in the more prosperous south-east. In these different places, followers of Calvin had different names. You will find them explained on page 59.

1 The Reformation might not have happened in the way it did if Luther and Calvin (and perhaps also Erasmus and Thomas More) had lived before the invention of printing. Read from page 53 again, and make a list of the times when new ideas spread through the printed word.

2 What teaching by both Luther and Calvin could only spread where people could read?

3 Write a description by a citizen of Geneva of life there in Calvin's time. Before you begin, make a list of things you might enjoy, and things which you would find unpleasant.

The Counter-Reformation

Horrified by the divisions caused by the Reformation, the Catholic Church began to reform itself, and try to win back Protestant 'heretics'. One of the most important people in this 'Counter-Reformation' was Ignatius Loyola (1491–1556), a Spaniard, who founded the Society of

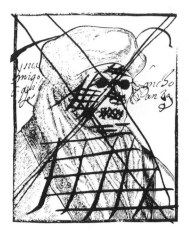

The tragic hatred between divided Christians is shown by what happened to this portrait of the gentle scholar Erasmus, who never left the Catholic Church. It has been vandalised by the Catholic Inquisition (see page 59), because of the criticisms he made. Yet Luther too condemned him — because he did not go far enough.

Jesus. He was a soldier; after he was seriously wounded, in battle, he began to have a vision of a new life entirely devoted to God. When he recovered, he began a long, hard training to prepare himself for this. In 1534, he and nine companions made solemn vows to dedicate their lives to God and the Catholic Church, in complete poverty, and to face any hardship. This was how the Society of Jesus, or the 'Jesuits' as they came to be called, began. Like Loyola himself, the Jesuits trained for long years, to prepare themselves for suffering. They were ready to be persecuted — harshly treated because of their religion in order to win heathens in distant lands, and Protestants in Europe, to the Catholic faith. The Jesuits had great influence in many ways. Their schools were famous, and their missionaries travelled as far as China and Japan. In Protestant countries, especially in England from the late sixteenth century, people feared and respected them.

The divided Christian Churches

The teachings of Luther and Calvin changed Early Modern Europe. Now there was no longer one Catholic Church. The Reformation created new Protestant churches; these put an emphasis on *personal* faith, and they differed from each other, as well as from the Catholic Church. Yet both Catholics and Protestants believed sincerely that they alone held the truth, and that those who held different views were doomed to Hell fire. So both sides were certain that religious persecution was right, and terrible religious wars divided Europe. Moreover, powerful national rulers believed there should be one uniform church within their kingdoms, and they should choose whether it would be Catholic or Protestant, to prevent strife and rebellion. It would be a long time before Christians began to learn toleration, and respect for beliefs different from their own.

The divided Christian Churches in the Early Modern Age

	Catholic	Protestant	
		Lutheran	**Calvinist**
Organisation	Pope, cardinals, archbishops, bishops, priests, monks, friars, nuns	No Pope Bishops and priests less powerful No monks, friars or nuns	Ministers chosen by their congregation, who shared in the organisation of their church
Church Services	The Mass in Latin, with the priest at the altar at the east end of the church wearing vestments	Communion amongst the people. The altar became a simple table; the minister wore a plain black gown. Long sermons to teach the Bible	
Buildings	Churches full of pictures, statues and candles, and as beautiful as possible to glorify God	Churches must be plain, without pictures or statues, which encouraged idolatry and superstition	

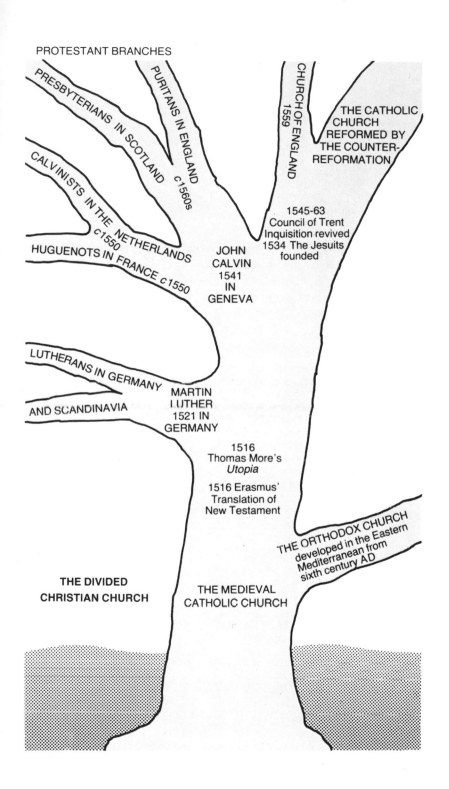

PROTESTANT BRANCHES

PRESBYTERIANS IN SCOTLAND

PURITANS IN ENGLAND c1560s

CHURCH OF ENGLAND 1559

THE CATHOLIC CHURCH REFORMED BY THE COUNTER-REFORMATION

CALVINISTS IN THE NETHERLANDS c1550

HUGUENOTS IN FRANCE c1550

JOHN CALVIN 1541 IN GENEVA

1545-63
Council of Trent
Inquisition revived
1534 The Jesuits
founded

LUTHERANS IN GERMANY

AND SCANDINAVIA

MARTIN LUTHER 1521 IN GERMANY

1516
Thomas More's
Utopia

1516 Erasmus'
Translation of
New Testament

THE ORTHODOX CHURCH
developed in the Eastern
Mediterranean from
sixth century AD

THE DIVIDED CHRISTIAN CHURCH

THE MEDIEVAL CATHOLIC CHURCH

Key words and meanings from this section

Use this list for reference later in the book.

REFORMATION The religious revolution of the sixteenth century, when Protestant Churches broke away from the Catholic Church.

CATHOLIC A Christian who accepts the authority of the Church and the Pope in Rome.

PROTESTANT A Christian who relies on the teaching of the Bible, and does not accept the authority of the Pope. There are several different groups of Protest-ants.

Note People still argue about these two words, but these meanings should help you to understand the problems over religion in the Early Modern Age.

HERESY Beliefs which are different from the official teaching of the Church. A heretic is someone with such beliefs.

INQUISITION A special court of the Catholic Church, used to condemn heresy.

RECANT To go back on one's beliefs, and admit they were false.

EXCOMMUNICATION Being expelled from the Church.

BULL An official announcement by the Pope, with his seal attached (*bulla* is the Latin word for seal).

THE LAITY, LAYMEN, LAY-WOMEN Everyone who belongs to the Church, who is not one of the clergy.

4 The Renaissance Prince

In the Early Modern Age, the word 'prince' was used of any ruler, male or female (though there were very few females). It was a word that meant power and strength. Many of the ideas of what a great prince should be like are in a well-known book written in Florence in 1514 by Niccolo Machiavelli. It is called, simply, *The Prince*. Machiavelli lived through a time when France and Spain were threatening much of Italy. He was distressed by this; he wrote his book of advice for rulers to help them avoid such threats. He believed that sometimes cruel or harsh actions might be necessary to keep a ruler in power; if a prince was strong, then all his subjects benefited. His book soon had a bad reputation, because it was so frank about the ways he thought a ruler should keep power. Here is some of his advice to 'princes'.

A A prince should always seek advice. But he should do so when he wants to, not when others want him to

B Nothing brings a prince more prestige than great campaigns and striking demonstrations of his personal abilities . . . above all a prince should endeavour to win the reputation of being a great man of outstanding abilities.

open
character

C A prince . . . need not necessarily have all the good qualities I have mentioned but he should certainly appear to have them . . . He should appear to be compassionate, faithful to his word, *guileless* and devout. And indeed he should be so. But his *disposition* should be such that if he needs to be the opposite, he knows how.

1 What does the word 'prestige' mean in passage B? What sort of personal abilities does Machiavelli say will bring a ruler prestige?

2 In passage C, write down the words which describe the good qualities a ruler should have; write their meaning beside them. Use a dictionary if you need it. Then, in the margin, write the *opposite* of these good qualities: e.g. compassionate — harsh.

3 Make a list, using A, B, and C, of the other things a powerful ruler should do.

4 The word 'Machiavellian' is stilled used of a crafty action which helps someone's selfish ends. Do you think that is fair to Machiavelli?

Machiavelli's ideas of a successful Renaissance prince were not really new. But books like his show that people expected a great deal of rulers in the Early Modern Age. In Britain in the mid-fifteenth century, there were great problems.

Crown under threat

In the same year (1459) the realm of England was out of all good governance, for the King was simple, and led by *covetous* counsel, and owed more than he was worth. His debts increased daily, but payment there was none; all the possessions that *pertained* to the Crown the King had given away . . . so that he had almost nought to live on. And such *impositions* as were put to the people . . . all that came from them were spent in vain, for he held no household, nor maintained no wars. For these misgovernances and for many others, the hearts of the people were turned away . . . The Queen, with *such as were of her affinity*, ruled the realm as they liked, gathering riches innumerable.

greedy

belonged
taxes

people who supported her

■ This is a description of England under King Henry VI, and the writer finds a good deal wrong — a badly governed kingdom, with the 'hearts of the peopled turned away'. Start a list of wrongs by explaining the following:

> The King was simple, and led by covetous counsel.
> He owed more than he was worth.
> He held no household, nor maintained no wars.

Add to this list the other things the writer says are wrong. Underline anything which concerns money.

Henry VI's disastrous reign went wrong from the beginning. His father died when he was only nine months old (he was crowned with a bracelet). A minority — when a child is too young to rule — brings problems, and there was rivalry between the powerful nobles trying to control the kingdom for him. Some of them also had a claim to the throne, which made things worse. (Look at the family tree on page 63.)

When Henry grew up, it became clear that he did not have the personality people expected of a king. Most of his subjects agreed that he was 'simple', and easily influenced. He found it difficult to make up his mind, but could suddenly and unexpectedly be very obstinate. His appearance made matters worse. He did not bother how he looked; once in London the crowd jeered when he appeared in a shabby blue gown 'as though he had no more to change into'. Being a king seemed altogether too much for him. Several times during his reign, his mind gave way under the strain; and he would sit in dejected silence, refusing to make even the smallest decision. It is not difficult to see why a king like this 'kept no court', and had little interest in grandeur and magnificence. He did however build two great chapels, at Eton and Cambridge, which gave him a reputation for saintliness.

Henry VI by an unknown artist

This portrait is unlikely to be a realistic likeness of Henry VI, and it may not even have been painted in the King's lifetime. But it seems to reflect the general feeling that he did not have the dignity and majesty expected of a King.

A king was expected to 'live of his own', which meant he should manage on his own income, and not ask for extra taxes from his subjects. Look at what you underlined about money in 1459. It must have been an exaggeration to say *'all* the possessions, . . .' had been given away, but Henry had unwisely sold Crown lands. A king had other sources of income, the most important of which were customs duties on imports and exports; but these had to be collected efficiently, and Henry was obviously not the kind of king to ensure that happened. If extra money had to be found, then a king had to ask the consent of Parliament. No one ever likes paying taxes; if they have to, they expect the money to be spent efficiently. Do you get the impression Henry managed that? Undoubtedly a successful ruler had to manage money wisely.

Henry's marriage added to his problems. Royal marriages were made to increase a king's power, either by alliance with a foreign country, or to win the support of a powerful family at home. Usually the couple had not met before the wedding. Everyone expected a great deal of a queen. She had to be a dutiful wife — a king might be unfaithful and have a mistress, often quite openly, but if a queen behaved in a similar way, it was regarded as high treason, and she could be executed. She had to produce sons to carry on the line, and, since women were not regarded as capable of ruling a kingdom, she was not expected to interfere in state affairs. Henry VI married a forceful French princess, Margaret of Anjou. France was always seen as England's natural enemy, so this strong-minded French woman who quickly took control from her weak and gentle husband became very unpopular indeed. Many said (without any evidence) that the son she bore was not the King's, and this was a useful ←61 way of putting forward other claims to the throne. Look back at the description of England in 1459. What does the writer say about the Queen?

Since Henry VI did not measure up to what was expected of a king, it is not surprising that his reign was a turbulent one, and that he was challenged by the Yorkists — followers of Richard, Duke of York, who believed that he had as good a claim to the throne as Henry and the family of Lancaster. The family tree on page 63 shows the people involved.

A fifteenth-century battle scene

Although cannon were sometimes used, they were frightening rather than dangerous. Soldiers still fought in full armour, and battles usually became confusing hand-to-hand fights. What weapon is obviously causing most casualties to both men and horses?

This is how the Wars of the Roses began — a time of civil war, when the crown was often under threat. The name comes from the badges the two sides sometimes used: the red rose of Lancaster and the white rose of York. Although the wars lasted 25 years (1460—85), there were long periods of peace, and the times when there was actual fighting added up to only 13 weeks. Trade went on normally, with few interruptions. The Cely family carried on as usual, and so did other merchants.

However, for anyone actually fighting, the war was real enough. Yorkists and Lancastrians fought in several bitter battles, in 1460 and 1461. Richard, Duke of York was killed at Wakefield. His head was displayed with a paper crown on it on the gates of York, mocking his attempt to win the throne. The Yorkist cause seemed lost; but his 18-year-old son Edward claimed the crown, gathered his supporters together, and in a blinding snowstorm, won the battle of Towton, which give him control of the north. Henry VI and Margaret fled to Scotland, and Edward marched in triumph to London.

Edward IV's favourite badge was 'the sun in splendour'. It is carved here (with crowns and Tudor roses) below a window in St George's Chapel, Windsor, which he founded, and where he is buried. Later in this chapter you can work out Edward IV's link with the Tudor monarchs.

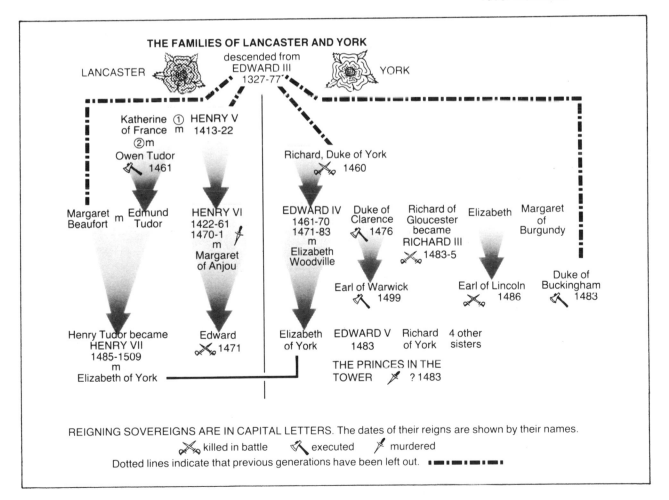

THE FAMILIES OF LANCASTER AND YORK

LANCASTER — descended from EDWARD III 1327-77 — YORK

Katherine of France ① m HENRY V 1413-22
②m Owen Tudor ⚔ 1461

Richard, Duke of York ⚔ 1460

Margaret Beaufort m Edmund Tudor

HENRY VI 1422-61 1470-1 🗡 m Margaret of Anjou

EDWARD IV 1461-70 1471-83 m Elizabeth Woodville

Duke of Clarence ⚔ 1476

Richard of Gloucester became RICHARD III ⚔ 1483-5

Elizabeth

Margaret of Burgundy

Earl of Warwick ⚔ 1499

Earl of Lincoln ⚔ 1486

Duke of Buckingham ⚔ 1483

Henry Tudor became HENRY VII 1485-1509 m Elizabeth of York

Edward ⚔ 1471

Elizabeth of York

EDWARD V 1483

Richard of York

4 other sisters

THE PRINCES IN THE TOWER 🗡 ? 1483

REIGNING SOVEREIGNS ARE IN CAPITAL LETTERS. The dates of their reigns are shown by their names.
⚔ killed in battle   ⚔ executed   🗡 murdered
Dotted lines indicate that previous generations have been left out. ▪━▪━▪━▪━▪

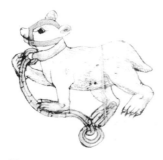

The emblem of the Earl of Warwick

He was nicknamed 'the Kingmaker' because his support helped to bring Edward IV to the throne in 1461, and to restore Henry VI briefly in 1470. He is a good example of how a powerful noble could become when the Crown was weak.

Edward IV

The new King, although he was of royal descent, had won his crown through victory in battle. This was dangerous, since others might challenge him in the same way. The defeated Henry VI was bewildered and depressed, but Margaret was determined to carry on the struggle for the sake of their son. The nobles who had helped Edward wanted their reward: power and lands. The powerful Earl of Warwick, especially, expected to dominate the young and inexperienced King. Edward was going to have to be a much stronger king that Henry VI, if he wanted to keep his throne.

What kind of king? Evidence about Edward IV

It is difficult to know what people in the past were really like. We need to look at as many different kinds of evidence as possible.

1. *Three descriptions of Edward,* written by foreigners who had seen him.

A French writer, who did not like him: He was a very handsome prince, and tall . . . I do not remember seeing a more handsome prince than he was.

A German: A person of most elegant appearance, and remarkable above all for the attractions of his person.

An Italian: Edward was of a gentle nature and cheerful aspect: nevertheless should he assume an angry countenance he could appear very terrible to beholders.

■ Are accounts by foreigners more likely to be truthful than those by his own subjects? If so, why?

2. *A portrait of Edward*

This portrait was painted at a time when there were few good artists in England. The unknown painter almost certainly did not paint the King from life. He may have only actually seen him once or twice — or perhaps not at all. All he was trying to do was to show an important man. What can you see that tells us this? Is there any clue that this is the portrait of a king? What impression does the portrait make on you? Does it match up with the written descriptions?

Since we know so little about how it was painted, do you think it is reliable evidence for Edward's appearance?

3. *Edward's skeleton*

In 1789, more than 300 years after Edward's death, his coffin was opened, and his skeleton measured. He was 1.92 metres tall, and broad in proportion. This was at a time when the average height of a male adult was about 25 cm less than Edward's measurements.

■ We have three different kinds of evidence about Edward's appearance. How far do they agree? What do you think of him so far? What kind of impression do you think he made on his subjects?

4. Edward's clothes and jewels

Edward spent an average of £2,000 a year just on clothes and furs, at a time when a great noble's household usually cost £1,000 a year to run.

A list of 1480 gives us an idea of the materials and colours used:

> Black velvet lined with purple.
> White damask lined with sable fur.
> Purple cloth of gold, lined with ermine.

At Christmas 1482, the King wore 'a great variety of costly garments of quite different cut which had usually been seen in our kingdom'.

Edward also bought jewellery regularly. One of his bills of 1480 includes:

> A flower of gold, garnished with a fleur-de-lis (lily) diamond . . . £6
> Another flower, with a pointed diamond, four rubies, four pearls . . . £4
> A toothpick of gold, with a diamond, a ruby, a pearl . . . £8 6s 8d
> Four rings of gold, garnished with four rubies at 10 shillings each.

■ Draw and colour your own version of some of the materials used for Edward's clothes, and of some of his jewels

The Court of Edward IV

Edward IV collected a fine Royal Library. The Queen's brother, Lord Rivers, was a patron of Caxton; here he is presenting a printed book to the King. The Queen, the eldest prince and perhaps Richard of Gloucester (wearing ermine as well as the King) are there. The other kneeling figure may be Caxton. The picture gives us a good impression of an important court occasion.

65

5. *Edward's management of money*

Edward obviously enjoyed fine clothes, and being at the centre of a grand court, but all this cost a great deal of money. Here are some facts to show how he managed this problem:

He kept a careful personal check on his accounts, so he knew how much money he had.

He made sure the royal lands were properly run, so his income increased.

The customs duties were efficiently collected, and he also traded profitably himself in wool, cloth and tin.

After a brief invasion of France in 1475, he received a yearly pension in return for a promise to cause no further trouble.

He tried to avoid asking Parliament for taxes, and in the end he 'lived of his own'.

←61 ■ How does this compare with Henry VI's management of money?

6. *Edward's marriage*

Edward soon made his own independent decision on the important question of his marriage. The Earl of Warwick hoped to arrange a marriage for him with a French princess. The handsome young King, who already had quite a reputation where women were concerned, did not discourage him. However, on a May morning in 1464, Edward was in Northamptonshire, on his way north. He had told his courtiers he was going hunting, but he secretly rode to the home of a local gentleman. There, he married one of the daughters of the house, a young widow called Elizabeth Woodville. Her husband had been killed fighting against the Yorkists and she had little money. Meanwhile, plans for the French marriage went ahead; it was five months before Edward confirmed a great deal of rumour and gossip, and presented Elizabeth to his court as his Queen.

Elizabeth Woodville

Elizabeth seems to have been a fair-haired beauty, but there is little to show she had an attractive character. She and her family greedily made the most of her new position and, as a result, they were all unpopular. So many good marriages were arranged for the Woodville family that people felt there were none left for anyone else! A 20-year-old brother married the widowed Duchess of Norfolk, aged 65, who was an aunt of the Earl of Warwick. Elizabeth's son by her first marriage married a rich heiress who was already betrothed to a nephew of the Earl of Warwick. Four sisters were quickly married, one to the young heir to the Duke of Buckingham, who greatly resented it; he thought a marriage to one of the Woodville family was beneath his dignity.

■ In class discussion, work out your theories on the following problems:

a) Why Edward married Elizabeth Woodville. Write down reasons why she was an unsuitable Queen, according to the ideas of the time.

b) Why Edward kept the secret for five months.

c) Why Elizabeth agreed to the marriage.

d) Why the great nobles, especially the Earl of Warwick, disliked the marriage.

e) What can be learnt about the way marriages of powerful people were arranged at this time? Look again at the section on marriage on pages 25—6.

7. *Edward and his enemies*

Edward had to face a serious rebellion in 1470—1, when he lost his crown to the Lancastrians. His ambitious younger brother, the Duke of Clarence, joined the Earl of Warwick — you should have no difficulty in seeing why the Earl was ready to rebel by this time. Together they put Henry VI back on the throne. Edward fled to the Netherlands, but it was only a year before he made a comeback: he won two major battles at Barnet and Tewkesbury, and returned in triumph to London. This table shows the people who fought against him, and how he dealt with them.

	Aims and motives	Fate
Henry VI	He was probably too depressed to have any aims, and was completely controlled by his Queen.	Almost certainly murdered in the Tower on the orders of Edward IV, when he returned to London in 1471
Margaret of Anjou	To win back the crown for her son at all costs	Fled into exile in 1471; died 1482
Their teenage son, Edward		Killed during or after the battle of Tewkesbury, 1471
The Duke of Clarence	Probably hoped to gain the crown	Edward IV forgave his brother at first, but when he plotted again in 1476, he was executed, it is said through drowning in a butt of malmsey (barrel of wine).
The Earl of Warwick	Hoped to gain control over Henry VI and Margaret, since he had failed to dominate Edward IV	Killed escaping from the battle of Barnet, 1471, though Edward tried personally to save his life

■ Would you defend the way in which Edward acted towards his enemies?

8. *The end of Edward's reign*

By 1483, Edward was 40 years old, and his kingdom was peaceful. The Lancastrian cause seemed dead. The only remaining leader was a young man in exile called Henry Tudor; and his claim to the throne was a shaky one. The King was not popular with everyone, and people resented the Woodvilles and their supporters, but no one questioned his authority. Moreover, he had two healthy sons of 12 and 10, so the succession was secure. He was not so good-looking now, and an Italian visitor Mancini, reported the gossip about the King's life style:

a medicine that causes vomiting

> In food and drink he was most immoderate; it was his habit, so I have learned, to take an *emetic* for the delight of gorging his stomach once more. For this reason, and for the ease which was specially dear to him after the recovery of his crown, he had grown fat in the loins.

Such unhealthy habits cannot have helped when at Easter, 1483, Edward suddenly fell ill. By 9 April, he was dead.

■ You now have different kinds of evidence about Edward IV. Arrange the information in two columns, headed *Successes* and *Failures*. Then use your conclusions to write a description of Edward and his court in March 1483, by someone old enough to have been at Henry VI's court. Decide whether you support Edward, and bring in as much information about his reign as possible.

Margaret Beaufort and Henry Tudor

Margaret Beaufort was descended from a famous and admired son of Edward III, John of Gaunt. Her first marriage was to Edmund Tudor; he was the son of a Welsh gentleman who had married the widow of Henry V. He was therefore Henry VI's half-brother. Margaret's only child Henry Tudor was born just after her husband's death, when she was still only 14 years old. She was a woman of great character, who helped to found three colleges at Cambridge University, and was a patron of Caxton the printer. She married twice more. Her third husband, Lord Stanley, was a Yorkist supporter in 1483.

The statue of Margaret Beaufort on her tomb in Westminster Abbey

1 Had Henry Tudor a claim to the throne through his father?

2 Who had the better claim to the throne, Henry or his mother?

3 Why did no one at the time consider Margaret's own claim, but only her son's? (For all these questions use the family tree on page 63.)

Challenges to power

Unexpectedly, England now had a boy King of 12, Edward V, who was not old enough to rule. On his deathbed, Edward IV had made his youngest brother, Richard of Gloucester, Protector, to rule for the new young King until he was an adult. This was an obvious choice. Richard, unlike the treacherous Clarence, had been unswervingly loyal. He had governed the north of England efficiently for his brother. He had, however, always distrusted the Woodvilles, and the young King was in the care of the Queen's brother, Lord Rivers, at the time of Edward IV's death. The Protector quickly found an ally — the Duke of Buckingham. The Duke had been married to the Queen's sister and had resented it. He had now inherited his father's title. The Queen, meanwhile, was also obviously worried, and took sanctuary in the monastery in Westminster with her other children. Two months later, the Protector made himself King Richard III. By August, both sons of Edward IV had completely disappeared.

This story and what happened afterwards is puzzling. There are two big mysteries.

The first mystery: What kind of man was Richard III?

The character of Richard III is unclear. His reign ended in defeat and death, and the Tudor monarchs who displaced him destroyed his reputation. Accounts written in his lifetime tell us he was quiet and shy, slightly built, and may have had a crooked shoulder. After his death people began to describe him as an evil-looking hunchback. This portrait was painted soon after his death (we do not know exactly when) and there is no proof that the artist ever saw him. The right shoulder was altered later to make it look higher than the left one. Why do you think this was done?

What would you say to someone who commented on this portrait that they did not like the look of him? Or if they said the opposite — that he did not look like a bad man?

A portrait of Richard III

The second mystery: What happened to the princes in the tower?

Some Facts	Problems
Spring 1483 Richard and Buckingham took Edward V from Lord Rivers, who was soon executed. The young King was taken to the Tower to prepare for his coronation. Elizabeth Woodville allowed her younger son to join his brother.	Why did Elizabeth allow her younger son, Richard of York, out of the safety of Westminster Abbey, if she feared Richard of Gloucester?
June 1483 The two princes were declared illegitimate and Richard of Gloucester was crowned King Richard III.	Did Richard take the crown for selfish, ambitious reasons? Or because he could see no other way of keeping the country peaceful?
August 1483 Rumours spread that the two princes had been murdered. Richard III took no notice of them. The Duke of Buckingham was Constable of the Tower at this time, so he could control everything that happened there.	If Richard did not murder the princes, why did he not deny the rumours, and produce the boys? If he had decided to hide them, where would he have done so? On the other hand, if he really believed they were illegitimate, did he need to murder them?
October 1483 The Duke of Buckingham made contact with Henry Tudor, and rebelled. He was captured and executed. Henry tried to land, but quickly retreated to safety in Brittany.	Did the Duke rebel because he had found out about the princes? Or was he claiming the throne? (He also was descended from Edward III.)
7 August 1485 Henry Tudor landed with a small army at Milford Haven in west Wales, where his family had much support.	Did he too have a motive for murdering the princes?
22 August 1485 Henry Tudor defeated the army of Richard III at the battle of Bosworth; and Richard was killed. So the first Tudor, Henry VII, became king. He married Edward IV's daughter, Elizabeth of York, and so united the families of Lancaster and York.	If the princes were still alive in 1485, they were a threat to Henry. He married their sister to strengthen his position, so he could not admit they were illegitimate. But they both had a much better claim to the crown than he did. So could he be the murderer? It is odd that he accused Richard III of many evil deeds in 1485, but not of these two murders.
Twenty years later, in 1502 A man called Sir James Tyrell confessed to suffocating the two princes in the Tower in 1483, on Richard's orders.	Why did he wait so long to make this confession, if he was going to make it at all?
1674, in the reign of Charles II Bones of two children of about 12 and 10 were found under some stairs in the Tower, and buried in Westminster Abbey as the remains of the two princes.	Experts do not agree about these bones, which were examined in 1933 by a surgeon and a dentist. Not all of them were human bones. They are not necessarily male. They do not establish the cause of death, and even if they were examined again, it is probably not possible to establish the exact age of the children, nor how long the bones had been there.

Power-building again: The first Tudor

In August 1485, Henry VII, the first Tudor King, faced the same problem as Edward IV had done at the beginning of his reign. He had won his crown in a battle. Now he had to show his subjects he was a strong king, and that no one else could do the same to him.

The battle of Bosworth had not been a very glorious one. This did not help Henry for it meant he owed his victory to luck rather than skill. Henry's stepfather, Lord Stanley, controlled a useful number of troops; he had kept out of the early stages of the battle, although he had promised to support Richard III. He was probably waiting to see which way things would go. When he finally joined in, it was on Henry's side. During the fighting with these fresh troops, Henry's other piece of luck occurred. Richard plunged into the thick of the battle, probably in a desperate attempt to kill his Tudor enemy. But it was Richard who was killed, and the leaderless Yorkists fled.

Many people were doubtful about this new King and yet another change on the throne. They waited to see what would happen.

Henry had no doubts — or he did not show them. He ordered that Richard's naked body should be slung over a mule, and taken to nearby Leicester so that everyone could see that he was defeated and dead. He issued proclamations that law and order must be observed. He was crowned with great ceremony; and when Parliament was summoned, it was agreed to date his reign from the day before Bosworth. This meant that he could, if he wished, accuse those who had fought against him of treason.

The Tudor rose — the most famous emblem of Tudor monarchs

The red rose of Lancaster was united with the white rose of York. Henry's claim to the throne was strengthened by his marriage to Edward IV's eldest daughter, Elizabeth of York.

Some powerful enemies:
The Howard family

John Howard, Duke of Norfolk, and his son, the Earl of Surrey, fought for Richard III at Bosworth. Henry had to decide how to deal with powerful nobles like these men; he needed them to help him run the country. The Duke was killed in the battle; but his son was a skilled soldier and still very much alive. Henry punished him by putting him in the Tower; and removing the title of Duke which he should have inherited. He also took some of his lands. Four years later, Henry restored most of the lands, and sent him to keep the north in order, and defend it against the constant danger from the Scots. If the Earl had wanted to cause trouble, he could easily have done so. Instead, he loyally and efficiently carried out the King's wishes. In the reign of Henry's son, he would do even more for the Tudor King.

The Yorkist family

The Earl of Warwick, a nephew of Edward IV, was ten years old in 1485. He was kept prisoner in the Tower. He may have been mentally handicapped; he certainly lived a lonely, boring life, starved of affection.

The Earl of Lincoln, also a nephew of Edward IV, was the only adult male Yorkist alive in 1485; he was a great danger to Henry, who hoped for the best and took him on his council.

Margaret of Burgundy, Edward IV's sister, and widow of the Duke of Burgundy. She lived in the Netherlands and was prepared to help any enemy of Henry.

Two serious challenges: The Pretenders

Loyalty to Henry was soon tested. Only a year after Bosworth, a clever, ambitious priest in Oxford decided that a fair-haired pupil called Lambert Simnel could be passed off as the Earl of Warwick. Although few believed the boy was the Yorkist Earl, Henry's enemies were quick to make use of him.

In Ireland, the leading noble, the Earl of Kildare, proclaimed him King. Margaret of Burgundy provided money and 2,000 German troops. The Earl of Lincoln left Henry's court and gave his support. In 1487, Henry won a hard-fought battle at Stoke. He was lucky, as he had been at Bosworth. He survived; the Earl of Lincoln, who might have remained a serious threat, was killed.

Henry decided he could afford to be merciful. The Earl of Warwick was paraded through the streets of London to show that he was still alive. The priest who began it all was imprisoned, but not executed. Lambert Simnel was put to work in the royal kitchens, and later promoted to be falconer.

Imagine you are a fair-haired 17-year-old boy, apprenticed in the Netherlands to a merchant who sells fine silks, which you sometimes wear. Decked out in your finery, you are in Ireland on your master's business, and you are impressed by how much everyone seems to dislike the Tudor English King. Everyone starts telling you that you have the fine Yorkist looks . . . you begin to get ideas. This is what happened to Perkin Warbeck in 1491. Before you read on, decide what *you* would do next, if you were Perkin Warbeck.

1 Which Yorkist are you going to pretend to be? The Earl of Warwick is not a sensible choice. You want someone who cannot be produced to prove you are a fake. Go back to the family tree on page 63.

2 Who will provide you with money and give you information which will help you seem genuine? Who will help you to cause trouble for Henry?

This was what actually happened: Perkin decided to pretend to be the younger of the two princes in the Tower, Richard of York. He obtained money, and useful information about the family from Margaret of Burgundy, who *said* he was her nephew. The Irish Earl of Kildare helped him, as he had done Lambert Simnel. James IV of Scotland provided him with a high-born wife, and in 1496 briefly invaded the north of England. The King of France and the Emperor of Germany also supported him for a short time. To add to Henry's difficulties, there was a rebellion in 1497 in Cornwall against taxes, just before Perkin landed there. However, when he came face to face with Henry's forces, he fled and was soon captured. Two years later, Henry ordered his execution — and also of the unfortunate Earl of Warwick, although he had done nothing; but alive, he remained a danger to Henry.

1 Look at the way Henry treated his enemies. Make a list of them, and put a tick or a cross against each, to show whether you agree or disagree with the way he dealt with them. Then compare your verdict with the rest of the class.

2 Why do you think people in Scotland and Ireland were so ready to support Henry's enemies?

Henry VII, by Sittow

Henry VII at the end of his reign

This portrait is different from the ones of the other kings in this chapter. We know the name of the artist, a talented Flemish painter, called Sittow, and that the portrait was painted from an actual sitting in 1505. The artist is skilful enough to give us a good idea of what Henry looked like towards the end of his reign.

■ Write down some words to describe the impression this portrait makes on you. Then compare your ideas with this description written at about the same times as the portrait:

His body was slender but well built and strong ... his face was cheerful, especially when speaking; his eyes were small and blue, his teeth few and blackish; his hair was thin and white; his complexion sallow. His spirit was distinguished, wise and prudent; his mind was brave and resolute and never even at moments of greatest danger, deserted him. He had a *most pertinacious memory* ... His hospitality was splendidly generous ... He knew well how to maintain his royal majesty ... He cherished justice above all things ... But all these virtues were obscured *latterly* by *avarice* ... in a monarch indeed it may be considered the worst vice, since it is harmful to everyone.

a very good memory

in the later part of his reign, greed

Perpendicular architecture

Important English buildings which date from the beginning of the Early Modern Age were built in a style called 'Perpendicular'. You can recognise it by looking at the windows and roof in this picture of the great chapel which Henry began to build at the east end of Westminster Abbey for his own tomb, and which his son finished after his death.

Glass was more easily available (though it was still expensive), so windows were set in wide arches, with vertical (or perpendicular) supports which reached the top, however much decoration may be between them. The roof is supported by delicate fans of tracery, called fan vaulting.

There are several famous and beautiful royal buildings in the perpendicular style: Henry VI's chapels at Eton, and King's College, Cambridge; Edward IV's foundation of St. George's Chapel, Windsor; and Henry VII's Memorial Chapel at Westminster which you can see here.

Marriages, money, and peace

While this was going on, Henry was quietly making his government work. His marriage at the beginning of his reign certainly helped. Elizabeth of York, Edward VI's eldest daughter, was a pleasant, quiet girl who became devoted to her husband and bore him several children, including two sons, Arthur and Henry. She never interfered with state affairs. In other words, she did what was expected of a queen at that time, unlike her two unpopular predecessors. Henry was grief-stricken when Elizabeth died in 1503.

Henry also arranged two good marriages for his children. His eldest son Arthur was married to the daughter of the King of Spain, Catherine of Aragon. He was only fifteen, and a weakly lad; five months later, in 1502, he died of a sudden infection. Henry did not want to lose the advantage of such a good match, and got special permission from the Pope for his second son, the future Henry VIII, to marry Catherine. However, the two fathers spent so much time wrangling over the dowry, that the unfortunate Catherine was still waiting to re-marry when Henry VII died.

The fine carving of Elizabeth of York on her tomb in Westminster Abbey

The other marriage was also important. The two ancient enemies, England and Scotland, made a 'perpetual (everlasting) peace' after the troubles over Perkin Warbeck; to seal the agreement, James IV of Scotland married Henry's eldest daughter, Margaret. From this marriage, the Stuart Kings who ruled both England and Scotland in the seventeenth century were directly descended. From now on, the fortunes of the two countries were even more strongly linked; though not sadly in 'perpetual' peace.

One part of his kingdom was more in the centre of affairs than it had been. The Tudor King was Welsh; Welsh gentlemen were welcomed at court, and began to take more part in English affairs.

Where money was concerned, Henry was sensible enough to learn from Edward IV. His methods were very similar; he even managed to get a pension from the King of France. By the end of his reign, he was managing to 'live of his own' (see page 66), but he was rather too fond of using fines as a way of keeping his powerful subjects in order. This was not popular; look at the last sentence of the description of Henry on the previous page.

Henry personally signed each entry in his accounts. These two entries show the place where he began to write his initial in a different, and perhaps quicker way.

Few in 1485 expected Henry VII to last long as King. But, although he never seems to have been very popular, he managed to be a successful ruler. When he died 25 years later, he left his kingdom peaceful at home and had avoided expensive wars abroad. There was one last piece of luck. He died when his son Henry was almost 18 and could be counted as an adult. This meant there would be no repetition of the events which followed Edward IV's death. The young Henry VIII succeeded peacefully, amid general rejoicing.

James IV of Scotland
(1488—1513)

He is of noble stature, neither tall nor short, and as handsome in complexion and shape as a man can be ... His knowledge of languages is wonderful. He is well read in the Bible ... He fears God, and ... says all his prayers. He is active and works hard. When he is not at war, he hunts in the mountains ... I have never seen a man so temperate in eating and drinking ... He is courageous even more than a king should be. I have seen him undertake the most dangerous things in the last wars ... His deeds are as good as his words. For this reason, and because he is a very humane prince, he is much loved.

This is how the Spanish ambassador to Scotland, Ayala, described James IV when he wrote to his own king, Ferdinand of Spain, in 1498. Ayala had been in Scotland for at least two years, and was very friendly with James; he accompanied him on the raid into England in 1496. He also may have wanted to persuade his king that James was a suitable husband for Ferdinand's third daughter; and further his own career in doing so. Therefore this is likely to be a flattering account.

We know a good deal more about James. He came to the throne at the age of 16 — when his father was murdered. He needed all the strength of a Renaissance prince to control his unruly nobles; he ruled firmly, even keeping the independent Highlands and the border with England reasonably peaceful. He encouraged trade, and did his best to improve the value of the Scots coinage. He also encouraged printing and education: in 1496 a law was passed ordering all 'lairds and freeholders' (property owners) to send their sons to school. This was intended to train more lawyers; there was a £20 fine for disobeying.

■ It is difficult to know how a law like this worked. There is no evidence that there were soon more lawyers in Scotland, nor of any fines being paid. But it was a very unusual law for the time. How important do you think it was?

James's accounts tell us a good deal about his interests. There are payments for jousting tournaments, and to jugglers, jesters, and musicians. The poet William Dunbar worked at court. An extraordinary Italian, John Damien, was another favourite. (In 1507 he received 4 litres of 'aqua vitae' — whisky — amongst other gifts.) Damien was sure he could turn cheap metal into gold. James helped him when he attempted to fly to France from the walls of Stirling Castle, using artificial wings. Unfortunately he fell straight to the ground, and broke his thigh. James was fascinated by medicine, and could pull out a tooth, and set a broken leg. He also spent money for a surgeon to help one of his sailors who fell from the rigging, and an injured boy in the royal kitchens.

There are regular payments to the Church too, for prayers to be said, and to help the poor. James spent money on building, especially at Stirling, and in Edinburgh, where he built Holyrood Palace.

By far the greatest sums were spent on the navy and army. Two great warships were built — the *Margaret*, in 1505, costing over £10,000 (James's whole income was not more than £30,000), and the *Great Michael*. Cannon (including the famous big gun 'Mons Meg') and other artillery were built. We know that James dreamed of going on crusade; but, in spite of his marriage to Margaret Tudor, it was rivalry with her brother, the young Renaissance prince, Henry VIII, that really led to these expenses, and would finish in tragedy.

■ Do you agree with Ayala's description of James? Should you add anything?

The Renaissance Prince in person

An English nobleman interested in the New Learning wrote a letter to Erasmus when Henry VIII came to the throne in 1509. In it he said:

> Heaven and earth rejoices; everything is full of milk and honey and nectar. *greed* *Avarice* has fled the country. Our king is not after gold, or gems, or precious metals, but virtue, glory, immortality.

The new young king seemed to fulfil everyone's expectations. This is what was written about him a few years later by the Venetian ambassador:

> His majesty is twenty-nine years old and extremely handsome . . . He is a great deal handsomer than the King of France; very fair and his whole frame admirably proportioned . . . He has a beard that looks like gold. He is very accomplished, a good musician, composes well, is a most capital horseman, a fine jouster, speaks good French, Latin, and Spanish, is very religious, hears three masses daily when he hunts, and sometimes five on other days. He hears the office every day in the Queen's Chamber . . . He is very fond of hunting . . . He is extremely fond of tennis, at which game it is the prettiest thing in the world to see him play, his fair skin glowing through a shirt of the finest texture.

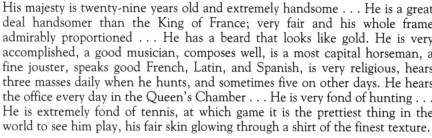

Like English kings before him, Henry proudly displayed the lilies of France on his coat of arms, as well as the lions of England. He soon went to war to claim the French crown — in vain.

■ Make a list of all the things the Venetian ambassador says Henry is good at. Who was Henry VIII's grandfather? Do you think he is like him?

Henry jousts proudly before Queen Catherine, displaying both their initials on the elaborate trappings of his horse. This tournament celebrated the birth of a son, but the little prince soon died.

In Chapter 6, you can find out more about Henry's interests.

Henry VIII began his reign as he felt a Renaissance prince should. He married Catherine of Aragon, saying he was carrying out his father's deathbed wishes. The Spanish princess was six years older than her husband. She had spent seven difficult years as a widow in England. These years had turned her into a wise and sensible woman. Henry was devoted to her, and though some people grumbled that he was too much under the influence of Spain, Catherine's goodness and care for the poor made her popular. She bore a son; the baby died soon after birth, but everyone hoped a healthy male heir would soon follow.

←74

Henry also soon showed that he could be ruthless. His father's two financial advisers at the end of his reign were Richard Empson and Edmund Dudley. They had become very unpopular as they carried out Henry VII's orders to bring in fines. They were immediately put in the Tower, and executed.

Then the young King sought glory in war. He revived the old rivalry with France, claiming the French crown as so many English kings had done in the past. This revived the 'Auld Alliance' and the other old enmity, with Scotland. In 1513, Henry won a small skirmish in France, which was given the grand name of the 'Battle of the Spurs'. Meanwhile, the Earl of Surrey faced a Scots invasion over the Border. James IV brought a large, well-equipped army, including his great cannon 'Mons Meg'. His big warships went to sea too. At Flodden, a terrible battle was fought: 10,000 Scots were killed, including James himself, and 13 earls. The town of Selkirk sent a company of spearmen: only one returned. After this English victory, the widowed Margaret Tudor had to try to rule Scotland for her two year old son, James V.

←2

←71

The great Cardinal

As Henry had so many interests to follow, and he enjoyed playing the role of Renaissance prince, he had little time or inclination for the boring day-to-day business of government. So he looked around for the right kind of adviser. Like many kings before him, he chose an experienced and efficient churchman, who had already helped to organise the French war with success. His name was Thomas Wolsey.

Wolsey was energetic and loyal. The son of a butcher, he enjoyed the wealth and power that his position brought him; but he worked hard to ensure that the King's government was effective. 'He alone transacts all state affairs ... He has the reputation of being extremely just: he favours the people exceedingly, and especially the poor,' wrote the Venetian ambassador. Not everyone agreed. Many people thought Wolsey was arrogant and superior. It was said that he walked around with a pomander (an orange stuck with cloves) to ward off the smells of the

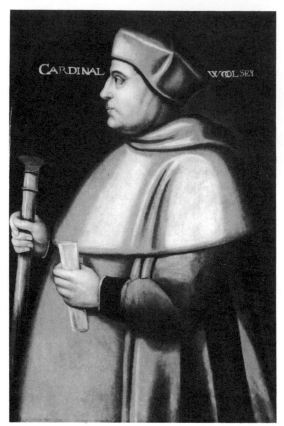

Cardinal Thomas Wolsey at the height of his power, painted by an unknown artist

common people. This was perhaps true; even if it was not, it tells us how some people felt about Wolsey.

Polydore Vergil wrote a history of his own times; this is what he said about Wolsey:

> Wolsey with his arrogance and ambition aroused against himself the hatred of the whole country, and by his hostility towards the nobility and the common people, caused them the greatest irritation through his vain glory. He was indeed detested by everyone, because he assumed that he could undertake nearly all the offices of state by himself.

We know that Vergil disliked the Cardinal; Wolsey imprisoned him for a time which cannot have improved their relationship.

There is no doubt that by the 1520s Wolsey was very unpopular. By then, he had probably taken on too much anyway. In spite of his great energy, he could not do all his work properly. The situation was made worse by the fact that neither Wolsey nor Henry was good at managing the Crown's money, and Henry's wars in 1512—13 had been expensive. Nor did the King and his minister bother to get on well with Parliament, which had to approve the badly needed extra taxes.

Wolsey was by now richer than all the nobles in England; and none of them was happy about that. Also, it was easy to blame Wolsey for anything that went wrong, and far less dangerous than blaming the King. Perhaps that is why Henry did not seem to mind the way in which Wolsey paraded his wealth. If he wanted

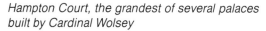

Hampton Court, the grandest of several palaces built by Cardinal Wolsey

to turn against the Cardinal, there were plenty of people waiting to trample on his unpopular minister. One thing is certain: Wolsey knew his power depended on the King. If he lost Henry's favour, he was doomed.

A description of Cardinal Wolsey, Lord Chancellor, going to hear cases in Westminster Hall:

He would issue out all apparelled in red, in the *habit* of a cardinal . . . the best money could buy . . . There was borne before him, first the *great seal* of England, and then his Cardinal's hat, by a nobleman or some worthy gentleman . . . Thus he passed forth, with two great crosses of silver borne before him: . . . and his sergeant-at-arms with a great mace of silver gilt . . . his mule *trapped* together in crimson velvet and gilt stirrups . . . with his cross-bearers . . . upon great horses trapped with red scarlet . . . having about him four footmen with gilt pole-axes in their hands.

robes
see page 82

harnessed

In 1520 Wolsey arranged a magnificent occasion nicknamed 'The Field of the Cloth of Gold' between Henry VIII and Francis I of France. On the left, Henry's grand procession arrives. Elsewhere you can see the two Kings feasting and jousting (rather competitively) in great splendour, and even the local people doing rather well out of the fountains running with wine. It was an empty splendour — the two Kings were soon at war again.

1518

THE POPE made him
PAPAL LEGATE with full
power to act for him in
England.

1515

THE POPE made him a
CARDINAL.

THE KING made him
LORD CHANCELLOR.

1514

Became ARCHBISHOP
OF YORK; held other
rich bishoprics as well

1513

Organised the successful
military expedition
in France

1507

Became a royal chaplain

1497

Gained a degree at
Oxford University
Went into the Church

about 1475

Born the son of an
Ipswich butcher

Wolsey's coat of arms

Coats of arms began as a way to identify knights in battle, when they were wearing full armour. Since only high-ranking people became knights, coats of arms soon became family badges, which showed importance and noble birth. By the sixteenth century, it was the sign of a gentleman to have a coat of arms; anyone who got on in the world would make sure he had one. He would proudly display it in his house, on his belongings, and in portraits.

Cardinal Wolsey, the son of a butcher, made his coat of arms into a kind of 'thank you letter' to all those who had helped him in his rise to power:

The Tudor rose referred to his King.

Two black Cornish choughs referred to Thomas Becket, his 'name saint' (Wolsey was called after him). It was thought that these two little birds were on Becket's coat of arms, though in fact Becket lived before it was the custom to have coats of arms.

The red lion referred to Pope Leo X, who made Wolsey a cardinal.

The four blue leopards, and the white cross on a black ground refer to the two noble familes in Wolsey's native Suffolk.

Wolsey allowed 'Cardinal's College', which he founded in Oxford, to use his coat of arms with the tasselled Cardinal's hat above it. After his downfall, when Henry VIII refounded the college and called it Christ Church, Wolsey's coat of arms was kept. It is still the College coat of arms to this day.

Success as a Renaissance Prince

In this chapter, we have been looking at what subjects expected of their rulers. You will probably have noticed that it was the powerful people in the kingdom, whether in England or Scotland, who had to be convinced that their ruler was a success — the nobles and gentry. Ordinary people were too busy making sure they had enough to live on; when times were hard they too expected the monarch to solve their problems, but it was not easy to make their voices heard.

To sum up, copy the table below, and award each ruler a score out of five for the qualities expected of a Renaissance prince. Make the last column a bit bigger; as well as the total, add three or four words to describe each king. You can choose from the words below the diagram, or better still, think of your own.

	A Magnificent Court	A Wise Marriage	Successful Wars	Well Organised Finances	Total
Henry VI 1422—60 1470—1					
Edward IV 1461—70 1471—83					
Richard III 1483—5		*			
Henry VII 1485—1509					
James IV of Scotland 1488—1513					
Henry VIII 1509 up to 1529					

ruthless	weak	decisive
gentle	sensible	indecisive
greedy	pleasure-loving	tactful
unworldly	impressive	merciful
miserly	handsome	practical

* Richard III's marriage: The chapter gives no information about this because it did not really affect his position as King. He was already married to Anne Neville when he took the Crown; their son died in 1484, and Anne in 1485. As far as we know, both deaths were from natural causes.

THE WORKING OF POWER IN EARLY MODERN ENGLAND

Money

The King was expected to 'live of his own' money from:
Royal Lands
Customs
Loans from rich merchants

He was only expected to ask for taxes in an emergency

KING

QUEEN

A wise marriage increased the King's power

Fighting Men

The King had no regular soldiers, and had to rely on the nobles when he needed an army

THE COUNCIL
Close advisers

The Lord Chancellor was usually the most important. He held the Great Seal which had to be used on all the most important documents.

Nobles   Churchmen   Country gentlemen

Tasks: To give advice and carry out the King's decisions

Ruling classes

PARLIAMENT

LORDS

Met where and when the King decided — usually at Westminster

Tasks

Nobles
Bishops
Abbots
Judges

To make Acts of Parliament — the laws which everyone must obey. COMMONS, LORDS AND KING all had to give their consent

The Lord Chancellor presided sitting on the 'Woolsack'

To vote taxes when the King needed them – since no one liked paying taxes, the King and Parliament did not always agree when a tax was necessary.

To give advice – the King did not have to take this advice, but it was a useful way of seeing how the ruling classes felt.

COMMONS

Gentlemen elected from counties and the more important towns

To vote in an election you had to be able to rent land worth 40 shillings or more, usually from the local landowner.

The Speaker decided what was to be discussed, who should speak, and for how long. He informed the King on what happened and delivered his instructions.

Ruling classes

RULING   CLASSES   IN   THEIR   OWN   COUNTIES

Collected taxes – they decided how much everyone should pay, and how the tax should be collected.

Many were Justices of the Peace

Raised troops when the King needed them

Maintained LAW AND ORDER

Decided what should be done about THE POOR and UNEMPLOYED

Fixed WAGES and APPRENTICESHIPS

Licensed ALE HOUSES which they often owned themselves

Repaired ROADS and BRIDGES

THE   REST   OF   THE   POPULATION

5 Crown and Church

Both monarchs and churchmen were powerful people in the Early Modern Age; and they relied on each other. Henry VIII prided himself on being a religious man. How many church services did he attend each day? For about 15 years he also chose to depend on the churchman Cardinal Wolsey, to whom he gave great power.

←76

In this chapter, we shall see how this Tudor king, who seemed so loyal to the Pope and the Catholic Church, began a quarrel that divided the English Church from the Pope, and in the end linked up with the Reformation in Europe. This Reformation in England increased the power of the Tudor monarchy, and affected both the ruling classes and ordinary people, whose parish church was so much part of their lives.

←55

The King's 'Great Matter'

By 1527, most people knew of the King's concern over what he called his 'Great Matter'. Two remarkable and very different women were at the centre of the problem.

Catherine of Aragon

Henry's marriage to Catherine (left) had now lasted 20 years. The devout and learned Queen was popular and respected. She had borne many children, several of them boys, but only one had lived: a daughter, Mary, now 11 years old. The Queen's age was beginning to show, and no one expected her to have any more children.

Anne Boleyn

Anne Boleyn (right) was a lady at court; she was the niece of the Duke of Norfolk, head of the powerful Howard family, who all hated Wolsey. Anne may have particularly disliked him because he prevented her marriage to the son of the Earl of Northumberland. She was a sharp, lively girl of 20, who had been educated at the sophisticated French court. No one seemed to think she was beautiful, but she knew how to make the best of her glossy dark hair and large eyes. In this portrait she is wearing the new French hood. It was more fashionable and becoming than the heavy old-fashioned Spanish hood worn by Catherine.

Henry VIII, by Hans Holbein

Henry was at the height of his powers: in his mid-30s, active, and not yet very overweight. He respected his wife, but he had not been a faithful husband — kings were not expected to be. He and most of his subjects were quite certain that the future security of his kingdom depended on a healthy male heir, and he had only one weakly daughter. He was also displeased with the Emperor Charles V, who ruled Spain, the Netherlands, most of Germany, and part of Italy (see page 39), and was Catherine's nephew. He had not backed Henry's last unsuccessful attempt to invade France in 1523, and now Henry was considering an alliance with his old enemy, the King of France. This did not make him feel warmly towards his Spanish Queen.

The King had also fallen deeply in love with Anne Boleyn. This was no ordinary affair, mainly because Anne probably saw her chance to become Queen; she refused to become his mistress. Henry too may have been unusually cautious if he saw her as the mother of his longed-for son — who must be legitimate. But his letters to Anne show his strong feelings; Henry did not often bother to write letters himself. These are two excerpts: the first was written in 1527:

tell

> I have put myself in great distress . . . praying you with all my heart that you will expressly *certify* me of your whole mind concerning the love between us two. For of necessity I must ensure me of this answer, having been now above one year struck with the dart of love.

Henry then goes on to say that if she will only promise herself to him, he will be utterly faithful 'rejecting from thought and affection all others save yourself, to serve you only'. Two years later, in 1529, he is more sure:

> No more at present, mine own darling, for lack of time, but that I would you were in mine arms, or I in yours, for I think it long since I kissed you.

This is the initial Henry often used to sign his letters. He used a French phrase to finish one of his letters to Anne. It means 'Henry looks for no one else but Anne'. And he surrounded the heart and Anne's initials with the royal HR (Henry the King):

H autre (AB) ne cherche R

These three reasons made Henry decide to embark on his 'Great Matter' — to divorce Catherine and marry Anne. He began to think his first marriage had been wrong. Surely those dead baby boys were God's judgment on his marriage to his brother's widow. There was a verse in the Old Testament which forbade it. He now believed that Pope Julius II, who had given permission for the marriage so long ago, had been wrong. So the present Pope, Clement VII, must undo the wrong, and grant the King his divorce.

Divorce was not unusual for high-ranking people, but they needed to get special permission from the Pope. So Henry, as usual, expected his Cardinal to solve this problem. Wolsey certainly tried his best, but he was in a very difficult situation.

84

Wolsey's problems over Henry's divorce

1. The Pope would have to cancel the permission to marry granted by Julius II. this meant admitting that another Pope had made a serious mistake, which was difficult at the best of times.

2. This was not the best of times. In 1527, the Emperor Charles V had captured and sacked Rome, and made the Pope a prisoner. As Charles V was Catherine's nephew, he saw the divorce as an insult to his aunt and his whole family.

3. Catherine steadfastly refused to accept the idea of divorce. She burst into bitter tears when Henry finally summoned up courage to tell her his plans; then she appealed to Rome. Her marriage to Arthur had been a mere formality since he had been so young; she was Henry's true and faithful wife. She also refused to solve the problem by going into a nunnery.

←78

4. Wolsey's own position was very dangerous. His unpopularity did not matter as long as he had the King's support. But the longer the problem remained unsolved, the more unreliable Henry became. Everyone knew what happened to people who failed to carry out the King's wishes, and Henry had never wanted anything more than he wanted this divorce. But if Wolsey succeeded, and Anne Boleyn became queen, she would not want him to stay in power. He seemed doomed, whether he failed or succeeded.

Finally, in 1529, the Pope allowed a special court to be held at Blackfriars in London, presided over by Wolsey and Campeggio, an envoy sent from Rome. Catherine, who had been sent away from court and separated from her daughter, was summoned to appear. Henry sat on a throne under a golden canopy, and told the court of his 'great scruple'. Suddenly, and unexpectedly, Catherine knelt before him and pleaded that he should not cast aside his own true wife, and their daughter. She then left the court; she was called back three times but did not return. She never saw Henry, or their daughter Mary, again. One bishop, John Fisher, was brave enough to defend her. She was imprisoned; Anne meanwhile continued to appear at Henry's side. Soon the Pope, a sick man and still much under the influence of Charles V, sent orders to close the court; the case was to be heard in Rome.

The fall of the great Cardinal

The divorce problem had now dragged on for two years and got nowhere. This was the end of Wolsey. He desperately tried to see the King, and even gave him his great palace at Hampton Court. Perhaps Henry did feel sorry for the minister who had served him so long. He sent him to carry out his duties as Archbishop of York, a post he had held since 1514, though he had never been to York till now. It was better than being sent to the Tower, but Wolsey could not get used to his banishment. Although he was ill, he still tried to meddle.

Even at the height of his quarrel with the Pope, Henry still thought he was a loyal churchman. He continued to use the title 'Fidei Defensor' (Defender of the Faith) which the Pope had given him in 1521 because he wrote a book condemning Luther. The title is still used by British sovereigns: find the initials FD on this modern 10p coin.

In 1530, Henry suddenly pounced. The sick and weary Cardinal was arrested and started on the long journey to London. On the way, he became so ill that he was taken to Leicester Abbey, where he died, and so avoided the executioner's axe. As he lay dying, he said:

I see the matter against me how it is framed. But if I had served God as diligently as I have done the King, he would not have *given me over in my grey hairs.*

■ Write a class play with four short scenes:
1. Henry explains to the Duke of Norfolk and other important nobles why he wants a divorce.
2. Catherine and her ladies talking just before the Blackfriars court.
3. Anne Boleyn meets Henry just afterwards.
4. Wolsey's last meeting with Henry — who saw him once after the court failed; Anne prevented a further meeting by taking the King out for a picnic.

New men and a new plan

The King soon found another able and hard-working servant. Thomas Cromwell, like Wolsey, came from a very ordinary family; he was the son of a Putney blacksmith. But unlike Wolsey, this ambitious young man did not become a churchman. There were now other ladders to success. In his early days, he was a soldier and a businessman in Italy and the Netherlands. He became interested both in the New Learning and in Protestant teaching, though in Henry VIII's England, he kept quiet about the latter. Then Wolsey employed him, and gave him his first step upwards. When Wolsey fell, Cromwell managed, with the help of the Duke of Norfolk, to become a Member of Parliament and then of the King's Council. By 1532, he was the King's chief adviser.

We do not know exactly how and when Henry decided to appoint this clear-headed, cool and efficient man. They probably worked out together a new plan: that if Henry took complete power over the Church in England, he would have no need of the Pope to give him a divorce. Everything must of course be legal. England had an accepted, legal way of making laws through Parliament. Henry had summoned Parliament in 1529, when Wolsey fell, and he could now use it to give him a divorce and the new powers he would need as Head of the English Church.

Matters were now far more urgent. Since 1529, courtiers had become used to paying respect to Anne as if she was Queen. Early in 1533, she was pregnant. Since this child must surely be the longed-for son, there must be no doubts about his legitimacy. A secret marriage took place. Henry was lucky that here too he found a new servant to do his will. The old Archbishop of Canterbury had died in 1532, and in 1533 Thomas Cranmer, a quiet scholarly chaplain to Anne Boleyn, was appointed.

deserted me when I was old

This close copy of Holbein's portrait of Thomas Cromwell shows him soberly dressed, and surrounded by what he needs for his work. How many writing implements can you see? What were the scissors used for? Holbein's picture almost certainly gives a true impression of this man. What words would you use to describe him?

←82

The old and the new Archbishop

The weary 80-year-old Archbishop, William Warham (below left), had faced great difficulties. For years it had been hard to do his job as the most important churchman in England, in the shadow of the powerful Cardinal Wolsey. He was deeply worried about the divorce, and the attack on the Church which the King was obviously planning. Probably his death in 1532 saved him from much greater troubles.

Thomas Cranmer (below right) had long been interested in Protestant teaching, and had even married, although this was forbidden for Catholic priests. He knew such beliefs were not acceptable to Henry, so, like Cromwell, he kept quiet about them, and about his wife. He also believed strongly in obedience to his King. Cromwell once said to him: 'You were born in a happy hour. Do or say what you will, the King will always take it well at your hand.' Cranmer was indeed the only royal servant who kept Henry's favour, and did not run into real trouble.

1 Look carefully at the portrait of William Warham, by the great artist, Hans Holbein. Write down some words that describe the impression it makes on you.

2 In the portrait of Thomas Cranmer, find as many things as you can which tell you he is an important person. (Clues: glass, fur, cotton, and Turkish patterned rugs were all luxury objects.)

3 The ring he is wearing has on it his initials backwards: ƆT, and the coat of arms of the Archbishop of Canterbury. What does this tell you it was used for?

4 What do you think of this portrait? Is the artist as gifted as Holbein?

William Warham, by Holbein

Thomas Cranmer, by Gerhardt Flicke

In May 1533, Archbishop Cranmer held a special court at Dunstable, and granted the King his divorce. On 1 June, Anne was crowned Queen. In September, her baby was born — a girl, Elizabeth. Henry was so disappointed that he does not seem to have bothered to attend the christening. He could not know that his daughter would grow up to become a great Queen. However, Anne was young, and there was still hope for a son.

Supreme Head

Meanwhile, Cromwell made sure that Parliament passed laws which gave the King new powers over the Church, whatever the Pope might do. Henry had already said 'Even if His Holiness should do his worst by excommunicating me and so forth, I shall not mind it, for I care not a fig ←59 for all his excommunications.' And when the Pope 'did his worst' in the summer of 1533, Henry took no notice at all.

The Reformation Parliament

This Parliament lasted from 1529 to 1536. The many laws it made ensured that the Pope had no more power in England; and that the monarch was now head of the Church there. These five Acts deal with the things which mattered most to the King.

Money
1532 Annates Act No more taxes were to be paid to the Pope. Henry did not put this into force immediately. Can you see how useful it was to have it as a way of bargaining? It was finally enforced in 1534.

The Law
1533 Appeals Act This forbade English law cases to take place in Rome. Catherine wanted her case to be heard there.

The King's power over the church
1534 Act of Supremacy The King was made **Supreme Head** of the Church of England

The heir to the throne
1534 Act of Succession Henry and Anne's children were to succeed to the throne. Catherine's daughter Mary was declared illegitimate. All important people had to take an oath declaring they accepted this.

Obedience
1534 Treason Act Treason — plotting against the King — was the most serious crime. It was now treason to *say* the King was a *tyrant* or a *heretic* (see page 59). Why were those two words such a threat to Henry?

The end of the monasteries

Henry VIII, Supreme Head of the Church of England, was now much more powerful. But he still could not control one part of the Church — monasteries and nunneries. When men and women became monks and nuns, they made three solemn vows: *poverty* — to give up all their possessions; *chastity* — to have nothing to do with the opposite sex; and *obedience*, which meant they had to obey the Pope and the head of their order (the group of monasteries or nunneries to which they belonged). Which vow interfered with Henry's new powers?

In spite of their first vow, monasteries and nunneries had become very rich over the centuries; they owned about a quarter of all the land in England and Wales, as well as a great deal of treasure. As Henry was always short of money, this wealth was very attractive.

It also looked as if good reasons could be found for destroying (or dissolving) the monasteries and nunneries. As well as keeping the rules of their order, monks and nuns were expected to serve their local community; and monks often acted as priests for nearby parish churches. These services were not always done very efficiently.

It was not that monks and nuns were wicked. More often they were just rather worldly. Abbots lived the lives of great landowners. For instance, William More, Prior of Worcester from 1518 to 1536, owned four manors; they kept him so busy that in most years he only spent about ten weeks at his monastery. He also had to attend the King in London. He had many household and outdoor servants, and he spent large sums furnishing his manors comfortably, running his estates, and entertaining the local people (not just the rich ones). He seems to have been a generous, rather jolly character, but he was hardly living the life of a monk. With men like these to lead them, ordinary monks did not always live strictly.

So in 1535, Thomas Cromwell was given an important new job — Vicar General. He was now responsible for supervising the church for the King, and he set about organising an efficient inquiry into all monasteries and nunneries. A team of lawyers visited every single one in England and Wales — about 800 — in six months. In those days of slow travel this was an achievement in itself. They demanded answers to a long list of questions, and not surprisingly, sent back a good deal of useful evidence to Cromwell in London.

Nuns singing in their convent church

The three knots in their girdles represent their three vows of poverty, chastity and obedience.

QUESTIONS AND ANSWERS

Some questions asked:

Were the correct number of church services attended? Did the abbot and the monks stay in the monastery? Were they well educated? Did they over-eat?

■ Work out some other questions which must have been asked from this part of the report on Bury St. Edmunds, Suffolk, sent to Cromwell:

As for the abbot, we found nothing suspect (about) his living, but it was detected that he lay much forth in his *granges*, that he delighted much in playing at dice and cards, and therein spent much money . . . there was here such frequence of women coming to this monastery . . . Amongst the relics we found much vanity and superstition, as the coals (which) to St Lawrence was toasted, the paring of St Edmund's nails, and . . .*skills* for the headache.

house owned by the abbot, separate from the monastery

charms used to cure headaches

Once again, the King used Parliament for this important step in giving him complete control over the English Church. In 1536, an Act dissolving the smaller monasteries was passed and they quickly disappeared. In 1539, all the large ones were destroyed as well.

Three pieces of evidence on the end of the monasteries

A A letter to Cromwell from the Abbot of Combermere in Cheshire, 10 May 1538:

> Right honourable . . . good lord, I meekly have me commended to your good lordship . . . It please your lordship to send me your honourable letters willing me . . . (to) surrender the monastery to the King's Grace, I beseech you for God's sake to be my good lord. I had my office by the King's Grace . . . and when it shall please His Grace and your lordship to take it again, I shall be ready . . . trusting that I and my poor brethren may continue in the monastery . . . and we shall continually pray to God for the prosperous state of his most noble reign, and the long continuance of your lordship's good health

1 Look at the date of this letter. Was Combermere a small or large monastery?

2 What does the abbot mean when he asks Cromwell to be his 'good lord'?

3 What does he hope his letter will achieve? Is he likely to be successful?

4 What do you think of this letter? Read it aloud in a suitable voice.

B A letter written from the famous monastery at Glastonbury to Cromwell by three of his officers, 22 September 1539.

It begins with an account of an unsatisfactory examination of the old abbot. His study was searched, and a book written against the King's divorce, some papal bulls, and a life of Thomas Becket were found. A second examination of the abbot showed 'his cankered and traitorous heart against the King's Majesty . . . and so with as fair words as we could, we have conveyed him from hence into the tower (of the monastery), being but a weak man and sickly'.

They then describe the treasure they have found in the monastery and ask for instructions on what to do with it. They say they are so impressed with its wealth that they are sure 'your lordship would judge it a house meet for the King's Majesty and no man else '.

1 Look back at the Acts passed by the Reformation Parliament (page 88) and give reasons why the abbot will be convicted of treason.

2 Use this letter to make a list of instructions which Cromwell must have given to his officers before they paid their final visit to Glastonbury.

3 The Abbot of Glastonbury was executed soon after, on Tor Hill, above the abbey, and 'took his death patiently, asking pardon of God and the King for his offences'. What kind of man does he seem to be?

C Some of the values of the possessions of St Osyth's Priory in Essex:

> 261 wagonloads of lead, from several buildings including the steeple and roof of the church £1,044

> Treasure sent to the King, including a silver gilt crown for the skull of St Osyth, a famous relic £175 18s 6d

> Treasure, corn, cattle, household goods, awaiting the King's decision £250

> Bells £40

■ What was the most valuable item from this monastery? Where was it used? Why, when it was removed, were the monastery buildings likely to fall down?

Reminder on money values:
The annual cost of running a noble household — about £1000. The daily wage of a labourer — about 5 pennies.

What happened to the monasteries and nunneries?

Lands The King now had vast extra lands. He kept some; he gave some as rewards to people at court, such as the Duke of Norfolk and Cromwell (who received St Osyth's amongst others). A great deal was sold to raise ready money when the King went to war again in 1543. Nobles and gentry bought these lands, and some went up in the world as a result.

Buildings Some great monastery churches became cathedrals, for example Durham, Canterbury and Gloucester. Others, such as Tewkesbury Abbey, became parish churches of busy towns. Some were turned into grand private houses — an example is Forde Abbey in Dorset. Some fell into ruins, and local people took the stones for their houses, barns and walls. We can still see today these 'bare ruined choirs' as Shakespeare called them: Fountains in Yorkshire, Valle Crucis in Wales, Hailes in Gloucestershire are three examples, but there are many more.

People There was some help for the people involved. Abbots who co-operated received a large pension, and some became bishops. Six did not co-operate and were executed. Monks received about £8 a year; this was the same income as a poor priest, which most of them seem to have become. Servants were either found employment, or were given money. Nuns probably did worse. Their pension was smaller, and they were forbidden to marry, which was the only way a woman could gain status in the Early Modern Age.

←25

It is difficult to tell how much difference the disappearance of the monasteries made. In the north people complained that the sick, the poor, and weary travellers suffered. Some schools disappeared; the King gave some money to improve education — for instance the 'King's Schools' at Canterbury and Worcester were founded. What is certain is that a very big part of the Church's life had disappeared, and it would be difficult ever to restore it. The new owners of the monastic lands were not likely to give them up.

The Bible in English

By 1539, Cromwell and Cranmer were strong enough to persuade the King to agree to an official translation of the Bible in English, to be read regularly in every church. This was an important change, for Protestants believed everyone should read the Bible in their own language. So far, Henry's actions had given him power over the Church, but he had not changed Catholic services or teaching. Soon the King took fright over this new English Bible too; in 1543, he ordered Parliament to pass an Act forbidding 'women, apprentices, journeymen, servingmen . . . and labourers' to read the Bible themselves, because 'that precious jewel, the Word of God, is disputed, rhymed, sung and jangled in every alehouse'. Only gentlemen could read it, at home.

For those who had discovered the Bible, the Act was too late. William Malden of Chelmsford, Essex, later recalled the time when he was an apprentice, and the Bible was first read in English:

Poor men brought the New Testament . . . and on Sundays did sit reading in the lower end of the church, and many would flock to hear their reading . . . then I saw I could not rest. Then thought I, I will learn to read English, and then I will have the New Testament and read thereon myself.

His father strongly disapproved, but he and another apprentice saved up; they bought their New Testament, and 'hid it in our bedstraw' so they could read it whenever possible — in spite of a serious family row in which his father threatened to hang him with a noose.

We have no way of knowing how many were reading the English Bible like this, but it is certain that it gradually became an important part of English life for ordinary people as well as educated ones.

This is the front page of the Great Bible in English, which was printed largely at Cromwell's expense. Its design is carefully planned. At the top the King sits enthroned, handing out Bibles to his important subjects. It is not so easy to see God, though He is there, above Henry's head. Below him, Cranmer in his Archbishop's mitre, and the soberly dressed Cromwell, also hand out the Bible. At the bottom, a preacher tells ordinary people to pray for all men, especially the King, and they answer (in Latin) 'Long live the King!'.

1. How does the picture opposite show that the King wanted his subjects to understand that it was more important for them to obey him over Church matters, than to read the Bible?

2. Why did Henry become worried when ordinary people began to read the Bible?

3. What does William Malden's story tell you about the difficulties facing ordinary people if they wanted to read the Bible?

4. Why did William's father disapprove so strongly?

5. Why is it difficult to enforce law telling people what they should or should not read?

Opposition

The break with Rome was a kind of revolution. The disappearance of the monasteries, and the reading of the English Bible in churches, meant that everywhere in the country people knew about the change. Anyone important had to swear the oath accepting the Act of Succession. There were bound to be some who disapproved, but the risks involved in open opposition meant most kept quiet. Some, however, were braver.

←88

←54

Sir Thomas More Henry VIII admired Sir Thomas More and made him his Chancellor when Wolsey fell in 1529. Perhaps he was trying to persuade More to support the divorce, for More openly disapproved; he resigned in 1532, and soon refused to swear the oath. In spite of 17 months' imprisonment in a small cell in the Tower of London, and continuous questioning, he remained silent.

In the prayer book which he used during this time, he added in his own writing 'Give me grace, Good Lord to set the world at nought, to set my mind fast upon thee.' Finally, he was put on trial, found guilty, and executed in July 1535.

Bishop John Fisher The King did not forget Bishop Fisher's defence of Queen Catherine at Blackfriars. When he refused to swear the oath, he too was imprisoned in the Tower. The Pope did not help. He made Fisher a Cardinal to show his support. Henry flew into a rage, and swore that Fisher would wear his red hat on his shoulders, for he would never leave him a head to set it on. The threat was soon carried out; Fisher was executed just before Thomas More.

The Monks of the Charterhouse in London The monks of the Charterhouse were rather unusual: they lived strict and disciplined lives, devoted to God. Most of them refused to swear the oath; they were imprisoned in dreadful conditions in the Tower, tied to posts with no food or drink.

The pictures on the next page show them being dragged to their deaths on hurdles, and being hanged, drawn and quartered. The imprisoned Thomas More, who admired them greatly and knew some of them,

Bishop John Fisher by Holbein

He was a tall, imposing man, though by the time of his execution, he was old and ill. But he never wavered in his opposition to the King's divorce.

watched as they went to their deaths. He said to his daughter, who was visiting him: 'Lo, dost thou not see, Meg, that these blessed fathers be now as cheerfully going to their deaths as bridegrooms to their marriage?' The Prior's severed arm was nailed to the monastery gateway, and the few remaining monks gave in.

The Pilgrimage of Grace Late in 1536, the citizens of Louth (see page 50) who had spent so much on the new steeple for their parish church, were very worried by all kinds of rumours. If the King was going to destroy the monasteries, what else might lie ahead? Taxes on christenings, marriages and burials? Would the parish treasure be taken? Would their parish church be in danger? Their priest preached a fiery sermon; there was a riot, and the rebels marched to Lincoln. When the Duke of Suffolk appeared with armed men, the rebellion soon collapsed. But a Yorkshire lawyer, Robert Aske, who was travelling home from London full of grievances about the Church, sympathised with the Lincolnshire men. He began to win support in the north of England from both gentry and ordinary people. Robert Aske was a religious man, and the name he gave his movement was not a warlike one. He called it a 'Pilgrimage of Grace' to persuade the King to restore the monasteries, to make Princess Mary legitimate, and to get rid of 'heretic' advisers like Cromwell and Cranmer. There were other demands which showed the local feeling that government in London neglected the north. They demanded that Parliament should be held in York, for instance; and there were complaints about high rents and enclosures (see page 10).

Soon the north had risen, and the 'Pilgrims' marched south. The Duke of Norfolk faced them at Doncaster: Aske was persuaded that if he told his followers to go home, and he went to London, the King would listen to his demands. At first, Henry appeared quite sympathetic. But he had gained the time he needed to raise more troops, and further unrest in the north gave him the excuse he wanted. Aske was sent to be hanged in chains from York Castle, and nearly 200 others were also executed. There was no more trouble from the King's northern subjects.

■ Why did the Pilgrims' demands receive support in the north?

Wives

Everyone knows that Henry VIII had six wives. But not everyone realises that the story of each wife is closely linked to the great religious changes which took place in his reign.

Jane Seymour

The loyalty Henry promised Anne Boleyn when he was courting her in 1527 did not survive her failure to produce a son. After the birth of Elizabeth, she had a still-born son — she 'miscarried of her saviour', as

was said at the time. Henry was tiring of her sharp tongue too, but while Catherine of Aragon was still alive, he could not get rid of Anne. That would mean he admitted he had been wrong over his 'Great Matter'. However, in 1536, Catherine died. Anne was accused of unfaithfulness (probably unjustly) and sent to the block. As a sign of 'mercy', she was executed with a sword, not an axe.

This took place as the monasteries were disappearing, and Henry seemed to look more kindly on Protestant ideas. Jane Seymour, a quiet and gentle lady at court, was a welcome contrast to Anne, and Henry already favoured her family, in spite of its Protestant leanings. It was Queen Jane who in 1537 bore the son and heir Edward, for whom Henry had waited so long. She did not survive the dangers of sixteenth-century childbirth, and died 12 days later. The King was grief-stricken.

Jane Seymour, by Holbein

Anne of Cleves

The Duke of Norfolk had been in a difficult position when his niece, Anne Boleyn, was executed, and he left court for a time. But the King could not do without such a powerful noble, and the Duke was restored to favour when he helped to crush the Pilgrimage of Grace. The Duke was now determined to get rid of Cromwell; he resented Cromwell's power and believed he was pushing the King too near to Protestantism. At the same time, there were great dangers abroad. The Emperor and the King of France, usually such bitter rivals, were together planning a Catholic crusade against the heretic King of England. Cromwell's answer to both these threats was an alliance with the Protestant princes of Germany, who were fighting the Emperor. A new marriage to a Protestant German princess, Anne of Cleves, would seal the alliance.

The artist, Holbein, was sent to paint her, and the marriage took place by proxy. When Henry met his new wife, he was said to be horrified, and he compared her to a Flanders mare — a clumsy, stocky beast. But probably he was also tired of the idea of a Protestant alliance. A divorce was speedily arranged.

Catherine Howard

Cromwell's position was now very dangerous, because the Duke of Norfolk had brought another young and attractive niece to court, Catherine Howard, and the King was paying her a great deal of attention. The Emperor and the King of France were quarrelling again too, so the dangers from abroad were less; and Henry felt free to act as he pleased. The King was also worried that all the changes in the Church might destroy the old beliefs, so the Act of the Six Articles, which stated the six most important Catholic beliefs, went through Parliament in 1539. In June 1540, Cromwell walked into the Council Chamber to find officers from the Tower waiting with a warrant for his arrest. He never saw the King again, and was executed a month later. Henry soon married Catherine

Anne of Cleves, by Holbein

Since Holbein does not seem to have got into trouble for flattering her, perhaps this quite attractive portrait is a realistic view of her — and Henry had already made up his mind he did not want the match before he ever saw her.

Howard. It was not long before the King regretted both these events. He soon began to miss the most able minister of his reign, who had served him faithfully for eight years. And Catherine was unwise enough to be unfaithful to Henry, who was now unhealthy and overweight, with a painful ulcer on his leg. It is said that Hampton Court is haunted by her cries as she was taken to the Tower to be executed for treason.

Catherine Parr

This time, the Duke of Norfolk realised the situation in time, and survived the fall of another niece by helping to accuse her. Henry still seemed to favour the old beliefs too. But there were other straws in the wind. Archbishop Cranmer had survived, though in 1543 he only escaped arrest in the Council Chamber like Cromwell, because he had a ring from the King which guaranteed his safety. He was still quietly loyal, but he was beginning to work on an English Prayer Book which was undoubtedly Protestant. Also, Henry's last marriage was to a sensible learned woman, Catherine Parr, who was also interested in the Protestant religion. She brought Henry's three children to court, and at last they were for a time a reasonably happy family. When the Duke of Norfolk tried to poison the King's mind against her, she managed to win Henry over. It was Norfolk who spent the last months of the reign in the Tower, and he only escaped execution because the sick old King died the night before the appointed date.

Catherine Parr, by an unknown artist

She tactfully cared for the King in his last years.

The end of the reign

No one really knows what Henry believed by 1547, the end of his reign. A Catholic said soon after his death that the King was like 'one who would throw a man headlong from the top of a high tower, and bid him stay where he was half way down.' The Act of the Six Articles (see page 95) was still in force. But the disappearance of the monasteries, and the English Bible, had changed English life. It is hard to know how many English Protestants there were by now, but since the 1520s, Protestant teachings had quietly crept into England, brought by merchants and scholars who travelled in the Netherlands and Germany. Cranmer's Protestant Prayer Book was nearly finished and Henry's nine-year-old son Edward had Protestant teachers.

The formidable, bulky old King — a portrait probably copied from Holbein in about 1540

1. Make a list of the important people in Henry's reign. Using different colours, for Catholic and Protestant, underline the names to show their beliefs.

2. Today, TV interviewers ask politicians searching questions about what they are doing and why. Imagine you could interview Henry VIII at the end of his reign in this way. In class discussion, work out the questions you would like to ask him, and how he might answer. You could then choose actors, and tape the interview.

The Protestant Court of Edward VI

This imaginary picture (which could hardly have actually taken place) shows the young King Edward VI receiving his power from his dying father. Edward was only nine in 1547; though one writer described him as a 'marvellous boy' who could speak Latin and French, and he was so religious that 'he receives into his own hand a copy of every sermon he hears', he obviously could not rule the country himself. So, with a child King too young to rule, the problems of a 'minority' were added to the difficulties over religion. This is a propaganda picture, intended to put the Government's point of view. What has the artist been told to do to show the power of the new King?

By the King's side stands his uncle, the Duke of Somerset, who made himself Protector, with full powers to rule. He was inefficient and unpopular with his fellow councillors around the table; he fell from power when he failed to quell two serious rebellions in 1549. Next to him (almost certainly) sits the man who then replaced him; the Duke of Northumberland, a more efficient and equally ruthless character. On the left is Archbishop Cranmer, who kept out of the power struggles, and now put his Protestant beliefs into practice serving the young Protestant King.

The picture shows clearly what Protestants believed to be important: ←58

The English Bible falls threateningly on the Pope's head, doing him no good at all. Two monks hastily escape in the bottom left-hand corner. The words on the Pope's chest say 'All flesh is grass', and to his right, 'Feyned (pretended) holiness', and 'Idolatry'. Why have these words been chosen as labels for Edward's enemies?

Statues and pictures in churches had to go: a government proclamation in 1549 ordered all images to be destroyed, and in the top right-hand corner soldiers pull down a statue of the Virgin Mary.

Cranmer's English Prayer Book is rather surprisingly not shown in the picture. It first appeared in 1549, and though it kept the shape of the old Latin service, it was simpler. Cranmer hoped Protestants would accept it because it was in English. But for many, it was too much of a compromise; and in 1552 it was altered to make it closer to Protestant beliefs.

THE TUDOR FAMILY

HENRY VII 1485-1509 m ELIZABETH OF YORK

| Arthur d1502 m Catherine of Aragon | HENRY VIII 1509-47 m | | | Margaret m JAMES IV of Scotland | Mary m the Duke of Suffolk |

① Catherine of Aragon

MARY I 1553-8 m Philip of Spain

② Anne Boleyn

ELIZABETH I 1558-1603

③ Jane Seymour

EDWARD VI 1547-53

JAMES V m Mary of Guise

Frances m Henry Grey

④ Anne of Cleves

⑤ Catherine Howard

⑥ Catherine Parr

Mary, Queen of Scots (Mary Stuart)

Lady Jane Grey "The Nine Days' Queen" 1553

JAMES VI of Scotland and I of England b1566 The Stuart line begins in 1603.

REIGNING SOVEREIGNS ARE IN CAPITAL LETTERS.
The dates of their reigns are shown by their names.

Princess Elizabeth, aged 13, by an unknown artist

The two daughters of Henry VIII

Before he died Henry VIII laid down that both his daughters should be recognised as legal heirs to the throne if Edward died. Mary, now aged 31, was next in line. She was firmly Catholic, loyal to her Spanish mother's memory. She refused to attend Protestant services, and no one seriously tried to make her do so. It was difficult to force someone as important as the heir to the throne. Her relationship with her younger sister had always been uneasy. She had been 12 when she was banished from court and her mother, Catherine of Aragon, humiliated. Mary did not forget that Elizabeth was the daughter of Anne Boleyn.

Elizabeth was 13 when her father died. At first she remained in the care of Catherine Parr, the last of Henry VIII's wives. Catherine married Thomas Seymour, the ambitious younger brother of the Duke of Somerset. Perhaps he soon tired of Henry VIII's widow. He certainly flirted with the young Elizabeth; and when he was accused of treason, she quickly learned that such involvements were dangerous, for she was threatened herself for a time. She remained cautious after that — both about people, and about her beliefs. Self-contained and well-educated, she chose at this age to be painted holding a book to emphasise her learning — and perhaps to show her long, slim hands as well.

The Nine Days' Queen

After all Henry's efforts to ensure he had a son to succeed him it was nevertheless women who remained at the centre of the changes in religion. By the time he was 16, Edward was desperately ill with tuberculosis. The new Protestant Church would be doomed if Mary became Queen, so the sick young King, and the Duke of Northumberland who was ruling for him, decided on a 'Device' to set aside Mary and Elizabeth. They chose as the new Queen Lady Jane Grey, a quiet, learned girl, firm in her Protestant beliefs, and very unwilling to become involved in power struggles. What relation was she to Edward? Her parents were ambitious for her; and to ensure his own position, Northumberland arranged a marriage between Jane and his son, Lord Guildford Dudley, which she almost certainly did not want. When Edward died in 1553, Jane ruled as Queen for nine days, until support for the rightful Queen built up, as Mary firmly claimed her crown. When Mary rode into London in triumph, Northumberland was already awaiting execution. Mary wanted to save Jane, and left her and her husband in the Tower.

Lady Jane Grey, aged about 13

This artist, Master John, has painted her clothes skilfully, but he has not attempted to provide a solid, realistic figure. You could turn it into a pattern of triangles — and then use your pattern to create your own copy of the portrait.

Mary I at the beginning of her reign, painted by Hans Eworth

She wears the great pearl drop brooch probably given to her by Philip as a wedding present.

Catholic Queen

For the first time for centuries, England had a reigning Queen. She had one clear aim: to bring her kingdom back to the Catholic Church. Everyone took it for granted that she would marry, for no one thought that a woman could rule on her own. But there was much disagreement over who her husband should be. An Englishman like Edward Courtenay, a descendant of Edward IV, would make the other nobles jealous; a foreigner would tie England to another power. Mary however had no doubts. The only husband she would consider was Philip of Spain, the son of the Emperor Charles V. If she was closely linked to her mother's country, she would be strong enough to restore the true faith. And God would surely grant a son to succeed her, so that her younger sister Elizabeth, whom she did not trust, would never become Queen.

Even before the marriage took place, a rebellion led by a Kentish gentleman, Sir Thomas Wyatt, showed what some of Mary's subjects thought of it. The rebels reached London, but surrendered when Mary firmly roused the citizens, to support their Queen. Although Elizabeth was much too cautious to be directly involved, she was in great danger; for a time she was sent to the Tower and then to semi-imprisonment in Woodstock. Lady Jane Grey, whose father supported the rebellion, was executed, and so was her husband. She was just seventeen, a pawn in other people's ambitious schemes.

Mary and Philip were married in July 1554 in great pomp. The wedding took place at Winchester Cathedral, because Mary's advisers feared there

A Spanish view of the English in 1554

One of Philip's Spanish attendants wrote home:

> The Queen is not at all beautiful — small and rather flabby than fat, she is of white complexion and fair, and has no eyebrows. She is a perfect saint, and dresses badly. . .

> This match will have been a fine business if the Queen does not have a child and I am sure she will not . . .

> (English women are) neither beautiful nor graceful . . . not a single Spanish gentleman has fallen in love with one of them, nor takes any interest in them, and their feelings for us are the same.

Philip of Spain, at the time of his marriage to Mary

be riots in London. The Spaniards who came with Philip were very unpopular, and except for an attempt to drink English beer, Philip does not seem to have made much effort to please.

From every point of view, the marriage was a disaster. Mary was pathetically in love with her much younger husband; but he was only interested in returning to Spain, which he ruled for his father, and which he would soon inherit. He stayed in England just over a year, and returned briefly once, in 1557, not to see his wife, but to win support for his war in France.

The war was disastrous too, for England lost Calais, her last important possession on the mainland of Europe. Although Calais had been an expensive luxury to maintain, and in the end the results were not serious, at the time the loss seemed to be national disaster, and one more bad result of the Spanish marriage.

Finally, the marriage did not produce the son for whom Mary longed. She twice mistakenly thought she was pregnant. Midwives were engaged, a cradle prepared, and Elizabeth in Woodstock tactfully made some baby clothes. In fact, Mary was already suffering from the disease which would kill her; her disappointment was one more sadness amongst the many she suffered.

Persecution

When Mary became Queen, about 400 prosperous English Protestants, mostly gentry, fled to Germany and Switzerland because they could worship safely there. They were right to fear what might happen if they stayed, for Mary was determined not only to bring back the Pope's power, but also to stamp out Protestant belief. She genuinely believed the Catholic faith was the only true way to God, and that persecution would save the souls of heretics.

←59

Mary was an idealist: she believed in following the right course, whatever the difficulties. But there was one practical difficult that even she understood. The monasteries were part of the old Church and must be restored. But would all those who had bought monastic lands give them back? Mary restored the monastery at Westminster at her own expense, and hoped her subjects would follow her example. They did not. But most of them realised the old faith would return, and were probably not too sorry to go back to familiar ways, as long as their lands were safe.

Mary had an Archbishop of Canterbury as zealous as she was. Cardinal Pole had spent years in exile in Italy because he disapproved of the break with Rome, and had just returned to an England he hardly knew. Together Mary and Cardinal Pole urged their bishops to hunt out Protestants, and burn them as heretics.

Four Protestant bishops were burned, three of them at Oxford. Hugh Latimer, famous for his preaching, suffered with Nicholas Ridley on the same wet day in October 1555. Seeing his friend in agony as the damp faggots smouldered, Bishop Latimer said: 'Be of good comfort, Master Ridley, and play the man. We shall this day light such a candle, by God's grace, in England as I trust shall never be put out.'

←24

Above all, Mary was determined to punish Archbishop Cranmer who had served Henry VIII so faithfully in his 'Great Matter'. He was old by now; and unlike many people in the Early Modern Age, he had taken a long time to work out his Protestant beliefs, perhaps because he could see the other side of the argument. He also believed strongly in obedience to his sovereign — but should he obey a Catholic Queen? He was kept in prison: Spanish friars constantly urged him to deny his faith, and he was made to watch his friends, Latimer and Ridley, go to their deaths. Finally, six months later, he gave in and signed a recantation saying he gave up his Protestant faith and accepted Catholic beliefs. But Mary still felt he should suffer for all the years when he was a heretic. She ordered the execution to go ahead. Cranmer now realised what he had done. He was

←59

The burning of the two Protestant bishops, Latimer and Ridley — an illustration from Foxe's 'Book of Martyrs'

brought to the stake 'with a cheerful countenance', accompanied by two friars, still trying to convert him. However he firmly stated his Protestant faith. This is how a Catholic eye-witness described his death in March 1556:

> Fire being now put to him, he stretched out his right hand and thrust it into the flame, and held it there a good space, before the fire came to any other part of his body . . . crying out with a loud voice, 'This hand hath offended'. As soon as the fire was got up, he was very soon dead, never stirring or crying . . . Surely his death much grieved every man . . . his friends sorrowed for love, his enemies for pity, strangers for a common kind of humanity whereby we are bound one to another.

■ How do you think the Catholic eye-witness felt about Cranmer's death? Give reasons for your answer.

Apart from the four bishops, and 16 priests, it was ordinary people who suffered: tradesmen, weavers and other clothworkers, farm labourers, and more than 50 women. One poor woman gave birth to a baby just as she was brought to the stake, and the baby was thrown into the fire along with her.

These figures show where there were most burnings:

> London, 67; Middlesex, 11; Essex, 39; Kent, 58; Sussex, 23; Suffolk, 18; Norfolk, 14; Gloucestershire, 10; Wales, 3; Devon and Cornwall, 1; the North, 1. The full total was just under 300.

When we think of the burnings, we need to remember that people watched public executions as a matter of course in the Early Modern Age; also that hanging, drawing and quartering for treason, which many of Henry VIII's opponents suffered, was just as horrible a death as burning. However, in Europe, and especially in Spain, burning was more common than in England, so once again (and probably unjustly) the Spaniards were blamed. Because it was mostly ordinary people who suffered, Protestants won sympathy because of a 'common kind of humanity', even from those who did not share their beliefs. But it was a best-selling book, which was not published till 1563, after Mary's death, which made sure that the burnings were never forgotten in England. John Foxe, an enthusiastic Protestant, collected together the stories of the martyrs. The facts were accurate, and illustrated the pictures like the one on page 101. Like the English Bible, Foxe's *Book of Martyrs* became part of English life.

1 Look at the figures given of the burnings on this page. In what parts of England was Protestantism obviously strong? In these areas, there were more towns, there was more trade with Germany and the Netherlands, and there were more people who could read. Think of reasons why these things might help the spread of Protestantism.

←96

2 Do you think Mary was a cruel person? Think about all her actions, not just the burnings.

The middle way

Mary died at Westminster on 17 November 1558; Archbishop Pole, with whom she worked so closely, died the same night. Her husband was in Spain, and she had no son to follow her. Persecution had not brought dramatic conversions. Two bad harvests and a killer influenza epidemic had brought great suffering to her subjects; and Calais was lost. It was not a happy end to her reign.

There was a great welcome for the 25-year-old Elizabeth when she rode into London as the new Queen, but there were many worries too. The greatest seemed to be divisions and confusion in the country, caused by the changes in religion over the last 30 years. Could another woman ruler find a settlement? The cool-headed and realistic Elizabeth had kept her views to herself as far as she could, especially during her sister's reign. But now she knew a decision had to be made quickly. Can you see why the daughter of Anne Boleyn could not be the obedient servant of a Catholic Pope, as her half-sister had been? Elizabeth and her councillors set out to make a settlement that was a 'middle way', which they hoped would unite a deeply divided country.

The coronation of the young Queen

Her red hair flows loose under her crown, and she holds the sceptre and orb, the other two symbols of her power.

The middle way of the Church of England

To please Catholics The old organisation of bishops set over the ordinary clergy remained.
The same buildings were used, many of them old and beautiful.
The order of services was still quite like the Catholic service.

To please Protestants Cranmer's Prayer Book was based on Protestant beliefs. It was written in clear, dignified English.
There were no monks, shrines or relics, and fewer pictures and statues in churches.
The English Bible was read regularly in every church.
The Pope had no power over the English Church.

Look back at the table on page 58.

This was all enforced by two Acts of Parliament in 1559:

The Act of Supremacy Elizabeth I became Supreme Governor of the Church of England. Perhaps it was hoped that Catholics would find this title easier to accept than Supreme Head.

The Act of Uniformity Cranmer's Prayer Book of 1552, with a few alterations, had to be used in every parish church. If anyone refused to go to church, they had to pay a shilling fine. This was a lot for the poor, but a small sum for the rich.

The Queen and her Church

A 'middle way' very often pleases neither side. The new Church needed time for loyalty to grow. Elizabeth I made it plain that there were to be no more changes, and that in Church matters everyone must obey her. She could be harsh. This is a letter she wrote to the Bishop of Ely who had refused (quite rightly) to give some of his church lands to one of Elizabeth's courtiers, when she had ordered him to do so:

Bishop

dismiss

Proud *Prelate*,

You know what you were before I made you what you are now. If you do not immediately comply with my request, I will *unfrock* you, by God.

Elizabeth

Elizabeth's flowing confident signature

■ How many things can you find that make this letter particularly rude?

The Queen also strongly disapproved of some of her Protestant subjects who wanted to 'purify' the Church of England. Many of them had been in exile in Mary's reign in Protestant centres in Europe like Calvin's Geneva. They were soon given the nickname of 'Puritans'.

Puritans and Parliament

English Puritans wanted these changes:

Less power for bishops — perhaps even no bishops at all.
No special clothes (vestments) for clergy in church.
Services and church buildings to be as simple as possible.
More Bible reading and sermons to explain the Bible.

■ What kind of lifestyle did Calvin expect of his followers in Geneva? Think of reasons why shopkeepers and craftsmen in towns were more likely to follow this lifestyle than fashionable people, though some rich people who agreed with Calvin's ideas did so too.

←88, 103 Since Parliament had been used to change the Church already, and many Puritans were rich enough to be MPs, they tried to push through more changes when Parliament met. Elizabeth was determined to stop them, so there were several quarrels. In 1587, for instance, Peter Wentworth, a fiery Puritan who had already spent time in the Tower for criticising the Church, said:

We will pass nothing before we understand what it is, for that were to make you popes. *Make you popes who list* [others can make you a Pope if they wish] . . . we will make you none.

He was sent to the Tower again, but not for long. The Queen did not crush her opponents in the way her father had done, even if she did not like their actions. Puritans did not give up, however, though they achieved nothing in Elizabeth's reign. They were loyal too, and saw Catholics as a great threat to the Queen. In 1579 John Stubbs, a Puritan lawyer, wrote a pamphlet against the marriage she was considering with a Catholic French prince. He too was punished — very severely — by having his hand cut off. As the terrible sentence was carried out, he cried: 'God save the Queen!' and then fainted. The publisher who had printed the pamphlet suffered the same way, and lifted his mutilated arm, shouting: 'I have left there a true Englishman's hand.'

Some Puritans chose to dress plainly, but clothes were more likely to indicate a person's wealth and position, rather than their religious opinions. To what social class do you think these women belong?

Virgo Anglica.

Mercatorum uxori

Elizabeth hoped too that Catholics would be loyal subjects, and attend the services of the Church of England. Most English Catholics just wanted to be left in peace to practise their faith. Some went to the parish church, and then secretly held Mass when they got home. Others paid their shilling for non-attendance, though if they lived in areas such as Lancashire where most of the gentry were still Catholic, the fine was often not enforced. But all this soon changed because of another Queen who became a very great danger to Elizabeth. Once again two women were at the heart of a serious religious crisis, and once again Scotland played an important part in the affairs of the whole of Britain.

←103

The Northern Kingdom

There had been difficult times in Scotland since the terrible defeat at Flodden, when Henry VIII's victory had left his sister a widow, and Scotland with a two-year-old King, James V. Until James grew up, the turbulent, independent Scots nobles were unchecked. He became a harsh ruler: he also strengthened his position in the usual way. He married a French princess, Mary of Guise, and revived the Auld Alliance. 1542 was another bad year for Scotland. Henry VIII sent an English army over the Border which won a victory at Solway Moss. James V, already sick and depressed, seems to have lost the will to live; as he lay dying, he was told of the birth of his baby daughter, another Mary. Once again, there was a tiny child on the Scots throne, and this time it was a girl.

←2

The English continued to take advantage of Scots weakness: first Henry VIII, and then the Duke of Somerset, in Edward VI's reign, ravaged southern Scotland. They saw the chance to swallow up the northern kingdom by this 'rough wooing'; the baby Mary, Queen of Scots, could be married to Edward of England, and the two thrones united for ever. Few Scots were ready to accept that; neither were the French. When Mary was five, she was taken to the safety of the French court, where a glittering future awaited her; she was betrothed to the heir to the throne of France. Her mother, Mary of Guise, remained in Scotland to rule the kingdom.

Another problem further divided the Scots. The royal family was firmly Catholic, but they had been unable to prevent Protestant teachings, especially those of Calvin (see page 57), reaching Scotland. In the Lowlands, and especially Edinburgh, they began to win followers, who were not prepared to obey Mary of Guise and her councillors.

John Knox

John Knox first began to preach in Scotland in 1547, and became one of the most fiery leaders of the Scots Reformation. He was soon captured by the French, and spent eight terrible years working as a prisoner at the oar of a galley as a punishment for disloyalty. He already hated Catholics; he

John Knox

also became convinced no good could ever come from a woman ruler. However, Elizabeth and her advisers felt that Mary of Guise was dangerous so they gave help to the Scots Protestants who were rebelling against her. It was English help, from an English Queen, which made it possible in 1560 for the Scots Parliament to establish a Protestant 'Kirk of Scotland'. This Church was strongly supported in the south of Scotland, and John Knox was its most powerful preacher. But Mary of Guise still ruled, and the more remote Highlands remained firmly Catholic.

Mary, Queen of Scots: Threat to Elizabeth

Born 1542. Died 1587.

Queen of Scotland by birth.

Queen of France by marriage. In 1559, the year after Elizabeth became Queen of England, Mary's young husband became King Francis II of France.

Queen of England in the eyes of those Catholics who did not accept the marriage of Henry VIII and Anne Boleyn. In any case she was Elizabeth's cousin, and the heir to the English throne, unless Elizabeth married and had a child.

Tall, athletic, red-haired and slender, Mary loved France and the French court where she had grown up. She was also, of course, a firm Catholic.

In 1560, as the Reformation took hold in southern Scotland, the young King of France died suddenly of an ear infection. The eighteen-year-old Mary was now a widow; and by 1561 she had sadly returned to her unfamiliar Scots kingdom. There were riots in Edinburgh on the first Sunday that Mass was celebrated in the royal palace; Mary had to listen to Knox's lectures on the evils of women rulers. To Mary and her subjects, a second marriage was obviously the next step.

Marriages, murders and rebellion

Mary's choice was Lord Darnley, a handsome young man, but arrogant and stupid. He, too, was descended from Henry VII. Mary soon discovered her husband's unpleasant character, and sought comfort (probably quite innocently) from her Italian secretary, David Riccio. One evening, Mary, who was pregnant, held a supper party, at which Riccio was present. Suddenly, Darnley and several armed lords burst in. Riccio clung to the Queen's skirts, but he was dragged out of the room and brutally murdered.

Mary's son, James, was safely born three months later, in June 1566. She never trusted Darnley again, and began to rely on a Protestant noble, Lord Bothwell. But she kept up appearances, and nursed her husband through smallpox. One night, as he lay recovering, she left him to attend a courtier's wedding party. While she was away, the house blew up, and

The young Mary, Queen of Scots

Darnley was found strangled in the garden. Although many suspected Bothwell, and perhaps even Mary as well, there was only a show trial. Mary soon married Bothwell (who had divorced his wife) in a Protestant ceremony. Can you see why most of her subjects now neither supported nor respected her? She faced a serious rebellion, and was defeated and imprisoned. Bothwell fled to Denmark and died miserably after years of imprisonment there. In 1568, after another defeat at Langside, Mary fled over the border into England. Her baby son was made James VI by the nobles who had brought down his mother. Once more Scotland faced years of difficulty under a child king. Meanwhile in England, both Elizabeth and her Catholic subjects had a major problem to face.

The royal cousins

In 1568, Elizabeth I faced these facts about Mary:

> Mary was still a firm Catholic, despite her marriage to Bothwell.
>
> She was still closely linked to France, who remained unfriendly to England.
>
> She was still heir to the English throne, and, to some, the rightful Queen.
>
> She was Elizabeth's cousin, and a Queen as well.
>
> She was possibly involved in the murder of Darnley.

Elizabeth's problem

> She knew that some of her Catholic subjects might support Mary.
>
> She knew that the French might help Mary.
>
> She disapproved of Mary's behaviour, but she also disapproved of rebels.

Possible courses of action

> Mary could be sent back to Scotland — where the 'rebels' would imprison her.
>
> She could be sent to France — where she might be given a dangerous amount of help.
>
> She could be imprisoned in England — where she might become the centre of plots.

1 Take a class vote on which course you would choose if you were Elizabeth. Then discuss the reasons why you voted as you did.

2 Elizabeth in fact imprisoned Mary in England; she held an inquiry into Mary's possible guilt, which settled nothing. What do you think were Elizabeth's reasons for the decision she took? Could she have safely done anything else?

It was obvious that imprisoning Mary in England was not safe either. The North rose in rebellion in 1569, partly at least in support of her. Then there followed a series of plots to put her on the English throne, though these involved only small groups of English Catholics. Soon the actions of two powerful foreign rulers made the situation far more dangerous and difficult, not only for Elizabeth, but also for her Catholic subjects.

Both these miniatures are by the Elizabethan painter, Nicholas Hilliard. Elizabeth I's portrait is realistic, and the flowing golden writing on it tells us that it was painted in 1572, when she was 38. Mary (below) was painted at about the same age, when she had been imprisoned for more than ten years. Why does Elizabeth wear a rose, and Mary a crucifix?

The Pope and the King of Spain

Though France seemed a danger, in fact she soon became torn and weakened by civil war. Two other rulers became a far greater threat.

The Pope issued a Bull in 1570. In this he declared Elizabeth a heretic whom her subjects need no longer obey. Do you see what he expected English Catholics to do, when he said this?

Philip II of Spain had been friendly toward Elizabeth when she first became Queen, and even considered marrying her for a time. His attitude changed for several reasons. From the late 1560s a serious rebellion broke out in the Netherlands, where many of his subjects were Protestants. After much hesitation, Elizabeth helped these Protestant rebels. In 1585 she sent an expedition there, commanded by her favourite, the Earl of Leicester. It achieved little, but it certainly did not ←46 please the King of Spain. He also ruled the Spanish Empire in the New World, and Spanish galleons regularly brought valuable cargoes of treasure back home. English sailors had begun to sail into 'The Spanish Main' in the 1560s, first in search of trade, but soon to attack the Spanish treasure ships. By 1580, Francis Drake had completed his three-year voyage round the world, and his ship *The Golden Hind* had returned laden with Spanish treasure. In 1580 too, Philip became stronger because he took over Portugal. He had already decided that the old friendship with England was at an end, and had begun to plan a Catholic crusade against the Protestant Elizabeth, in which English Catholics must play their part. He wrote this as early as 1565:

> The Pope and I will consider the manner in which we may aid . . . the cause of God which now the Queen of Scotland upholds, since . . . she is the gate by which religion must enter the realm of England, all others now being closed.

Traitors or martyrs?

So three foreigners, the Pope, Philip II of Spain and Mary Queen of Scots, completely altered the position of English Catholics. Since they were now expected to plot against the reigning Queen, and support a foreign invasion if it came, they were faced with a terrible choice: were they to be loyal to their faith, or to their Protestant Queen?

By 1580, Catholic priests especially trained in the Netherlands, and Jesuits (see page 58) trained in Rome, began to come secretly into England. Some sailed into hidden bays and creeks, and were guided to 'safe houses' by local sympathisers; others arrived at busy ports in disguise. Most of them were hidden in gentlemen's houses, such as Stonor and Mapledurham in the Thames Valley. Were they coming to hold services and teach the faithful, or to organise plots to assassinate Elizabeth, and put Mary on the throne?

Catholic 'safe houses' often had secret place like this one in Sawston Hall near Cambridge, where priests could hide when the house was being searched. Sometimes this took so long that a priest had to survive for several days in a tiny space — and some, like Edmund Campion, were caught in their hiding place.

Elizabeth and her councillors believed they could take no risks in this dangerous situation, with growing fear of plots at home, and of a Spanish invasion from abroad. In 1581, Parliament passed a law making it treason to *be* a Catholic priest, or to help one in any way. Fines for not going to Church of England services were increased from one shilling to £20, which, Sunday by Sunday, could soon add up to a crippling sum, even for a rich man. All over the country too, gentry and nobles swore an oath, or 'Bond Association' to defend their Queen against Catholic plots, by violence and murder if need be. Were they right to fear Catholics so much?

Historians still argue whether this was a religious persecution like Mary's burnings. About 250 Catholics were executed for treason — how close is that to the number of Protestants who died under Mary (see page 102)? Some were tortured to make them give evidence of plots and many bravely refused to tell. They died because they were Catholics. Some were involved in plots against Elizabeth. Why is it difficult to tell how many?

The 'monstrous huge dragon'

There is no doubt there were plots to put Mary on the English throne after the Pope's Bull of 1570. Only a year later the Ridolfi plot was discovered. This was backed by Spain, and the aim was to marry the Duke of Norfolk (grandson to the Duke of Henry VIII's time) to Mary. The Duke was executed, and the family lost the title. Parliament petitioned Elizabeth to execute the 'monstrous huge dragon', as they called the Queen of Scots, and councillors tried constantly to persuade her. But Elizabeth disliked executions, and the execution of a Queen who was also a relative filled her with horror. For nearly 20 years, she would have none of it.

— Campian

In 1581 the well-known Catholic priest, Edmund Campion, was caught hiding in a country house in Berkshire after celebrating Mass. He was captured and tortured to try to make him confess that he was involved in plots against the Queen. Right up to the moment of his execution, he firmly said he had come only 'to teach the Gospel'.

Sir Francis Walsingham and the Babington plot

In 1585, Walsingham began to employ a double agent, a priest in touch with Mary, who gave him copies of all letters she received and sent. A local brewer, also in Walsingham's pay, smuggled the correspondence in the false bottom of a beer barrel in and out of Chartley Manor, where Mary was imprisoned. A group of Catholic gentlemen, led by Anthony Babington, a rash and romantic youth, plotted to kill Elizabeth, and wrote to Mary to plan her escape. Mary replied, and the letters provided evidence to hang the plotters and involve Mary too. Walsingham's secretary in London drew a gallows on the outside of Mary's letter when it reached him.

■ Why do you think some historians distrust these letters which Walsingham passed on to the Queen to persuade her to execute Mary?

Elizabeth could now delay no longer. Mary was tried at Fotheringay Castle in Northamptonshire, found guilty of conspiracy, and her death warrant

was signed. On a cold February morning in 1587, the local gentry gathered in the great hall of the castle to witness the death of the Queen of Scots. Soon after 8 o'clock she was brought in, carrying a crucifix and wearing black with a crimson petticoat, with a white veil on her auburn hair. She was middle-aged now, and lame with rheumatism, but she moved with great dignity. She refused to join in English prayers, and said her own Latin ones loudly and firmly. Then her ladies removed her black outer dress, to reveal the petticoats of crimson, the colour of martyrdom. After the axe fell, the executioner held up the severed head for all to see. It fell from his grasp, revealing short grey hair, and he was left holding the white veil and an auburn wig. Her little dog had hidden under her skirts, and could not be coaxed away.

■ This description is based on eye-witness accounts. Find as much evidence in it as you can to show that Mary meant everyone to know she died as a Catholic martyr.

This contemporary drawing of the execution of Mary, Queen of Scots, shows three stages in the final scene: on the left, Mary enters the crowded hall; in the centre, she stands on the scaffold with the low block nearby, and her ladies take off her black outer dress, ready for execution, which then takes place.

The Enterprise of England

For Philip II of Spain, the execution of Mary, Queen of Scots was highly convenient. He could make the most of this death of a martyr, which shocked him and the rest of Catholic Europe, for it was yet another good reason why heretic England should be invaded and conquered. Also, Mary had passed on her claim to the English throne to Philip. If she had lived, her presence in a conquered England might have been awkward for him; as it was, her death strengthened Philip's right to be the Catholic ruler of the kingdom he now set out to capture — his great 'Enterprise'.

When Elizabeth was told of the execution:

> her countenance changed, her words faltered, and with excessive sorrow she was in a manner astonished . . . she gave herself over to grief, putting herself into mourning weeds and shedding abundance of tears.

She also sent Secretary Davison, who had dispatched the death warrant (which she had signed), to the Tower for a time.

■ Why do you think she behaved like this? Do you think her reaction was genuine? Could she also be trying to impress Philip? If so, why?

Philip's plan for the Enterprise of England

1. The Spanish invasion fleet — or Armada — was to sail up the Channel, and possibly seize a beach-head on the coast of England (perhaps near Margate).

2. The fleet was to join forces with the Duke of Parma who commanded the formidable Spanish army in the Netherlands.

←108

3. The army was to be transported across the Channel to invade England.

4. A rebellion by English Catholics would ensure the success of this invasion, and lead to the conquest of England.

The artist who painted this scene of the Spanish Armada may not have watched the battle, but he knew what English and Spanish ships looked like. Though some English ships were bigger, many were like these — speedy and low in the water, which made their fire power more effective from a distance. The bigger Spanish galleons carried soldiers as well as sailors (unlike the English ships), and their high forecastles were a great advantage in fighting and grappling at close quarters.

In 1587, Sir Francis Drake, the English sailor most feared by the Spaniards, sailed right into the harbour of Cadiz, where the Armada was being prepared. He destroyed most of the ships, and also the seasoned wood stacked up waiting to be made into storage barrels. A new fleet had to be built; when it sailed, the barrels which held vital supplies were made of unseasoned wood, so they were unsound and leaked.

'The Invincible Armada' was the Spanish nickname for their invasion fleet. The Spanish government published details of the Armada just before it set sail in 1588. They were printed and sold all over Europe, including England:

> *Ships*: Galleons, other light fast ships, and supply ships — 130.
> *Men*: Sailors, soldiers, officers of noble birth and their servants, gunners, doctors, 180 friars and priests — over 30,000.
> *Equipment*: Cannon, field guns, small arms, powder, cannon balls (123,790), bullets, pikes, armour of all kinds, swords. Over 1,900 guns in all.
> *Food and drink*: Biscuit, bacon, fish, cheese, rice, beans, wine, oil, vinegar, water.

1 This sort of information about an invasion force would be Top Secret today. Why do you think the Spaniards took such trouble to publish it?

2 Protestant printers in England published it too, adding such things as whips, thumbscrews, racks and pincers. Why did they do that?

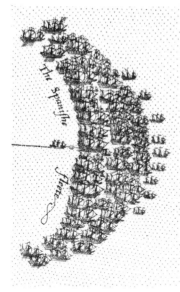

The Armada sailed in a formidable crescent-shaped formation which was difficult to attack. The strongest ships sailed on the outer 'rim', and on the horns. If, as here, they were attacked from the rear by the English, the horns closed in on the attacking ship, and protected the heavy, slow supply ships in the centre.

Diary of the Armada's journey, 1588

Late spring Delays to departure caused by storms, lack of supplies, and sickness. The longer the fleet waited in port, the more supplies were consumed.

20 May Armada set sail from Lisbon. Unreliable weather made progress slow.

19 June Stop at Corunna for food and water supplies. More storms.

19 July The English first sighted the Armada off Cornwall. Beacons were lit from hilltop to hilltop, to warn the whole country.

21 July English ships, led by Drake and John Hawkins, sailed out of Plymouth, and began to chase the Armada. They could not break the crescent formation; nor could the Spaniards shake them off. A running fight up the Channel.

27 July Armada anchored off Calais. No meeting point had been arranged with Parma's army, and there was no harbour deep enough to take the Spanish galleons on this coast. The English sent in 'hellburners' — fire ships which were very frightening, but in fact caused no damage. However, the Spanish cut their anchors to escape, and the crescent formation was broken.

The next six days A desperate battle followed. Both sides fought fiercely, but English guns in the end proved more effective.

Probable Spanish losses:

> 3 ships sunk, many badly damaged, 600 men killed, 800 wounded.

Probable English losses:

> No ships, 50 men killed; number of wounded unknown, but considerable.

The fighting gradually petered out. As both the wind, and the English fleet, made it difficult for the Armada to turn southwards, they had to continue north round Scotland and Ireland to get home.

August to the end of September Storms wrecked many Spanish ships off Scotland and Ireland. Probable Spanish losses, about 44 ships. (Accounts vary greatly.)

Meanwhile in England: 29 July Queen Elizabeth visited the troops collected at Tilbury, waiting to face the Spanish invasion. No one knew then what was happening at sea. The Queen wore white velvet, with a breastplate and sword. She said:

> I . . . am resolved in the midst and heat of battle to live and die amongst you all . . . I know I have the body of a weak and feeble woman, but I have the heart and stomach of a king, and a King of England too, and think foul scorn that Parma or Spain, or any prince of Europe should dare to invade the borders of my realm.

The troops who loyally cheered Elizabeth's speech in the end did not have to fight. There was no Catholic rising, and some Catholic troops were at Tilbury, ready to fight the Spaniards.

The English fleet limped back to port, not so badly damaged as the Armada, but full of wounded and sick men. Most of the sailors did not even get the pay due to them.

1 Make your own map. Show Philip's plan in one colour, and the actual route of the Armada in another.

2 Look at Philip's plan again, and decide how realistic each stage was. Use the diary to work out where it went seriously wrong.

3 Work out how important you think each of the following were in the defeat of the Armada:

Failures of Philip's plan; shortage of supplies; English guns; the weather.

4 Write an eye-witness account of the Armada by either an Englishman or a Spaniard, making the best of your side of the story. Make sure both sides are covered in the class, and compare your different versions.

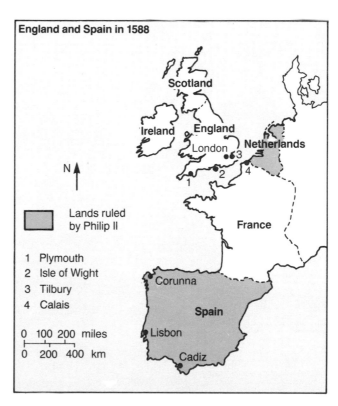

England and Spain in 1588

Lands ruled by Philip II

1 Plymouth
2 Isle of Wight
3 Tilbury
4 Calais

0 100 200 miles

0 200 400 km

113

Lectern

Statue of the Virgin Mary

The Spanish war dragged on till after Elizabeth's death, but the danger of a Spanish invasion was never so great again. However, the events of the 1580s, along with the memories of the burnings of Mary I's reign kept alive by Foxe's *Book of Martyrs,* had lasting effects on English attitudes to Catholics. From now on they were seen as 'Papists' — traitors who supported a foreign Pope, and Catholic Spain. The nickname, and the hatred behind it, stuck, although most Catholics still remained loyal Englishmen and women, as their behaviour in 1588 had shown.

■ Nicknames can be affectionate, or they can be cruel to people or groups who differ from the majority in some way. Think of nicknames you know, and perhaps use: of family or friends, or of groups. Try to work out the attitude behind them. Is it right to avoid using some kinds of nicknames?

The parish church

A great deal of this chapter has been about the attitudes of powerful people to the split in the Christian Church, called the Reformation. It is much harder to find out what ordinary people felt about the changes in their familiar parish church.

■ In the box (and illustrated in the margin) is a jumbled list of things ordinary people would have seen in their parish church before and after the English Reformation. Sort them out into two columns, one headed 'Before the Break with Rome', the other 'After Elizabeth I's Settlement'. Use a dictionary if necessary. Then make your own pictures of the old and the new look of the parish church.

Altar with crucifix and candles. Pulpit. Priest wearing vestments. Royal coat of arms on the walls. Lectern. Wall pictures. A plain table with a cross. Statue of the Virgin Mary. Bible texts painted on whitewashed walls. Rood screen.

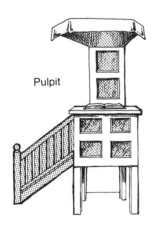

Pulpit

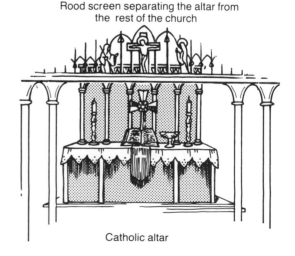

Rood screen separating the altar from the rest of the church

Catholic altar

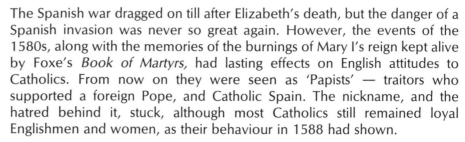

Protestant 'Lord's table'

It probably took a long time for people to feel comfortable about the changes, and some never did, especially in places distant from London, like the north and west of England; there it was easier to ignore what the government was doing. In 1549, ordinary people in Devon and Cornwall rebelled against the new English Prayer Book. They said it was like a 'Christmas game', and that they did not understand it because it was in English! Some of them did speak Cornish, but it was hardly likely that they really did not understand English, so what do you think they meant when they made those two statements?

In parish churches today, there is usually a list of vicars, and if the church is an old one, the list goes back a long way. If you can find one like this, it is worth looking to see if there were many changes in the reigns of Edward VI and Mary, and in 1559. Sometimes the same vicar remains the whole time. Think what the changes must have been like for him and his people, and the kind of reasons he might have had for staying. When perhaps might he have been allowed to marry, and when would he have run into difficulties if he had done so? As late as 1576, 40 per cent of the clergy in the big bishopric of Lincoln had been there before 1559. What big change would these clergy have had to accept?

When clergy were firm Protestants, they sometimes had difficulty with their people, especially over long sermons — perhaps not surprisingly. In 1598, a Nottinghamshire vicar scolded his parishioners by saying:

> Some came to church more for a sleep than for the service of God, and others had more in mind of going home to dinner than to hear God's word.

In 1601, Henry Hasellwood of Essex was in trouble because when a sermon was still going on after $2\frac{1}{2}$ hours, he went out and started throwing stones noisily on to the church roof.

Relics disappeared and so did other familiar ways for ordinary people to get comfort and help in church when they were troubled. This may have been a reason why witchcraft seems to have increased in some places in Elizabeth's reign. Anyway, people were anxious about witches, for there were more prosecutions. You could try to find out more about this.

←37

However, Elizabeth was a successful Queen, and her reign lasted for more than 40 years. By the end of it, there were still people who did not accept the new Church, but there were many to whom it was now familiar, and dangers at home and abroad had helped to make people more loyal to it. There were still ignorant and lazy vicars, but there were also committed and caring ones, with congregations who supported them. The Church of England was there to stay, even though many still wanted to improve it.

Today, we think of religion as a private matter, which people work out for themselves. In the Early Modern Age, when obedience to the ruler was thought to be so important, it was kings and queens who decided what people should believe. Differences, it was thought, would lead to trouble and rebellion. Yet some did follow their private conscience. Even Thomas Cranmer, with his firm belief in obedience, in the end disobeyed his Catholic Queen; and Edmund Campion would not betray his faith, although he was a loyal subject to Elizabeth I. The courage of these people, and many others like them, helped to bring toleration in the end — but it took a long time.

←109

You have seen some examples of propaganda in this chapter, when the Government of England puts over its viewpoint in words and pictures. This picture is propaganda too. It is called 'The Protestant Succession' *and it shows Henry VIII, Edward VI, Mary I, Philip of Spain and Elizabeth I. There are also two goddesses, of peace and plenty, and Mars, the god of war.*

1 Work out where all these people are in the picture.

2 Give reasons why this must be an imaginary scene, which could not have taken place in real life.

3 Work out the reason for the position of Mars and the two goddesses.

4 In whose reign must this picture have been painted? Give reasons.

5 Is it Catholic or Protestant propaganda? Give reasons.

6 Crown and people

Changes in the Church affected the lives of people in Britain, and made Tudor monarchs more powerful. The two monarchs most skilled at keeping in touch with their people were Henry VIII and Elizabeth I. Now we shall look at other ways in which royal power was used during their reigns.

Royal favour

Henry VIII had over 50 palaces. The most famous — Whitehall, Greenwich, Nonsuch and Hampton Court — were very large. Hampton Court had over 1000 rooms. Each palace had a Great Hall for ceremonies and banquets, but the most important room of all was the Privy Chamber. This was usually on an upper storey beyond the Great Hall, and approached through a number of ante-rooms and passages. Here the King spent most of his time when he was indoors, usually seated grandly on a throne with a richly embroidered canopy over it. He would consult his advisers, make decisions, receive important visitors from abroad, or just chat informally with those he chose to have around him.

It was those high in the King's favour who went into the Privy Chamber. At the Tudor court, the only way you could reach the King was through some high-ranking courtier who had the right to enter the Chamber. This was also often the only way in which to gain a post at court, or to be rewarded for some service done for the King. A regular wage packet, even for the most important jobs, was very rare in the sixteenth century. So ante-rooms like the ones in Hampton Court were thronged with people hoping to win rewards, or to gain influence with the favoured few who were allowed into the King's presence.

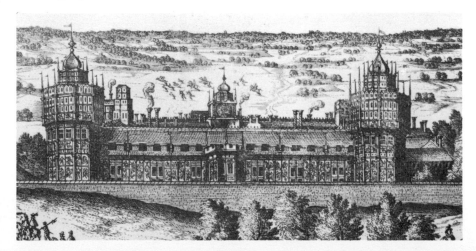

Henry built several palaces, but none was grander than Nonsuch, as it is name implies. A village was swept away to make room for it, and its towers rose more than 60 metres high. The exterior was painted and gilded in brilliant colours, and it had beautiful gardens. Nothing remains now to show where it was, except a small notice beside the busy Kingston by-pass, near the River Thames.

A portrait of Henry VIII

Holbein drew the plan (or cartoon) for his life-size wall-painting on paper, mounted on canvas. This half of it still survives today, more than 500 years later. It is possible to see, on the original drawing in the National Portrait Gallery, the pin holes in the outline which Holbein used to transfer the picture on to the wall, ready to paint. The wall-painting was destroyed when most of Whitehall Palace was burnt down in 1698.

This picture shows us Henry VIII in middle age, but still at the height of his powers. When it was drawn in 1537, Henry had already ruled England for almost 30 years; he had changed from the slim, athletic youth to the dominating figure shown here. He had survived the long-drawn-out anxieties over who was to succeed him, and had successfully ignored threats from the Pope, the Emperor, and the King of France. Recently he had crushed the only serious rebellion of his reign — the Pilgrimage of Grace (see page 94). Now at last, God seemed to have rewarded him, with the birth of his son and heir, Prince Edward. To celebrate this great event, Henry asked his Court painter, Hans Holbein, to make a big wall-painting in the new palace of Whitehall. It was to show the great Tudor family into which the baby prince had been born. Henry VIII stands on the left, solid and powerful. His father, Henry VII, is a gentle elderly figure in the background, very different from the shrewd and lively portrait on page 73. The other two figures were in the part of the picture which is now lost: Henry's mother, Elizabeth of York and Jane Seymour, the mother of the young prince, who died soon after his birth. The figure of Henry must have dominated them too, and he of course was the only one of the four people in the picture who was actually alive when Holbein was working on it. The King was so pleased with his own portrait that it was copied many times, by other artists as well as Holbein. It is the unforgettable image of Henry VIII which we all know.

King and courtiers

Henry VIII was not an easy man. He had an education fit for a king's son; from the age of 12, when his elder brother Arthur died, he had been treated with all the respect and honour due to the heir to the throne. He grew up surrounded by admiring courtiers, and seldom failed to get his own way. He was lively, and good company, but it was often difficult to know how he would react. He could be cruel and terrifying, and once he had decided that a person was his enemy, he would play with his victim like a cat with a mouse. Courtiers had to learn how to manage his moods, and they all knew how easily the King could be turned against them when they were not near him. The King's favour was the glittering prize which brought prestige and wealth. Everyone desired it, and competition was fierce. So courtiers had two worries: they worried about how to please the King, and they worried about who might be working against them to snatch the prize.

It is, however, important to remember than even a king like Henry could not govern the country by himself. He needed noblemen who had influence and power in the areas where they owned their lands. They were the people who could make sure the King's laws were known and obeyed, for there were no policemen in Tudor England. If Henry needed soldiers, he had to rely on his nobles to recruit and often to pay them. He also needed efficient advisers, who were good organisers. Two great servants, Thomas Wolsey and Thomas Cromwell, came from very ordinary families; but this was still unusual. Most people at Henry's court were the First Sort — the nobility and gentry.

■ Copy the timeline in the margin of this page, and draw two more columns beside it. Head one *Wives*, and the other *Ministers, courtiers and churchmen*. Then, using pages 76–96, put in each column at the right date, who was in favour, and if and when they fell.

Puzzles about Henry VIII

Take another look at Holbein's portrait of Henry VIII on page 118. Imagine what it must have been like to serve such a king, but remember too the respect and loyalty English people gave their sovereign in the Early Modern Age. Think about the following puzzles, using your completed time chart, and the index, for information on the people mentioned. There are no 'right answers', but these puzzles may help us to understand the real Henry a little better.

1 Why do you think that Henry appointed Sir Thomas More Chancellor when Wolsey fell in 1529, although he knew More did not approve of the divorce?

2 On pages 94–6, find the three occasions when the Duke of Norfolk had difficulties at court. Why do you think he was able to survive when Wolsey and Cromwell did not? Was it just luck?

Main events of Henry's reign

1509	Henry VIII became King
1510	
1511	
1512	
1513	Wars with France and
1514	Scotland ⚔ Flodden
1515	
1516	Birth of Princess Mary
1517	
1518	
1519	
1520	Field of the Cloth of Gold
1521	
1522	War with France
1523	
1524	
1525	Trouble in East Anglia over taxes
1526	Debasement of coinage
1527	Henry began to consider divorce
1528	
1529	Failure of Blackfriars Court, Parliament called
1530	
1531	
1532	Clergy submitted to Henry
1533	Birth of Princess Elizabeth
1534	Act of Supremacy / Oath to succession
1535	
1536	Dissolution of monasteries began
1537	Birth of Prince Edward
1538	Pilgrimage of Grace
1539	The Great Bible / The end of the monasteries
1540	Act of Six Articles
1541	
1542	
1543	Wars with France and Scotland
1544	Debasement of coinage
1545	
1546	
1547	Debasement of coinage / Henry's death

119

3 When was Archbishop Cranmer in danger? He was the only important servant of Henry VIII who survived the whole reign without losing the King's favour. Why do you think this was so?

4 Count how many people were executed in Henry's reign. Don't forget Empson and Dudley in 1509. Then find examples of times when the King 'played with his victim like a cat with a mouse'.

The centre of the court

The King was the centre of the court; what he enjoyed, everyone else enjoyed too. Henry VIII loved active sports. He was a fine horseman, and when he went hunting he would tire out eight or ten horses a day. He enjoyed hawking, royal tennis (played indoors), and throwing spears the

Holbein at the Court of Henry VIII

IOANNES HOLPENIVS BA⸱   SILEENSIS
SVI IPSIVS EFFIGIATOR   Æ: XLV.

The artist Hans Holbein was German; he worked as court painter to the King from the mid 1530s until his sudden death from plague in 1543. He painted this picture of himself just before that happened. It is the best evidence we have of his character. What kind of man do you think he was? Although he lived and worked in the Palace of Whitehall, he is dressed as a craftsman, not a courtier; artists, however talented, were not of high rank. We are fortunate that he spent these years at Henry's court, for his portraits are so lifelike that we feel we know personally the people he drew and painted. The courtiers opposite were not, except for the Earl of Bedford, very important, and we do not know much about them. So you can make up your own mind about the kind of people you think they are.

height of two tall men. When he practised archery with his guard, he 'cleft the mark in the middle, and surpassed them all'. His favourite sport was jousting. He seems to have been quite fearless as he thundered down the tiltyard in full armour, aiming to unhorse his opponent with his heavy lance. Once, he forgot to lower his helmet visor, and his opponent shattered it, covering Henry's face with metal splinters; but the King insisted on six more jousts. At the age of 44, he was knocked off his horse, which fell on top of him. It may have been a jousting accident which damaged his thigh bone, causing the infected ulcer which gave him so much pain in his last years. Even then, he took little rest, though he was so heavy that he often had servants carry him in a chair, or haul him upstairs by machinery.

THE EARL OF BEDFORD had been at court since the days of Henry VII; he held the important post of Lord Privy Seal. He lost an eye in one of Henry VIII's French wars, so this portrait may have been tidied up later by another artist.

WILLIAM PARR, LATER MARQUIS OF NORTH-AMPTON, did well at court once his sister Catherine became Queen. The round badge on his hat shows that he was a Gentleman Pensioner, one of the King's personal bodyguard. Holbein has noted details of his costume so that he can show them accurately in the portrait he is planning to do from this drawing.

GRACE, LADY PARKER was married at the age of eight. Her eldest son was born when she was 17, and a second son in the same year as Prince Edward. She attended Edward's christening, and Queen Jane's funeral; she died at about the age of 30. We know little else about her. What is your impression of her?

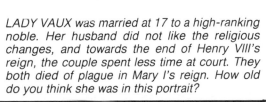

LADY VAUX was married at 17 to a high-ranking noble. Her husband did not like the religious changes, and towards the end of Henry VIII's reign, the couple spent less time at court. They both died of plague in Mary I's reign. How old do you think she was in this portrait?

The King was devout, and attended Mass regularly. He was interested in learning too. He knew Latin, French, some Spanish and Italian, and a little fashionable Greek. He enjoyed especially discussing these interests with scholars like Thomas More. Before More refused to co-operate over the divorce, the King would take him aside:

religion
on to the roof

> into his private room, and there some time in . . . astronomy, geometry, *divinity*, . . . and sometimes in his worldly affairs, to sit and confer with him, and other whiles would he in the night have him up *into the leads* there to consider with him the . . . courses, motions, and operations of the stars and planets.

Henry was a gifted musician. He collected musical instruments, including 26 lutes, trumpets, viols (an early violin), fifes, drums, harpsichords, virginals, and organs, several of which he could play. He enjoyed concerts, and employed foreign musicians. He listened to the visiting organist from St Mark's, Venice for four hours at a time. The King also composed church music and songs, though probably not the lovely traditional tune 'Greensleeves', which people often say he wrote.

Henry loved ceremonies and banquets, and the rich clothes that went with them: costumes of cloth of gold, silk and velvet, encrusted with jewels. Ambassadors often marvelled at them. The Venetian ambassador noticed that:

> His fingers were one mass of jewelled rings and round his neck he wore a gold collar from which hung a diamond as big as a walnut.

Talented, charming when he chose to be, impressive: the court revolved round Henry like planets around the sun. No one ever had any doubt that 'Bluff King Hal', as he was sometimes called, was a real king. And his terrifying rages, and unpredictable changes, were all part of the same picture.

This is the last suit of armour made for Henry at the special workshop at Greenwich dated 1540. His waist by then was 138 cm. At the Royal Armouries in the Tower of London you can see the suit made for the slim young King at the beginning of his reign (waist 82 cm). Why does tournament armour like this provide such heavy protection for the left arm and shoulder?

Money problems

Henry VIII was not short of money at the beginning of his reign; his father had left him about two years' supply. As long as he kept his spending under reasonable control, there should have been enough to run the country. This is exactly what he did not do.

Palaces Think about the cost of building a palace like Nonsuch, pictured on page 117. Henry built other palaces, including St James'. He transformed Wolsey's London house into the Palace of Whitehall, adding, among other things, a great tiltyard for his favourite sport. These palaces were decorated with fashionable and expensive ornamented ceilings, fireplaces, panelling and tapestries. Gardens were laid out, fountains installed, and trees and flowers planted. All this was very expensive, and hundreds of servants had to be employed, indoors and out.

Entertainments and pastimes Clothes, jewels, sumptuous food and wine, gifts for important visitors, musicians, acrobats, and actors all cost money. Work out what expensive equipment was needed for jousting. Henry started his own armour workshops at Greenwich, as well as importing the best foreign armour. How many good horses might Henry use in a day of sport?

Military and naval expenditure War was always the most expensive activity of all. How many times did Henry go to war? Raising troops, paying them, providing fighting equipment and food cost a great deal. Even finding enough carts was a problem. The risk of invasion from France or Spain — or both — during the quarrel with the Pope meant that fortifications had to be built along the south coast. The size of the navy was increased, with impressive warships whose sides were pierced with rows of heavy guns. Two new dockyards were built at Woolwich and Deptford, and Portsmouth was enlarged. In the last eight years of his reign, Henry spent 2 million pounds on war.

Henry spent money like water, and certainly enjoyed the things which money could buy. Unlike his careful father, however, he was bored with keeping accounts, and supervising how his money was spent. He left that to his ministers; one of them, Thomas Cromwell, tried to solve the problem, but was not given the time to do it.

The fort at Deal, one of Henry's defences against the French

What advantage did the curved walls give to the defenders?

Henry embarks at Dover for France. The ship in the foreground may be the 'Henry Grace à Dieu'. When this new flagship was launched in 1515, the King dined on board, wearing white silk and a big gold whistle encrusted with gems.

The way the King spent money affected the way he got on with his people. This table shows how this happened:

Ways in which extra money was raised	Effect on the King's subjects
Taxation, voted by Parliament	Taxes are always unpopular. Nobles and gentry had to assess how much people should pay, and collect the money. They disliked the job, even though they could make sure they did not have to pay much themselves.
Forced grants or loans, without consent of Parliament; for instance the 'Amicable Grant' of 1525, to pay for the French war, though this failed to bring in any money.	Ordinary people hated taxes. No one felt 'amicable' in 1525. In Suffolk, 'men that had no work began to rage . . . and there rebelled 4000 men . . . then the demand for money ceased throughout the realm, for well it was perceived that the commons would pay none.'
Sale of land from monasteries Thomas Cromwell had intended that most of the lands which the Crown gained from the monasteries should be kept, to solve the constant shortage of money. But after his death, when war began again from 1542, about ⅔ of the lands were sold.	Nobles, country gentlemen and merchants who bought the lands, made money from them, and did not want to see the monasteries come back. Ordinary people who paid rent for the land because they lived on it, were worried by the changes, though in the end, things were probably not very different for them.
Debasement of the coinage in 1526, 1544 and 1547 Gold and silver coins had to be melted down, and new coins with more cheap metal in them were issued. The government charged for doing this, *and* kept some of the gold and silver from the old coins, so a good profit was made.	The new coins were easy to recognise because they weighed less than the old ones, and the 'silver' ones were redder in colour. People distrusted them, so when they sold something, they asked for more coins in payment. What effect did that have on prices?

1 There was another money problem which affected everyone, not just the King. Prices were rising, especially for basic commodities such as food. They rose particularly steeply from about 1510–20, and in the 1540s. What was Henry doing in those years which might have helped to push prices up? (Look at the time chart on page 119.) Work out reasons for your answer. (Look back to pages 10 and 29.) Is it fair to blame Henry entirely for the price rise?

2 Work out whether these groups would gain or lose from the price rise, giving reasons:

People paying rents fixed by law, which could not be changed.

The landlords to whom these rents were paid.

People earning wages — also fixed by law, and could not be raised

People producing enough food to sell.

People with expensive life-styles.

The King owned a great deal of land. Would he lose or gain more from the price rise?

3 Write a letter from Thomas Cromwell to the King in 1539 about his expenditure, and possible ways of raising money. Use your time chart, and remember how tactful you must be.

The Court of Elizabeth I

Elizabeth I shared several talents with her father: she too could give the impression of awe-inspiring majesty. She too could sense how her people were feeling, and keep their loyalty and devotion, however much they might disapprove of some of her actions. Like her father, Elizabeth was the centre of her court.

Use the evidence of the descriptions by foreign ambassadors, and the portraits on the next page, to form your own impression of Elizabeth I through her long reign. Notice the date of each; she was 25 when she came to the throne in 1558, so where her age is not given, you can calculate it. Look back too at the Coronation portrait.

←103

1557 The Venetian ambassador described her as:
Comely rather than handsome, but she is tall and well-formed, with a good skin, although swarthy, she has fine eyes.

1558 The Spanish ambassador wrote:
She seems to me incomparably more feared than her sister, and gives her orders and has her way as absolutely as her father did.

1597 The French ambassador wrote:
She drew off her glove and showed me her hand, which is long and more than mine by three broad fingers. It was formerly very beautiful, but it is now very thin, although the skin is still most fair . . . as for her face, it is . . . very aged . . . her figure is fair and tall and graceful in whatever she does.

1598 Paul Henzner, another foreign visitor, described a royal procession:
Next came the Queen, in the sixty-sixth year of her age . . . very majestic; her face oblong, fair, but wrinkled; her eyes small, yet black and pleasant; her nose a little hooked; her lips narrow, and her teeth black . . . she had in her ears two pearls, with very rich drops; she wore false hair, and that red.

The Armada Portrait of Elizabeth I, by George Gower

There are many grand portraits of Elizabeth, like the one at the top of this page, painted to celebrate the Armada victory. Find as much as you can in the picture which tells you about the victory, and that Elizabeth is a great Queen. Now look at her face, and calculate her approximate age. Is this shown realistically? The Queen had strong views on her portraits, and this is one of the 'face patterns' artists were supposed to use. They were copied many times, in pictures, seals and coins. Why did she try to keep such strict control of her portraits?

This miniature of Elizabeth I was painted in 1600, and has a delicate jewelled frame. How old was the Queen? Compare it with the miniature by Hilliard on page 107. Why do you think the Queen stops growing old in her portraits?

Nicholas Hilliard was the leading miniature painter in Elizabeth I's reign. He was a goldsmith, and his miniatures (tiny paintings) were like jewels, in beautiful frames. People sometimes wore them around the neck, in a hat or even on the heel of a shoe. They were often no bigger than a 10p piece, painted under a magnifying glass in brilliant colours with a fine squirrel-hair brush. In this self-portrait you can even see the pattern of the lace ruff clearly. Hilliard painted the Queen many times, as well as other famous Elizabethans.

Elizabeth was active like her father, and loved hunting and dancing. She was musical too, and could speak Latin, French, Spanish and Italian 'very elegantly'. However, no one could have written the following of Henry VIII:

> She was in her diet very temperate, as eating but of few kinds of meat . . . The wine she drank was mingled with water . . . (she never ate) but when her appetite required it.

Probably her diet, and the exercise she took, were the reasons why she stayed healthy and active almost to the end of her long life. She had even survived a serious attack of smallpox in 1562. It is not certain whether she was scarred, but as time went on she wore a great deal of thick white make-up on her face, hands and chest; usually a mixture of white of egg, powdered eggshell, alum, borax, and poppy seeds mixed with mill-water — 'near half an inch thick' said one ambassador. What have you already read that tells you that the Queen wore a red wig? She may have lost her hair when she was ill.

The marriage game

The Queen at the centre of her court was a woman in a world of men. William Cecil, who became her most trusted minister and remained in her service till his death in 1598, was very doubtful at first that any woman could rule; he scolded a foreign diplomat for discussing 'a matter of such weight, being too much for a woman's knowledge'. He soon had to change his mind. Everyone expected the Queen to marry, so that (as Philip II of Spain wrote in 1558 when he was considering marrying her himself) her husband 'might relieve her of those labours which are only fit for men'.

What difficulties faced a reigning queen in choosing a husband which Elizabeth might have observed from her sister's experiences (see page 99)? Although her subjects expected her to marry, Elizabeth knew that few would approve of the men who sought her hand. There were certainly plenty of those; for a time each had the impression that the Queen was seriously considering his proposal. Skilfully she used their interest to keep friends when she needed them. She listened politely to the Spanish ambassador when he pressed Philip's claim at the beginning of her reign: she needed Philip's friendship while France was a great threat. When Philip married the French King's daughter, she kept the alliance going by considering his cousin, the Archduke Charles. That idea came to nothing when she decided she could not think of marriage if she had not seen her future husband. (Remember, royal marriages were usually arranged by ambassadors.) The Archduke decided it was beneath his dignity to be inspected, and then probably rejected. When a Protestant alliance seemed desirable, the Queen considered the King of Sweden's eldest son.

In 1579, when the Queen was 46, an age which many thought too old for marriage, she began a long series of negotiations to marry the French King's brother, the Duke of Alençon — she called him her little 'Frog'. The

William Cecil in 1560

When Elizabeth I appointed him, she said, 'This judgement I have of you . . . that you will be faithful to the state, and that . . . you will give me that counsel which you think best.' She later made him Lord Burghley. She did not always act on his advice, but she respected it.

127

Robert Dudley, Earl of Leicester

In the early years of her reign, the Queen constantly sought the company of Robert Dudley, her Master of Horse, whom she made the Earl of Leicester. How does his portrait show his wealth and rank. Why might other courtiers resent him? He had to leave court for a time because his wife, Amy Robsart, died in suspicious circumstances; but rumours continued that the Queen might marry him. We do not know how seriously she considered Leicester as a husband. He married twice more, and earned her wrath, but was later pardoned. In 1575, the whole court paid a visit to his castle at Kenilworth, which he had just enlarged. During all the elaborate entertainments, the clock on the castle keep was stopped, so that time should stand still while the Queen was there. When Elizabeth died, and her ladies opened the little box she kept at her bedside, they found a letter Leicester had written just before his death in 1588. On it, the Queen had written 'His Last Letter'.

1 How serious do you think Elizabeth was about marriage?

2 What was the great disadvantage if she did not marry?

nickname was an indication of his appearance, but most of her subjects thought she was serious, and he was very unpopular in England. But it was no accident that by that time, a French alliance was a help against the growing enmity of Spain.

Elizabeth used the fact that she *might* marry to great advantage. She also used the fact that she was a woman to dominate her ambitious courtiers. Her favour, like her father's, was a glittering prize; she carried on a kind of romance with them all. She was 'Gloriana' — a Fairy Queen, even when she was a middle-aged woman wearing a wig and a lot of make-up. Her anger was feared but she used charm and wit too. Those close to her had nicknames: the Earl of Leicester was her 'Eyes'; Sir Christopher Hatton, who charmed her with his dancing, her 'Lids'; Sir Walter Raleigh was 'Water', from his name. They were her favourites, good company, talented, and rather unreliable. She never made the mistake of giving them power, and relied on sensible William Cecil, her 'Spirit'; hardheaded Francis Walsingham, the 'Moor' (from his dark looks), and, later William Cecil's clever hunchback son, Robert, the 'Elf'. Only one favourite at the end of the reign was a real disaster: the Earl of Essex. He flattered the lonely old Queen, and in 1600 she gave him command in Ireland to deal with the serious rebellion there. He used it to try to seize power, and was one of the few during her reign executed for political reasons.

Sir Walter Raleigh, by Hilliard

128

The Elizabethan theatre

The Queen and her subjects enjoyed plays. For Elizabethan Londoners, going to the theatre was a new occupation; theatre buildings did not exist until her reign, and earlier plays had been performed in the streets, usually in guild pageants. One new London theatre was the Globe, where William Shakespeare and a band of professional actors performed the plays he wrote. From pictures drawn at the time we can get a very good idea of what going to the theatre, sixteenth-century style, was like. The Globe was open to the sky. The stage jutted out amongst the poorer part of the audience; they had to stand all the time in the 'pit', and got wet if it rained. The expensive seats were in the covered galleries round the sides, and the most fashionable members of the audience hired stools and sat on the stage; there they hoped they would be admired as much as the play. As you can see from the people who are getting a free view of the play outside the Globe, women were as interested in the theatre as men, but they did not act; boys took female parts. In the London theatres, rich and poor Londoners enjoyed themselves together, sympathising, laughing and grieving with the characters in Shakespeare's plays. The Queen did not join them, but actors came to court to perform the same plays which her subjects saw at the Globe, and they were often written to please her.

William Shakespeare, 1564–1616

The son of a Stratford-upon-Avon tradesman, he arrived in London in 1586 to seek his fortune. He acted in several of the new London theatres, and wrote many of the plays which delighted Elizabethan audiences, and which still fill theatres today.

1 Draw your own plan of the Globe theatre. Label it clearly to show where the cheap and expensive seats were, the entrance to the 'pit', the stage, and where the actors' dressing rooms were. Don't forget the flag to show the performance is taking place.

2 Why were the people in the cheapest area called 'groundlings'?

3 Describe a visit to the Globe in Elizabeth I's reign as a groundling. If you know any scenes from Shakespeare's plays, make them the performance you watch.

The outside of the Globe theatre with the flag flying to show a performance is in progress

A trumpet was often used to announce its beginning. The River Thames is in the background.

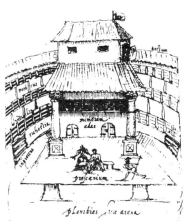

This is a contemporary sketch of another London theatre, the Swan. The Globe was very like it.

The Queen on a 'progress'

Money problems again

Henry VIII's extravagance had left a problem for all his children; Edward and Mary I had little chance to solve it. Elizabeth, unlike her father, was very careful over money, apart from what she spent on dresses and jewels. She did not build any more palaces, or buy new furnishings (it was hardly necessary). Although there were grand entertainments at court, she also went on 'progresses' round the country, visiting the houses of important courtiers like the Earl of Leicester. This had two advantages: she could see and be seen by her people; and she did not have the expense of her large household when she was an honoured guest. Also, she was not very generous with presents and rewards for those who served her. The Earl of Huntingdon, who was responsible for the whole of the north of England after the rebellion of 1569, and did the job well for many years, left serious debts when he died, because he spent so much in the Queen's service.

←107

←124

The Queen and her ministers restored the value of the debased coins that people disliked so much, and for a time prices did not rise so fast. She avoided expensive wars for as long as she could; when she finally went to war with Spain from 1585, she was as careful as possible. Sometimes she took this too far. Once she gave orders that her soldiers were to pick up all the cannon-balls they had fired, and use them again! Remember too how reluctant she was to pay the sailors who had fought against the Armada.

←113

The Queen and her Parliaments

←82

←88, 103

Although Elizabeth was so careful over money, she could not avoid taxing her subjects, and that meant that she often had to call Parliament. She also found it a useful way of finding out how her most powerful subjects felt on important matters. However, there were problems. Parliament was more important than it had been, because it had been used to make the great changes in the Church legal. In Elizabeth's reign, 53 more towns gained the right to have an MP. Gentry were now more willing to come to London to attend Parliament, not least because it gave them more prestige in their own local area.

Members now expected to be consulted on all important matters. They also insisted on their traditional privilege to be able to speak freely, without fear of arrest. But Elizabeth believed there were 'matters of state' which Parliament should not discuss without her express permission. These were: *religion, marriage, foreign affairs and money* — in other words, everything which really mattered. It is hardly surprising that the nobles and gentry did not always obey the Queen. Trouble was inevitable.

Religion On pages 103–4, we saw how Elizabeth with difficulty prevented the Puritans in Parliament from introducing changes in the Church of which she was head. The Puritans did not succeed in her reign, but they did not give up either.

Marriage and foreign affairs Elizabeth thought that the decision about marriage was her own personal affair. Her subjects worried about what would happen if she did not marry and produce an heir. Foreign affairs often came into the problem, because most of her suitors were from abroad; if Elizabeth had no children, after her death a foreigner, Mary, Queen of Scots, might become Queen of England.

A Royal answer to Parliament

In 1566, there was particular worry because Elizabeth had recently nearly died from smallpox, and still showed no signs of deciding upon a husband. This is how she answered Parliament's petition that she should marry:

> Though I be a woman, yet I have as good a courage as my father had. I am your anointed Queen . . . I thank God I am *endowed with such qualities that* if I were turned out of my realm in my petticoat, I were able to live in any place in Christendom . . . I will marry as soon as I conveniently can.

the kind of person who

She also called MPs a pack of ignorant schoolboys — but she reduced the sum of money she was asking them to raise in taxes.

■ What methods did the Queen use to deal with this petition? How much did she use her power as Queen? Did she play on the fact that she was a woman? Was she going to grant their wish? How do you think MPs felt about these methods?

Elizabeth apparently did not listen to Parliament's constant demands for the execution of Mary, Queen of Scots, the 'monstrous huge dragon', but they may well have influenced her final reluctant decision in 1587.

Money By the 1590s, the war with Spain was dragging on, and there was a serious rebellion in Ireland. The government was short of money, taxes increased, and prices rose sharply. MPs did not want the Queen to find ways of raising money without their consent. Do you see why? They particularly objected to a new system of rewards for important courtiers. They were granted or sold a *monopoly,* which meant they alone had the right to manufacture or sell certain goods. When the Earl of Essex was in favour, he was given the monopoly of sweet wines. Anyone who wished to buy and sell them had to have his permission, and pay for the privilege. In 1601, Parliament was in an uproar about monopolies — on everyday articles like salt, starch, fish, vinegar, iron, brushes, coal, currants, playing cards and dice.

1 What was likely to happen to *prices*, and the *quality of goods* controlled by a monopoly?

2 Why would fashionable Elizabethans object to the monopoly on starch?

3 Why would the monopoly on salt be hard on both rich and poor?

The old Queen had often been very firm with Parliament. 'Beware how you try your Prince's patience,' she once threatened. This time she knew she could not win. She issued a proclamation promising to abolish monopolies. When MPs came to Whitehall Palace to thank her, she said:

> Though God hath raised me high, yet this I account the glory of my Crown, that I have reigned with your loves . . . And though you have had, and may have, many mightier and wiser princes sitting on this seat, yet you never had . . . any that shall love you better.

Then she allowed them all to kiss her hand.

Queen Elizabeth I in the House of Lords

1 The speech which Elizabeth I made, quoted above, is often called her 'Golden Speech'. Why do you think it is called that? Why did she choose to make a speech like that, at that particular moment?

2 Make a list of the times Elizabeth I gave in to Parliament. Do you think her successor was likely to have problems?

3 Find out more about the modern ceremony of opening Parliament. Who writes the speech the present Queen makes?

The Queen sits enthroned in the House of Lords surrounded by her councillors. In front of her are the chief lords and judges. In the foreground is the Speaker of the House of Commons (see page 82), who is addressing the Queen; by him are other members of the House of Commons. When Queen Elizabeth II opens Parliament today, she too sits in the House of Lords, and MPs come in from the House of Commons to listen to her.

Sovereigns of Ireland and Wales

The two most powerful Tudor sovereigns did what they could to extend their sway over their Irish and Welsh subjects, to ensure the safety of their 'back doors'. After the break with Rome, Henry VIII was no longer content to be Lord of Ireland, especially as some of the Irish chieftains, urged on by the Pope and Emperor, rebelled in 1534. So in 1541, Henry gave himself a new title: *King* of Ireland. The change probably meant a great deal to him, but it made little difference to Irish loyalties. Both Mary I and Elizabeth tried another way to keep control: land in Ireland was given to

English gentry, who could make as much profit as possible from it, but also, it was hoped, to make sure that English laws were obeyed. Meanwhile, however, Jesuit priests rekindled loyalty to the Catholic faith; and in 1596 Philip II sent another Armada to break open this 'back door' into England. It failed, but was enough to spark off a major rebellion. The rebellion drained English resources, and also, in 1601, gave the Spaniards a chance to land 4000 troops. It was not finally crushed till 1603. The Irish remained fiercely loyal to their chieftains, and their Catholic religion — and resentful of English rule.

Wales meanwhile had come under Thomas Cromwell's orderly eye. In 1536, it was divided up into thirteen counties, and in the law courts and all matters of importance, English was used rather than Welsh. Many of the Welsh gentry did not mind this too much. They could become Justices of the Peace, which gave them influence where they lived, and Members of Parliament, which took them to London. They were as interested as any other members of the ruling classes in local power, and favour at court. Many sent their sons to Shrewsbury School, and in 1571, Jesus College at Oxford University was founded to provide the next step in the English education of a Welsh gentleman. However, the ordinary people of Wales did not forget their language; the Welsh Bible, published in 1588, also helped to ensure that it did not die, especially when in the early seventeenth century the cheaper Beibl Bach (the little Bible) became more widely available.

←82

1 Write down as many reasons as you can why an Irish peasant would resent a new English landlord.

2 A modern Welsh historian Gwyn Williams, has said that Thomas Cromwell's reorganisation sent the Welsh language 'into the kitchen'. What do you think he meant?

The Welshman, John Dee (1527–1608) was a mathematician, astronomer, geographer and expert in navigation. He influenced explorers like Richard Chancellor and Francis Drake, and was befriended by Walter Raleigh, Francis Walsingham (he may have worked for Walsingham as a spy), and the Queen herself. He was a mixture of magical and modern; he claimed a 'British Empire' in the New World, on the grounds that it had already been discovered by an imaginary Welshman, Owen Medoc, 300 years before — and he believed he could speak with angels.

The climb to the top

Bess of Hardwicke was born a simple yeoman's daughter in 1520. By the time she died, at the age of 87, she was Countess of Shrewsbury, and her granddaughter was of royal descent on her father's side. Bess achieved this extraordinary climb to the top of the First Sort by four careful marriages. There were ups and downs; she spent some time in the Tower because she displeased the Queen, but recovered favour, and married her fourth and grandest husband, the Earl of Shrewsbury. The couple had to guard Mary Queen of Scots for a time, and this led to many difficulties — Bess even accused her husband of having an affair with their important prisoner. They quarrelled so much that they finally lived apart. At a time when many of the gentry and nobles were building themselves grand houses, Bess seemed to out-build them all. Below is the front of Hardwicke Hall in Derbyshire. It has fashionable large windows (glass was cheap enough now to make it possible to build 'more glass than wall'), and a great Long Gallery, stretching the length of the top of the house, and hung with portraits and tapestries. How did Bess make sure that no one forgot the house was built by 'Elizabeth Shrewsbury'? There is a great deal more to find out about this great house, which has changed little since it was first built, and about the remarkable Bess of Hardwicke.

Bess of Hardwicke, when she was Countess of Shrewsbury

The problem of poverty

In 1570 a census was taken in Norwich. It gave details of all the poor who lived in the city. A record like this was unusual in the sixteenth century; the reason why the prosperous citizens of Norwich took this step was that they were worried. Poverty seemed to be growing — and not just in Norwich. Something should be done. These are three typical families described in the Norwich census:

money given to the poor

Ann Buckle of the age of 46 years, widow . . . hath two children, the one of the age of 9 years and the other of 5 years that work lace, and hath dwelt here ever — no *alms* but very poor.

John Burr of the age of 54 years, *glazier*, very sick and work not, and Alice his wife . . . 40 years, that spin, and have 7 children, (aged 20,12,10,8,6,4, and 2 who) spin wool and have dwelt here ever — in his own house, no alms, *indifferent*.

someone who puts glass in windows

not quite so poor as the other two families

John Findley, of the age of 82 years, *cooper* not in work, and Joan his wife, sickly that spin and knit, and have dwelt here ever — in the *church house*, very poor.

maker of barrels

a house provided by the church for the poor

1 What questions must the city authorities have asked these families?

2 Find a reason in each case why these families were so poor. Why was John Burr slightly better off?

3 How many children are mentioned? The census always says if children attended school, so we can be fairly sure that none of these did. They earned what they could instead.

4 How can you tell that Norwich was a centre of the cloth trade?

These three families were local Norwich people, who 'dwelt here ever'. But the ruling classes, in Norwich and elsewhere, were also worried about another kind of poor person.

Vagabonds and sturdy rogues

A All *strange* [not local residents] beggars now being within the city to the common nuisance shall avoid this city within 24 hours, and none of them there to remain, upon pain of punishment both in *scourging* [whipping] of their bodies and otherwise. (Regulations like this one made in York in 1530 existed in many cities, throughout the century.)

B And I may justly say that the infinite numbers of the Idle wandering people are the chiefest cause of the *dearth* [famine] . . . for they lie idly in the alehouses day and night, eating and drinking excessively. (From a report by a Somerset JP to Lord Burghley, Elizabeth I's chief adviser in London, in 1596, a year of great famine.)

C A rogue will speak in a *lamentable tune* [miserable way] and crawl along the streets . . . his apparel is all tattered . . .: not that they are driven to this misery by mere want, but . . . to be relieved with money, which . . . by night is spent merrily. (Thomas Dekker, writing a description of beggars in 1608)

D

Hark! Hark! the dogs do bark,
The beggars are coming to town.
Some in rags, and some in jags,
And one in a velvet gown.

A contemporary idea of what a vagabond family was like

1 In what ways are the poor people described in these four pieces of evidence, different from the ones in the Norwich census?

2 In B, do you think the 'Idle wandering people' were really 'the chiefest cause of the dearth'? (Read the first two paragraphs on page 136.)

3 In D, how can you tell that the artist does not want you to be sorry for these people? (For instance, do you think the man really needs a crutch?)

4 Why do you think York and other cities imposed such harsh punishments on beggars?

A beggar receiving his punishment

It was all too easy for the rich to say that the poor were idle, and had only themselves to blame for their misery. A 'Poor Law' of 1531 laid down that any idle person who was 'whole and mighty in body' convicted by JPs of begging should be 'tied to the end of a cart naked and be beaten with whips throughout the town . . . till his body be bloody'. He was then sent back to his birthplace to find work. In 1547, it was even ordered that idle persons should be made slaves, but this extraordinary idea was never put into practice.

These harsh measures did no good. The steadily rising population meant that there was not enough work for everyone, and often, not enough food either. The last years of Elizabeth's reign were particularly difficult. War and the Irish rebellion put taxes up; and unemployed soldiers and sailors increased the numbers of wandering beggars. A succession of cold, wet summers caused bad harvests in 1594 and 1595, and a terrible 'dearth' in the following two years. Prices rose sharply.

←54

Although the rich did not really understand the causes of poverty, they were not monsters without sympathy for less fortunate people. The Church had always taught that the poor should be helped and cared for; many could now read printed best-sellers like Thomas More's *Utopia* which condemned riches. In many towns, wealthy citizens founded almshouses to give shelter to the old and the sick, and more people gave private gifts of money. In 1601, Elizabeth's last Parliament passed a very different Poor Law:

> Special overseers of the poor were appointed in every parish.
> Money to help the poor was raised by a local tax, called a 'rate'.
> For the poor who were fit to work, raw materials for manufacture, such as flax, hemp, wool and iron, were to be provided.
> The lame, the blind, the old and children were to be given money and, if necessary, shelter in an almshouse or 'workhouse'.
> Anyone who refused to work was to be sent to prison.

This was the first time that the Crown and the ruling classes had organised proper help for the poor. The system lasted until the nineteenth century; it was not perfect, and poverty did not disappear, but it was a start.

■ What sort of difficulties might arise in making the Poor Law work? How does it compare with what the Government does now for the unemployed?

The end of an era

This unfinished miniature is the most realistic likeness we have of the Queen in old age. Compare it with the written descriptions of the Queen on page 125 and the pictures on page 126. Why do you think the artist, Isaac Oliver, did not stay in favour?

The Queen was getting old. In the cold spring of 1603, her vitality seemed to drain away. She sat on floor cushions, sighing heavily, and would take neither food nor medicine. She finally and reluctantly named her successor: James VI, the son of Mary, Queen of Scots. Then she quietly died 'as the most resplendent sun setteth at last in a western cloud'. There were regrets, of course. But most people looked forward to the new reign, and were glad to have a King again.

7 Power problems

Shall it ever be blotted out of my mind, how at my first entry into this kingdom, the people of all sorts . . . flew to meet me; their eyes flaming nothing but sparkles of affection, their mouths . . . uttering nothing but sounds of joy.

This is how the 37-year-old Stuart King of Scotland described his welcome as he rode south in 1603 to become King James I of England. Yet under the first two Stuart kings, divisions between their subjects in all parts of Britain became very serious, and finally led to war. We have already seen some of the ways in which monarchs used their powers, and the problems which could arise. These problems now grew greater.

The first two Stuart kings

James I (1603–25)

This famous description of James I was written by Anthony Weldon, who disliked the Stuart kings. He also once said of Scotland: 'The air might be wholesome, but for the stinking people who inhabit it.'

> He was of middle stature, more corpulent through his clothes than his body . . . the doublets quilted for stiletto proof, his breeches in great pleats and full stuffed. He was naturally of a timorous disposition . . . his eyes large, ever rolling after any stranger that came into the room insomuch as many for shame left the room . . . his beard was very thin: his tongue too large for his mouth and made him drink very uncomely . . . his legs were very weak . . . (which) made him ever leaning on other men's shoulders.

The description goes on to say that James was generous, but only with his subjects' money, and loved peace, but only because he was a coward. He was 'the wisest fool in Christendom . . . wise in small things but a fool in weighty matters'.

The portrait of the King was painted towards the end of his reign, when he was old, and probably rather ill. It is a formal, dignified picture.

James I, painted by the Dutch artist Daniel Mytens in 1621

1 How far do you think the artist has shown us the real James?

2 How much should you rely on the written description to give a true picture of the King?

←109

Henry, Prince of Wales, painted just before his death in 1612

His death was seen as a great loss, for he was popular and talented.

Robert Cecil, Earl of Salisbury, was trained by his father, Lord Burghley, and had also served Elizabeth at the end of her reign. He chose to be painted seated, facing the artist, to disguise his hunched back and small stature.

In 1603, there were many hopes of the new King. The King was known to dislike persecution. Catholics hoped that the harsh laws which made it difficult to practise their religion might be altered. Puritans hoped that at last the Church of England might be 'purified', for this King came from Scotland, where his Presbyterian subjects were strong followers of Calvin. The Scots hoped that they would gain from the fact that their King now ruled England as well. James's powerful subjects in Parliament hoped that now the imperious, unpredictable old Queen was gone, they could teach this King who did not know their ways to respect their privileges and allow them a say in matters of importance. It is not surprising that James did not live up to these high expectations. It was already obvious he was a very different kind of ruler from Elizabeth.

Anthony Weldon was not alone in finding James undignified, and physically unattractive. He allowed a good deal of drunken and immoral behaviour at his court. He could be lazy, often preferring to go hunting rather than deal with affairs of state. In spite of what he wrote about his arrival in England, he disliked going out to meet ordinary people as Elizabeth had done. He was very extravagant. In 1603, he spent £20,000 on his coronation alone, and £14,000 on gifts to favourites. He was probably lonely: he did not see much of his Queen, Anne of Denmark; she caused no trouble but was rather a stupid woman. His elder son, Henry, died suddenly at age of 18. His popular and attractive daughter Elizabeth was married in 1612 to a German prince, and left England. His younger son, Charles, was backward and shy. Perhaps as a result, James relied on favourites; handsome witty young men who seemed to everyone else to have far too much influence.

However, James had good points too. He had been a successful King of Scotland. He was sensible enough at first to rely on the practical and experienced Robert Cecil as his chief adviser. It was only after his death in 1612, that the favourites really gained too much influence.

The King genuinely disliked violence, and did all he could to encourage peace. The war with Spain was ended in 1604, and he tried to reduce the conflict between Catholics and Protestants in Europe, as we shall see. He also tried — unsuccessfully — to persuade the English Parliament that it would be sensible to unite with their old enemies, the Scots, now that he ruled both kingdoms.

James was an intelligent man. He wrote books, including a *Counterblast to Tobacco* in which he condemned the new fashion of smoking, which was spreading as the plant was imported from the New World. He said it soiled:

> the inward parts of men . . . with an oily kind of soot . . . loathsome to the eye, hateful to the nose, harmful to the brain, dangerous to the lungs.

Many people now would agree! He wrote a book on witchcraft too. In Scotland he seems to have been frightened and fascinated by witches, and encouraged prosecutions. When he arrived in England, William Shakespeare may have written the play *Macbeth* to please him. It certainly has some fearsome witches in it. But James seems to have decided that superstitions were foolish and often hurtful, and had the courage to change his mind. In his reign in England, there were few witchcraft prosecutions.

Like the Tudor monarchs before him, James believed that God had given him his kingly power. His subjects still agreed, but it was unfortunate that he was continually emphasising 'the divine right of kings', and wrote a book about that too. This is part of a speech to Parliament in 1610:

> The state of monarchy is the supremest thing on earth; for kings are not only God's lieutenants on earth, and sit upon God's throne, but even by God himself they are called gods . . . I will not be content that my power be disputed upon.

George Villiers, Duke of Buckingham (1592–1628)

George Villiers was the son of an unimportant Leicestershire gentleman, who gained 'greatness, honour, fame and fortune . . . (from) the beauty and gracefulness of his person', as a contemporary wrote. The King heaped honours on him, and from 1618 he was the most powerful man in England. James would have no criticism of him, and astonished his council by saying that 'Christ had his John, and I have my George.' Buckingham played up to this devotion, writing letters which began 'My dearest Dad and gossip [special friend]', and finished 'Your humble slave and dog.' The favourite became very unpopular, especially among the ruling classes; but they had to accept that to gain influence at court, or any kind of important job, they must please the Duke.

George Villiers, by the Dutch artist Miereveldt

As well as giving his favourite many honours, James made him Duke of Buckingham in 1623.

As the old King's health grew worse in the 1620s, so the Duke's power increased, for he seemed to be able to influence all royal decisions. When James died in 1625, Buckingham had already made sure he had won favour with his son Charles, the next king.

1 Write a flattering account of James at the beginning of his reign, by a courtier hoping for favour.

2 Make a list of reasons why James was likely to upset his subjects, especially the powerful ones in Parliament.

Charles I (1625–49)

Charles I was 25 when he became King. He had been a backward child; he did not walk till he was five. (He probably had rickets, a disease caused by diet deficiency — even royal children could suffer from it then.) He did not learn to talk until he was seven, and then it was with a stammer. He finally conquered this, but he was always slow of speech. He was overshadowed by his popular elder brother and sister. Then suddenly, when Charles was 12, Henry died, and he found himself heir to the throne. He was still weakly, and small for his age, but he was also very determined. He began a programme of physical training, and

The interior of the Banqueting House with Rubens's painted ceiling

became a good horseman. He also gained a natural dignity which made people forget how short he was. But he remained shy, and was isolated at his father's court, because he disapproved of much that went on there. His own court was to be very different.

Charles was very religious. He was the first English king to have been brought up in the Church of England, and he was deeply devoted to it. His religion strengthened his belief in the divine right of kings; nothing must weaken his God-given powers. The Earl of Clarendon, who knew him well, described Charles when he was King:

> He was punctual and regular in his devotions; he was never known to enter upon his recreations or sports . . . before he had been at public prayers . . . He was not in his nature bountiful . . . and he paused too long in the giving . . . He kept state to the full, which made his court very orderly . . . He saw and observed men long before he received them . . . and did not love strangers, nor very confident men.

1 Clarendon was a loyal supporter of Charles. Do you think he flatters him in this description?

2 From this description, what might courtiers respect about the King, and what might they resent?

Charles was also artistic. He spent large sums of money collecting works of art, and employed a great artist, Anthony Van Dyck, as his court painter. This artist's portraits of the King, his family, and his courtiers tell us much of the elegance and dignity of the court in the first part of Charles's reign. There was also a grand plan, begun in James's reign, to rebuild Whitehall Palace, which by now was a rather ramshackle collection of red-brick Tudor buildings. The whole plan was never carried out. However, the fashionable architect, Inigo Jones, designed a beautiful new Banqueting House in honey-coloured stone. The interior is perfectly proportioned because it is an exact double cube. Rubens, the most famous artist in Europe,

Van Dyck was treated as an honoured courtier when he arrived in England in 1632, unlike other artists who were usually looked on, and paid, as craftsmen. He was knighted, given a gold chain, a pension of £200 and a house in Blackfriars. This is one of his grandest portraits of the King; it was probably meant to go in an impressive position at the end of the Long Gallery in Whitehall Palace. Why is Charles shown on horseback? How much evidence can you find on this page that he used his artists to show him as a powerful king?

and Van Dyck's teacher, was paid £3,000 to design and paint the elaborate ceiling in memory of a James I, showing him as a great and powerful monarch. The Banqueting House provided a setting for grand court occasions, including masques. Masques were plays in verse, full of gods and goddesses with royal powers. The King, the Queen, and their courtiers often acted the main parts. Although the King disliked 'very confident men', it seemed that like many shy people, he needed to rely on one lively, outgoing and strong-minded person who was the opposite of his own character. Early in his life, he had admired and looked up to his brother Henry, and he may have learnt his artistic tastes from him. After Henry's death, the isolated young prince at first disliked the Duke of Buckingham, who dominated his father's court. However, Buckingham went out of his way to win Charles's affection, for this was the obvious way to keep power once James was dead. Soon his influence over Charles was as great as it had been over his father. Since the Duke was already so unpopular, Charles's reign began very badly.

Trouble with Parliament

(It will be helpful to remind yourself how Parliament worked from the chart on page 82.)

In spite of their good points, the first two Stuart kings were unpopular. The nobles and gentry especially expected to have more say in the affairs of the nation, and were soon disappointed that neither of these kings seemed able to work with them in Parliament.

James summoned Parliaments fairly regularly, though he managed without one from 1611 to 1621, except for the 'Addled Parliament' in 1614. This Parliament earned its nickname because it produced no money for the King, and sat for only six weeks. In 1621, Parliament claimed the right to

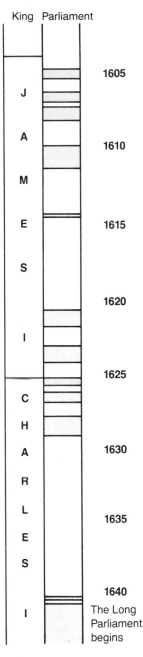

Parliaments 1604-40

King Parliament

J
A
M
E
S

1605
1610
1615
1620
1625

C
H
A
R
L
E
S
I

1630
1635
1640

The Long
Parliament
begins

(Shaded areas show when
Parliament was called.)

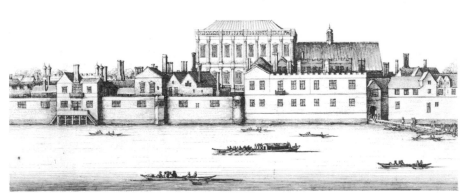

A seventeenth-century view of Whitehall Palace from the river

You can see the Banqueting House in the centre background.

discuss 'matters of state' (see page 130). James was so angry that he tore the page which recorded their claim out of the Commons Journal. In 1624, when he was old and ill, he gave in to their demands, because Buckingham and Charles sided against him in a bid for popularity.

Charles I started badly, because Parliament hated Buckingham, whom they felt they could not control. There were three Parliaments in four years, and nothing but quarrels. In the end, Charles decided he would manage without any Parliament at all. When he sent orders that Parliament should be dissolved, members locked the door, and held down the Speaker (who was in floods of tears), while they passed three resolutions disapproving of the King's actions. But the whole incident reflected their problem: once the doors were unlocked, the King's orders had to be obeyed, and they went home. Sir John Eliot, who was at the centre of the trouble, was sent to the Tower, where he died three years later. For 11 years, from 1629 to 1640, no Parliament was held at all.

Foreign affairs caused trouble up to 1629; but it was the old problems of money and religion which really divided the King from his powerful subjects. Finally, these difficulties brought about a situation which would lead to war. Inevitably, ordinary people were caught up in the troubles too.

Foreign affairs

Foreign affairs had always been the personal affair of the monarch; this caused trouble between the first two Stuart kings and their Parliaments, who wanted to play their part as well. When James's daughter Elizabeth married the German Protestant Prince Frederick, Elector Palatine, this was popular, although the wedding cost £9,000, and increased the royal financial problems. However, in 1618, the young couple became involved in the outbreak of the Thirty Years War in Germany, another terrible conflict between Catholics and Protestants. They accepted the crown of Protestant Bohemia, which was trying to break free from the powerful Catholic Emperor. However, they lost not only Bohemia, but also their own German lands of the Palatinate. Elizabeth of Bohemia, as she was known, went into exile in Holland, with her large family of growing children.

The English Parliament made James's daughter a great heroine, and were horrified that he did so little to help her. They were convinced that a naval war with Spain would force the Emperor (the Spanish King's cousin) to hand back her lands. However, they distrusted James, and were not prepared to vote a realistic sum of money to pay for the war. James had another solution, which Buckingham took up enthusiastically. His son Charles should marry the King of Spain's daughter; then Spain would persuade the Emperor to restore the lands of Elizabeth and her husband.

1 Do you think that either of these solutions was realistic?

2 Why would a Spanish marriage for the heir to the throne be unpopular?

Elizabeth of Bohemia was thought to be a great beauty in her youth. The poet Ben Jonson compared her with the goddess Diana. This portrait was painted when she was in exile, and had borne six children. She remained a strong, attractive personality.

Charles I's marriage

The arrangements for the marriage between Charles and the daughter of the King of Spain came to nothing, partly because Buckingham persuaded the shy young prince into a risky and romantic expedition to Madrid to woo her. The Spaniards were shocked (and probably not very serious about the idea anyway), for royal marriages were usually arranged very formally.

In 1625, when he became King, Charles married a French Catholic princess, Henrietta Maria. His subjects distrusted France almost as much as Spain, and of course, her religion was unacceptable. She was only 15 when she first arrived in Britain, and hardly spoke any English. She found her husband shy and distant, and she resented the Duke of Buckingham's influence. Charles found her shallow and spoilt. It was not a good beginning. However, after Buckingham's death, she comforted the King, and in the process, they seem to have fallen in love. It became a very happy marriage. Charles was a devoted husband, and his confidence grew. The children came quickly, and the succession was secure. Personally therefore, Charles's marriage was very good for him. Politically, it was a disaster. Henrietta never understood the English Parliament or the Church of England. Nevertheless, her influence on Charles was very great, and she was always urging him on to strong action to defend his powers. His subjects were quick to realise this, and she became more and more unpopular.

■ Write a poem, or draw a cartoon, opposing Charles's marriage in 1625 — or his Spanish adventure — or both.

Henrietta Maria in 1632, by Van Dyck

She was vivacious and elegant, and had the French talent for making the best of her looks; but Van Dyck's portraits almost certainly flattered her. A more truthful niece said that she had 'long skinny arms, and her teeth stuck out like defence works'.

When James I's last Parliament met in 1624, Charles and Buckingham had just returned from Spain. Members of Parliament shared the general relief that their future king was not married to a Spanish 'Papist' bride. For once they agreed with the two young men that a war with Spain would avenge the insult (as long as they did not have to pay for it); the reluctant old king was persuaded into a war he did not want, and knew he could not afford.

By the time Charles became King in 1625, the war was already going badly. Buckingham organised a naval expedition against Cadiz (just like Drake in 1587, he hoped), which was a disaster. When the ships returned to Portsmouth, their unpaid crews were disease-ridden and on the point of mutiny. The local people had to provide billets for the troops, without payment; they were often involved in brawls with them, and punished harshly. All over the country, forced payments were demanded to pay for this war, and for Buckingham's next idea: an expedition to help the French Protestants besieged in La Rochelle by the Catholic French government,

←111

which was trying to crush them in all parts of France. This meant that England was at war with the two great powers of Europe, France and Spain, at the same time; which was almost as crazy as it would be for modern Britain to declare war on the USA *and* the USSR. Once again this expedition ended in failure and suffering.

When Parliament met in 1628, a 'Petition of Right' was drawn up, demanding that billeting, unjust imprisonment and forced payments without Parliament's consent should stop. Charles appeared to listen, for he needed consent for new taxes. But he said: 'I owe an account of my actions to none but to God'.

Meanwhile, Buckingham was in Portsmouth, organising yet another naval expedition. A bitter and resentful officer, John Felton, who had been in the Cadiz disaster, stabbed him to death. The news was brought to Charles when he was at prayers. Clarendon said that:

> His Majesty continued unmoved, and without the least change of countenance, till prayers were ended, when he suddenly departed to his chamber.

Charles was alone in his grief. Outside in the streets, people were joyfully celebrating the end of the unpopular Duke.

When the King decided in 1629 to rule without a Parliament, foreign affairs became less important. Since he had to manage without taxes voted by Parliament, he could not afford war, or any other expensive activity abroad.

Money

■ Look back at the first section of this chapter, and make a list of the ways in which James I and Charles I were extravagant.

James also inherited debts of £400,000 from Elizabeth. So the Crown's shortage of money became much worse, and both kings needed to ask Parliament for extra taxes. Parliament saw this as a good way to force the King to listen to them — 'to redress their grievances'. They were very reluctant to vote money because they did not think it would be spent properly. They were also unrealistic about the costs of running the country.

It is not surprising that both Stuart kings found other ways of raising money. The Crown had the right to take some customs duties; these were called tunnage and poundage. At the beginning of James's reign, Robert Cecil imposed so many extra ones that they were called *Impositions,* and were much resented. John Bate, a currant merchant, challenged the King's right to ask for this money without Parliament's consent. He was prosecuted, and the judges (whose jobs depended on the King) said that he must pay. When Charles became King, Parliament would not vote tunnage and poundage permanently; but Charles continued to collect it — and even more impositions. *Monopolies,* the sole right to trade in or produce certain ←131 goods, had not disappeared either. There were about 700 monopolies by 1621. By the end of the 1630s they were bringing in about £100,000 a year to the Crown.

A modern historian's research on monopolies under the early Stuarts

This is what Christopher Hill has written:

> It is difficult for us to picture to ourselves the life of a man living in a house built with monopoly bricks, with windows (if any) of monopoly glass; heated with monopoly coal . . . burning in a grate made of monopoly iron . . . He slept on monopoly feathers, did his hair with monopoly brushes and combs. He washed himself with monopoly soap . . . he dressed in monopoly lace . . . linen . . . leather . . . gold thread . . . his clothes were held up with monopoly belts, buttons and pins. He ate monopoly butter . . . currants, red herrings, salmon, and lobster. His food was seasoned with monopoly salt, . . . pepper . . . vinegar. He smoked with monopoly tobacco out of monopoly pipes, played with monopoly dice, or monopoly cards . . . wrote with monopoly pens on monopoly writing paper; read through monopoly spectacles, by the light of monopoly candles, monopoly printed books . . . mice were caught in monopoly mousetraps.

1 What had Elizabeth done in 1601 that would make people particularly angry about these monopolies?

2 Find at least ten articles in the extract above which show (a) that monopolies affected the better-off as well as the very poor; (b) affected everyday life, not unusual activities.

3 Design an anti-monopoly poster, using as much information as possible from the list

---

After 1629, when Charles was ruling without Parliament, he had to find even more ways of raising money. He did this by using old methods which had long fallen out of use. For instance, he revived an old custom that those with incomes over £40 a year were fined if they had avoided the expense of becoming a knight. Those who had built within the boundaries of royal forests (some long since forgotten) were also fined.

A new tax called *ship money* caused the greatest trouble. The King had always had the right to make certain ports pay for ships. Now he made all parts of the country pay this tax. Most people felt that this was just another excuse to raise money without Parliament's consent. They were probably right, though Charles did spend most of it on the navy.

A powerful group of men who had been MPs decided a stand must be made. John Hampden, a rich Buckinghamshire country gentleman, was a sincere Puritan, and much respected; he was not at all the kind of person to act illegally. He refused to pay the tax of £1 11s 6d — a small sum for him — and was tried before 12 judges in London. Five of the King's judges were brave enough to acquit him, and although the other seven found him guilty, the King took the case no further. Hampden had really won.

For the time being, however, Charles had just enough money to avoid calling Parliament, provided he had no extra expenses. Above all, he had to avoid the most costly activity of all — war.

■ Make a list of the ways in which James I and Charles I raised money without Parliament, putting by each, one or more reasons why people would resent them.

Religion

Religion already divided the peoples of Britain. Catholics had had a hard time in Elizabeth's reign; they soon realised that their hopes of a better future under James were empty. Most of them sadly accepted the disappointment, but an extremist called Robert Catesby worked out a plot to blow up the Houses of Parliament when the King was present, to kidnap the royal children and to take over the government with Spanish help.

The Gunpowder Plot never had much hope of success, and in itself was not very important. But it added to the division between Catholic and Protestant in Britain, for it was never forgotten, and 'Papists' remained hated and feared. Special prayers were added to the English Prayer Book, and 5 November was celebrated each year as a time of special deliverance. We still celebrate it today, though most of us have forgotten who it is we burn on our bonfires and why we do it. Perhaps that is just as well.

James was pleased when a special petition from 1,000 Puritan clergy was presented to him, asking for changes in the Church of England, for it included sensible demands like better education for the clergy. Some of his bishops approved of these demands too. So in 1604 he summoned a special conference at Hampton Court to discuss it all. However, not all the bishops were happy, for some Puritans wanted to reduce their power; and ←59 when one of the Puritans began to praise the Scots Presbyterians, James decided he wanted no more talk of changes. The Presbyterians in Scotland did not allow bishops to have power in their church, and James had always found their ministers difficult to control. But he found the English bishops a very useful support, and did not want to see their power reduced. 'No bishop, no King', he shouted, and dismissed the conference, leaving the Puritans annoyed and resentful.

In fact some reforms went through. The most important was a new translation of the Bible, known as the Authorised Version, and finished in 1611. It is written in the beautiful language of Shakespeare, though it is sometimes difficult for us to understand now.

146

The Gunpowder Plot, 1605

Robert Catesby persuaded two leading Yorkshire Catholic gentlemen, Francis Tresham and Thomas Percy, and a Yorkshireman called Guy Fawkes to join him in his plot. In November 1605 the conspirators met in the Midlands. Guy Fawkes was given the task of waiting in a cellar under a house next to Parliament; he was then to set light to 36 barrels of gunpowder hidden under piles of wood, just as the King was opening Parliament. At this critical moment, Tresham chose to write the letter, part of which you can see below, to his relation, Lord Monteagle, warning him not to attend the opening — 'I say they shall receive a terrible blow this parliament and yet they shall not see who hurts them'. As a result, the cellar was searched, and Guy Fawkes was arrested.

There are several odd things about this story. The conspirators apparently first tried to dig a tunnel, but no one in the crowded streets of Westminster seems to have noticed anything unusual; nor have any traces of the tunnel ever been discovered. People could buy gunpowder only by government licence, which was unlikely to be granted to Catholics; and it is very odd that no one noticed such a large number of barrels being put so suspiciously near Parliament.

The letter may be a forgery. What do you think the words quoted meant? Lord Monteagle seemed to know for certain they meant there was going to be an explosion; he went straight to Cecil, who showed the letter to the King. It may be that Cecil discovered the plot quite early, and because he was afraid that the King might be too kind to Catholics, and encouraged it so that James would be thoroughly frightened. If that was his aim, he succeeded.

Guy Fawkes was tortured to make him name the plotters. He resisted bravely but eventually signed a confession. As soldiers arrested the other conspirators, Catesby and Percy were shot. (Did they know too much to be brought to trial?) The others were all found guilty and hanged, drawn and quartered — except for Tresham. He was imprisoned after the others were tried, and died suddenly and mysteriously in the Tower in December 1605.

■ Write out the plan Cecil might have made once he discovered the plot:

Most of the conspirators in the Gunpowder Plot are shown in this picture on the left, printed soon after the plot was discovered.

Part of the letter written by Tresham to Lord Monteagle is shown below. It is not too difficult to pick out the important sentence, in spite of the unreliable spelling.

Later in his reign, James appointed an Archbishop of Canterbury (George Abbot) who was more sympathetic to Puritans, but some still felt they could no longer stay in England. This led in 1620 to the voyage of the Pilgrim Fathers to the New World. (There is more about this in Chapter 10.)

The many Puritans amongst the powerful ruling classes were disappointed therefore that James had done so little to reform the Church of England. However, it was not until Charles's reign that they became seriously worried. Charles loved dignified services with beautiful music, in churches with candles, pictures and statues; this was much nearer the Catholic way of worshipping. His Catholic wife openly attended Mass at court; many people felt it was only a matter of time before their King accepted his wife's faith. Charles was in fact a firm member of the Church of England, as we have seen, but he did nothing to set his worried subjects' minds at rest; and he took no notice of the complaints in Parliament before 1629. As so often, he failed to understand how his subjects were feeling, and he chose exactly the wrong man to help him in church matters.

William Laud, Archbishop of Canterbury (1573–1645)

William Laud served the King from the beginning of his reign, and became Archbishop in 1633. He was the son of a tailor, who rose to power with the help of the Duke of Buckingham. He earned the nickname 'the Duke's earwig'. Clarendon said he was a man of great courage and resolution, who wanted all that was pious and just, but 'he never studied the ways to those ends . . . he did court persons too little'. In other words, he had the kind of personality that upset people. He could be pompous and fussy, and his enemies called him 'a little, low, red man'.

Archbishop Laud wanted an orderly and efficient church, with strong bishops to enforce his aims. People were often very casual in church. They brought in their dogs, wandered about talking in services, or leaned on the altar, which was often in the middle of the church. Laud made rules to stop this kind of thing. The altar must be railed off at the east end, decorated with candles, and it should be bowed to reverently. There should be pictures and statues. He tried to stop too much preaching because he felt it gave Puritans a chance to make trouble. His bishops punished those who disobeyed. Think of reasons why all this would upset Puritans.

←104

A harsh punishment

In 1637, a well-known Puritan, William Prynne, was prosecuted with two others for writing a pamphlet condemning the power of the bishops. The trial was not in the ordinary courts, but a special royal court called the Star Chamber, where Laud was one of the judges. The three men were sentenced to stand in the pillory, to have their ears cut off and their cheeks branded, and then be imprisoned in distant parts of the kingdom. They were also fined £5,000 each. All three behaved very bravely when the punishment was carried out in front of a large and sympathetic crowd in Westminster. So all the case did was to make the King and Laud even more unpopular.

■ Make your own cartoon by a Puritan in 1637, showing *all* the things you dislike about Archbishop Laud — not just the Prynne case.

This hostile Puritan cartoon shows Archbishop Laud eating ears for dinner.

A neglected kingdom

It was also in 1637 that Charles and his Archbishop turned their attention to Scotland. Since James VI of Scotland had become James I of England, the Scots had felt more and more neglected. They saw little of James or Charles, and felt they had no chance to share in England's prosperous trade. Charles favoured a few Catholic Scots nobles at the English Court. He distrusted the Protestant ones, who resented his neglect; these nobles strongly supported the Presbyterian Church. Scots Presbyterians were even more Protestant than English Puritans, and had run their Church in their own way since the days of John Knox. They allowed bishops no power, and did not use the English Prayer Book. But the King and Archbishop ordered them to do just that.

←105

A 'Solemn League and Covenant' promising to defend their Church was signed by thousands of people. Soon Scotland was in arms — and it was an efficient army, commanded by professional soldiers who had fought for the Protestants in the German wars.

←142

This is what happened in St Giles' Cathedral, Edinburgh, on the first Sunday the English Prayer Book was used. There was trouble elsewhere too, as all over Scotland, Presbyterians refused to accept the new service, and to obey Laud's rules which went along with it.

Charles had no intention of giving in, and began to raise an army to enforce his orders. He soon found that most of his English subjects sympathised with the Scots. There was a tax strike, and the ragtag and bobtail army he managed to collect ran away as soon as the Scots approached over the border. Charles now took the advice of another unpopular minister.

Thomas Wentworth, Earl of Strafford, (1539–1641) had criticised the King in Parliament in the 1620s, but later became a loyal minister. He was a great friend of Laud, and they both set out to help the King to govern the country efficiently. From 1633, he was Lord Deputy in Ireland, and kept the country under firm control, raising money for the King, and beginning to build up an army. 'Black Tom', as he was nicknamed, was not popular there or in England. He was usually fair, but he could be harsh; he made many enemies, and only a few loyal friends.

150

Strafford advised the King to call Parliament, so that enough money might be voted to raise a better army. In the spring of 1640, the Short Parliament met, so called because it lasted only a few weeks. Led by John Pym, a skilful and determined lawyer, they refused to vote any money unless Charles agreed to a whole list of demands, which would prevent him from ruling without Parliament ever again. The King sent them home.

Once again Charles tried to defeat the Scots; once again his army refused to fight. The Scots took Newcastle, and occupied the north of England. In league with Pym and the other leaders of Parliament, they insisted the King must pay them £850 a day for their army's keep. Charles was now powerless. There was only one way that he could find that kind of money: by calling Parliament and giving in to their demands. In November 1640, the Long Parliament met. Its name shows that Charles was not able to rid himself of this one quickly.

■ Copy the timeline on page 141, adding three more columns, headed Foreign Affairs, Money and Religion. Use the sections in this chapter to fill in the events in each column. Put Scottish affairs under Religion.

Steps to war

In November 1640, no one was thinking of going to war over the way Charles I was using his royal power. The leaders of the Long Parliament, Pym, John Hampden, and important peers like the Earls of Bedford and Warwick, and Lord Saye and Sele, wanted to ensure that the King could never again rule without Parliament. Almost all the MPs agreed with them, but they did not consider getting rid of Charles, let alone changing the way the country was ruled. They felt Charles had tried to introduce the new idea of an 'absolute' all-powerful monarchy, and they wanted to be sure he could not do this.

In the Early Modern Age, we have often seen that people felt very uncomfortable about blaming the King for things they disliked. It was always safer to blame his ministers. They still did that in 1640. Strafford and Laud were put in the Tower, accused of 'treason' — a difficult charge to prove against two loyal, hard-working servants of the King. Laud was not executed till much later, in 1645. People feared Strafford more, probably because he seemed to be the strongest person close to the King. Pym knew too that Strafford might accuse *him* of treason — for being in league with the Scots.

A proper trial failed to find Strafford guilty, so Pym introduced an Act of Attainder, which had to go through Parliament in the normal way. This simply stated he was guilty. Charles confidently promised that he would never sign such an Act. However, the London crowds, full of apprentices who were firm Puritans, came out into the streets round Whitehall, howling not only for Strafford's blood, but also the 'Papist' Queen's. Charles could not face a threat to his beloved wife, and Strafford wrote to him from the Tower, telling him to forget his promise. 'My Lord of

John Pym, the leader of the Long Parliament

←82

151

Strafford's case is happier than mine,' said Charles, as he reluctantly signed. Outside in the streets, the crowds were soon shouting jubilantly, 'His head is off, his head is off!' The King never forgave himself for agreeing to Strafford's death. It was the only time he ever admitted he was wrong.

Meanwhile Pym was busy pushing a series of Acts through Parliament which ensured that Charles could never again rule without Parliament. The most important was the Triennial Act (1641), which made it compulsory to summon Parliament every three years. Ship money, monopolies and impositions were all made illegal, together with the other ways in which Charles had raised money from 1629 to 1640. Royal courts like the Star Chamber, which had punished William Prynne, were also abolished.

So far, most MPs agreed with all this. However, many were worried about the way in which ordinary people were becoming involved in the crisis. The London crowds were bad enough, but the countryside was not peaceful either. Trouble seemed to be spreading and this had been encouraged by the King's disorderly army when it marched north to face ←10 the Scots in 1640. There were riots against enclosures, and in some places churches were broken into, and Laud's pictures and altar rails torn down. Gentlemen had not on the whole liked the situation in the 1630s, when the bishops were so powerful, but now there was talk of abolishing them altogether. Would that not increase all this disorder?

Crisis over power

In the autumn of 1641, a new crisis arose. The Irish broke out in rebellion, now that Strafford's firm rule had ended. Since the uprising at the end of Elizabeth's reign, even more Irish land had been taken away. In particular James I had given to Scots settlers most of the northern province of Ulster. They were zealous Presbyterians, and the Catholic Irish hated them even more than they did the other English settlers. It was these Scots Presbyterians who suffered most from violence and murder when the Catholic Irish chieftains and their people rebelled. The English were not slow to make the most of the terrible stories filtering back to London, as this playing card shows. There *was* a horrible massacre of Protestants on the bridge at Portadown; but how does the caption make it sound as if this happened all over Ireland?

Driving Men Women & children by hundreds upon Briges & casting them into Rivers, who drowned not were killed with poles & shot with muskets.

Now there was a new twist to the situation. An army was needed to crush the Irish — but who was to control it? It was always the monarch who commanded the army but perhaps this King would use it, not against the Irish, but against his English subjects in Parliament? Whoever controlled the army held the real power. Pym determined it should be Parliament.

152

To strengthen his hand, Pym drew up a long list of everything Charles had done wrong since he became King. He called it the 'Grand Remonstrance.' It included a demand to reform the Church and abolish bishops. The Church of England would then be like the Scots Presbyterian Church.

This was too much for many people, already worried by all the unrest and change. It was one thing to make sure that Parliament met regularly, and that the King could not impose taxes without its consent. It was quite another to rake up his past faults again, when everything seemed to be settled. Above all, to destroy the Church of England, of which the King was Head, was going altogether too far. There were violent scenes in Parliament as MPs debated the Grand Remonstrance, and it was finally passed by only 11 votes. Now at last, Charles had some supporters — Royalists, who did not wish to see any more change, and who believed that Pym and his followers were forsaking their duty and loyalty to the King.

The Five Members
During the long months when it seemed the King must give in, Henrietta Maria had been urging him to strong action. Now Charles listened to her, as she told him to arrest Pym, Hampden and three other Parliamentary leaders (the 'Five Members'), whatever their 'privileges'. Once they were gone, she argued, Charles could forget all the promises to rule with Parliament, and be a real King at last. 'Go pull those rogues out by the ears, or never see my face again!' she is supposed to have said. The Queen was not always careful about who was listening, and Pym knew one of her ladies-in-waiting, Lady Carlisle. Once he learned of the plan, Pym determined to make sure that the King actually walked into Parliament with his soldiers. This would break Parliament's traditional privilege of freedom from arrest, and put the King in the wrong. Surely ←130 that would bring back the Royalists, Pym thought, and he would have their support again. Also, of course, he was determined not to be arrested. A royal message to the Speaker demanding the five to be given up was ignored. On 4 January 1642, the King set out from Whitehall with nearly 300 men. It was only five minutes' march to Parliament, but a message reached the Five Members that the King was on his way to arrest them. The House gave them permission to go, and they slipped away by river to the City of London, where they had plenty of support.

Meanwhile, the King and his soldiers were entering the front of the Parliament buildings. Charles walked into the House of Commons, leaving his soldiers lined up near the doorway, and said to the Speaker, 'By your leave, I must borrow your chair.' He made a short speech asking for Pym and his colleagues, saying they had committed treason. He went on:

> Yet you must know that in cases of treason, no person hath a privilege. And therefore I am come to know if any of those persons that are accused are here.

There was silence as he looked round for them. Then he continued, rather forlornly:

'Well, since I see all the birds are flown, I do expect from you that you shall send them to me as soon as they return hither . . .' When the King was looking about the House, the Speaker standing below by the Chair, His Majesty asked him whether any of these persons were in the House . . . to which the Speaker, falling on his knee, thus answered, 'May it please Your Majesty, I have neither eyes to see nor tongue to speak in this place but as the House is pleased to direct me, whose servant I am here; and I humbly beg Your Majesty's pardon that I cannot give any other answer than this'. . . The King went out of the House, which was in great disorder, and many members cried out aloud, so that he might hear them, 'Privilege, privilege.'

1 This account was written by John Rushworth, a young clerk to the House of Commons, whose job it was to record what happened there in shorthand. From his shorthand notes he made a report for the King. Do you think he has put in anything in order to please him?

2 From page 82, make a list of the tasks of the Speaker. Then look at the incident on page 142. Why was the Speaker so upset on that occasion in 1629? Whose orders is the Speaker obeying in this incident in 1642 described here? (The Speaker in 1642 was not the same man as the Speaker in 1629.)

3 Use the map of London and Westminster on page 22 to make your own sketch map, which shows the King's march from Whitehall, and the escape route of the Five Members.

4 Imagine you are an MP writing home to your wife, and describe this scene. Decide whether you support Pym, or have become a Royalist. How might Royalists feel about the incident?

Charles had now tried force. Worse, he had tried it unsuccessfully. London, which had always favoured Parliament, was in an uproar, and was no longer a safe place for the King to be. The Queen left for Holland to sell her jewels and collect as much money as she could. Charles went north to raise an army. The Five Members came back to Parliament in triumph, and Pym too began to organise ways of building up an army. Talking had come to an end. Fighting seemed the only alternative.

A view of seventeenth-century Westminster, with Parliament House on the left and the river in the foreground

The familiar twin towers of Westminster Abbey were added in the early eighteenth century.

154

THE STUART FAMILY

JAMES I 1603-25 m Anne of Denmark

Henry, Prince of Wales
d1612

CHARLES I 1625-49 m Henrietta Maria

Elizabeth of Bohemia
m
Frederick, Elector Palatine

CHARLES II
1660-85
m
Catherine of
Braganza

Mary
m
William of
Orange

JAMES II
1685-8
m

Elizabeth
d1650

Anne
d1640

Henry
d1660

Henrietta
Anne
d1670

Rupert Maurice
(and 3 other
children)

Sophia
m
Elector of
Hanover

① Anne
Hyde

② Mary of
Modena

This marriage
produced the
Hanoverian
line from which
the present
Queen is
descended.

WILLIAM m MARY d1698
JOINT SOVEREIGNS 1688-1702

ANNE
1702-14

James Edward
b1688

REIGNING SOVEREIGNS ARE IN CAPITAL LETTERS. The dates of their reigns are shown by their names.

The five eldest children of Charles I, painted by Van Dyck in 1637. The heir to the throne, the future Charles II, aged seven, stands in the centre beside the big dog. His sister Mary, aged six, is on the left, and next to her is James, aged four. The two-year-old Elizabeth on the right carefully holds the baby Anne (who only lived three years). James and Elizabeth are still wearing long dresses, as children did till they were five or six; then they were dressed as miniature versions of adults. So the two eldest children are wearing the elegant fashions of their father's court. (How many differences can you see from Elizabethan fashions?) Van Dyck makes it quite clear that these children, however small they are, belong to a very important family; yet they also look like real children, who might actually fidget when they have to stand still for the artist to paint them.

8 The world turned upside down

Wars break out when people feel so strongly about their differences that all they feel they can do is fight each other. There is special bitterness and tragedy in a civil war, when people of the same country fight each other, and families and friends find themselves divided. The year 1642, when Royalists and Parliamentarians began to take up arms, was a time of great tension and unhappiness. Many Royalists joined the King's side for the kind of reasons which the Buckinghamshire landowner, Sir Edmund Verney, gave to his friend Edward Hyde, later Earl of Clarendon:

depression

> My condition is worse than yours . . . and will very well justify the *melancholic* that I confess to you possesses me. You have satisfaction that you are right; that the King ought not to grant that which is required of him . . . but for my part I do not like the quarrel, and do heartily wish that the King would yield and consent to what they desire . . . *I have eaten his bread* and served him near thirty years, and will not do so base a thing as to forsake him; and choose rather to lose my life (which I am sure I shall do).

I have been employed by the King

■ What shows that Sir Edmund Verney was depressed by the whole situation? Why did he nevertheless decide to fight for the King?

Edward Hyde was a lawyer who had disliked Charles's rule without Parliament, and had backed Pym until the crisis over the Grand Remonstrance. For him too, loyalty was a strong reason for supporting the King. However he felt happier about it than Verney, and had 'satisfaction that he was right', because he believed that enough had been done to limit Charles's actions. Any further change, he believed, would destroy the Church and the Crown. Parliamentarians like Pym and Hampden still believed that England should be ruled by a King; but they felt that *this* King could no longer be trusted. Promises and Acts of Parliament were not enough. They felt that they must make sure the checks the Long Parliament had put on the King's power would really work, by defeating him in battle. Pym had always been determined and ruthless. Clarendon described Hampden as wise, popular, and respected but 'after he was accused by the King of high treason, he was much altered; his nature . . . seemed much fiercer than it did before'. Parliamentarians were risking a great deal: if they were defeated, they would suffer the fate of all rebels. It is not surprising some of them were 'fiercer than before'.

Edward Hyde (1609–74) later became the Earl of Clarendon and is best known by this name. His history of his times tells us of the people he knew during his long career.
Although he was a strong Royalist, he was usually fair in what he wrote.

Many people found it very difficult to decide what to do in 1642. 'Both sides promise so fair, I cannot see what it is they should fight for,' wrote Lady Sussex, a friend of Sir Edmund Verney. A Norfolk gentleman wrote to

Cavaliers and Roundheads

When people begin to fight, words become part of the battle — especially nicknames. Royalists were soon called 'Cavaliers' by their enemies. 'Cavalier' meant a wild Spanish horseman (remember that Spaniards were always unpopular) who slaughtered and looted, and it gives a clue to the behaviour of some of their younger supporters. But Charles made the best of the nickname: 'The valour of Cavaliers hath honoured the name . . . it signifieth no more than a gentleman serving his King on horseback'.

Parliamentarians were called 'Roundheads'; Henrietta Maria may have given them the name in 1641, as she looked down from the windows of the Palace of Whitehall on the threatening mob of short-haired apprentices. Short hair was worn by poorer people; gentlemen wore their hair shoulder length at this time, as you can see from their portraits. So a good many Parliamentarians were not 'Roundheads', but the nickname stuck, and they made the best of it too: 'Though we be round-headed, we be not hollow-hearted.'

his wife in May 1642, on the day he had received orders from both the King and Parliament to raise troops: 'Oh sweetheart, I am now in a great strait [difficulty] what to do.' In fact, he did his best to keep out of the struggle, and there were many like him.

Lucy Hutchinson, who wrote the life story of her husband John, a colonel in Parliament's army, described how difficult it was in Nottinghamshire. Their home in Owthorpe was surrounded by Royalist supporters. John had to escape, to avoid capture by a Royalist troop of horse; and Lucy, 'somewhat afflicted to be left so alone', was relieved to find the officer in command was her own brother Allan. The Verney family was divided too. Although the eldest son Ralph was very fond of his Royalist father, Sir Edmund, he decided he must support Parliament. His younger brother Mun (Edmund) wrote:

> Brother, what I feared is proved too true, which is your being against the King; . . . it grieves my heart to think that my father . . . and I who so dearly love and esteem you should be bound . . . (because of our duty to the King) to be your enemy. . . . I am so much troubled to think of you being on the side you are that I can write no more.

Families were divided, and so were places. Buckinghamshire was divided between the followers of the Royalist Verneys, and the Parliamentarian Hampdens. In Chester, the city was split between King and Parliament. The rich and powerful University of Oxford was strongly Royalist, but many of the townspeople were for Parliament.

In August 1642, the King raised his standard at Nottingham and armies from both sides began to close in on each other.

■ Write the conversation Lucy Hutchinson might have had with her brother in the incident at Owthorpe in 1642.

The raising of the King's standard at Nottingham was a signal for all loyal supporters to join him. The weather was bad, and the standard soon blew down, which some people took to be a bad omen.

The two sides in 1642

The King	Parliament
Places The north of England, Wales, and the west	Mainly the south and east
Some important cities: eg York, Oxford, Nottingham, Shrewsbury	The capital, London, with its large population, its wealth and trade
	Several ports: eg Hull, Plymouth, Bristol
People 75 per cent of the nobility	25 per cent of the nobility
Gentry and rich merchants fairly evenly divided	
	More 'industrious sort of people': clothworkers, skilled craftsmen and shopkeepers and traders in towns
Country people tended to follow the local gentry.	
Military strength Prince Rupert, an inspiring cavalry leader	The Earl of Essex, a methodical, but uninspiring commander
Better cavalry More gold and silver plate to melt down for ready money	The navy, efficiently commanded by the Earl of Warwick

Parliament's standards were full of slogans. Captain Brown, a London draper, shows his disapproval of bishops; above the bishop is the Bible on which every Puritan relied.

Use the map and information on the opposite page and this table to work out the following:

1 The King's aim was to recapture his capital, London. Find as many reasons as you can why he decided on this, rather than any other plan. Do you think he was right?

2 Meanwhile, the King needed a headquarters, and he chose Oxford. Look at Oxford's geographical position, and find out what you can about seventeenth-century Oxford, to see whether you agree with his choice. What did a headquarters for the King and his court need to provide?

3 Why did the King have better cavalry, and more ready money in 1642?

4 Write down as many reasons as you can for the following two statements:

The King was likely to win a short war.
A long war might give Parliament the advantage.

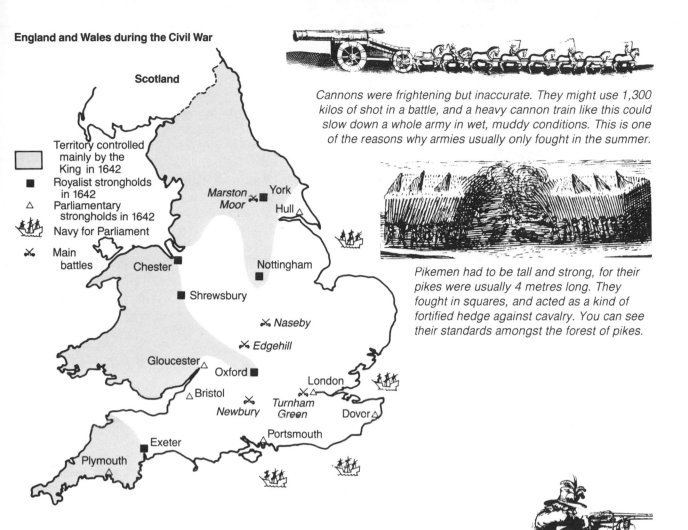

England and Wales during the Civil War

Scotland

☐ Territory controlled
   mainly by the
   King in 1642
■ Royalist strongholds
   in 1642
△ Parliamentary
   strongholds in 1642
⛵ Navy for Parliament
⚔ Main
   battles

Marston Moor ⚔ ■ York
Hull △
Chester ■
Nottingham ■
Shrewsbury ■
⚔ *Naseby*
⚔ *Edgehill*
Gloucester △
Oxford ■
London
Bristol △
⚔ *Newbury*
Turnham Green △
Dover △
Portsmouth △
Exeter △
Plymouth

Cannons were frightening but inaccurate. They might use 1,300 kilos of shot in a battle, and a heavy cannon train like this could slow down a whole army in wet, muddy conditions. This is one of the reasons why armies usually only fought in the summer.

Pikemen had to be tall and strong, for their pikes were usually 4 metres long. They fought in squares, and acted as a kind of fortified hedge against cavalry. You can see their standards amongst the forest of pikes.

In seventeenth-century England and Wales, there was no national army. When the Civil War broke out, local nobles and gentry organised and paid for their own troops. In the north of England, the Earl of Newcastle equipped his Royalist Whitecoats with tunics of unbleached white material, saying they would dye them with the blood of their enemies. John Hampden's troops were the Greenjackets, and Lord Saye and Sele, who controlled the Banbury area for Parliament, gave his men blue jackets.

Important cities like London had their 'trainbands' — local citizens trained and equipped by the city authorities. Ordinary country people sometimes felt strongly, and made up their own minds; sometimes they tried to keep out of the struggle; very often they followed the local landowner. A landowner like John Hampden had plenty of local support because he was respected and loved. Sometimes, however, villagers felt they must co-operate simply because they owed their livelihood and their homes to the local squire, and would lose both if they displeased him.

Firing a musket was a laborious business which took about a minute — a long time if facing a cavalry charge — and could often go wrong. At the beginning of the war, muskets were so heavy that they needed a stand; later they were made lighter.

159

Sir Edmund Verney, the King's standard bearer, was killed at Edgehill (as he foresaw). He was defending the standard so strongly that his hand was cut off. On it was this ring with a miniature of the King on it.

Main events of the Civil War

1642

The King began to march to London from the west Midlands. Essex's army caught up with him at *Edgehill*, about 30 miles from Oxford. Rupert swept all before him in a thundering cavalry charge, but his troops got out of control, and galloped off the field to loot a neighbouring village. Meanwhile, the rest of the two armies fought each other to a standstill. After the battle, the Parliamentarian Oliver Cromwell decided to withdraw to his home area, Huntingdonshire, to train cavalry to match Rupert's. The Royalists claimed the victory, because they were able to continue their march to London. On the way, the King occupied *Oxford* as his headquarters. His army reached *Turnham Green*, on the outskirts of London; there he was faced with the determined and well-equipped trainbands, drawn up in small fields and orchards. This was no place for a cavalry charge, so Rupert and the King withdrew to Oxford. It was the nearest the Royalists ever got to London.

1643

A three-pronged attack on London was planned by the Royalists:

1. The Earl of Newcastle would attack from the north. He was held up because he could not capture *Hull*.

2. Sir Ralph Hopton would attack from the south-west. He was held up because he could not capture *Plymouth*.

3. The King would attack from Oxford. He was held up because he could not capture *Gloucester*, whose Parliamentarian citizens stoutly defended it. After a difficult siege, the city was relieved by Essex and the London trainbands. At the first battle of *Newbury*, a Royalist army tried and failed to prevent Essex and the trainbands from returning safely to London. However, Rupert captured the important port of *Bristol*, and kept the area round Oxford safe. Parliament lost Hampden, killed at *Chalgrove Field*. Pym died, probably of cancer, in December; but not before he had organised the war effort, and made an alliance with the Scots, who had a good army. The King too sought an ally. He made peace with the Irish chieftains, to release his army trying to control the continuing rebellion in Ireland. In fact this was of little help. Meanwhile Oliver Cromwell's newly trained cavalry was gaining battle experience.

1644

The Scots marched south, and joined Parliament's armies threatening *York*. Rupert marched north to help the beleaguered Royalists. At the battle of *Marston Moor* he was decisively beaten for the first time, and the north was lost to the Royalists. However, they still held Oxford and the west.

1645

Parliament's New Model Army was organised on a national basis, and was commanded by Thomas Fairfax and Oliver Cromwell. The battle of *Naseby* was a decisive victory for Parliament, though the war dragged on for another year. The King lost the west, and Parliament's troops began to close in on Oxford.

1646

The surrender of *Oxford* brought the end of the war. The King had escaped beforehand, and surrendered to the Scots, at Newark. They sold him to Parliament.

1 Make two columns headed *Royalist Successes* and *Parliamentarian Successes*. Enter the main events in the appropriate column, keeping them in the right order.

2 When you have done this, in class discussion work out what you think are the most important reasons why Parliament won the war.

Cavalry wore the lobster-tail or pot helmet. Work out why this is such an effectively designed helmet for a man in the thick of battle, and why it was nicknamed thus.

Experiences of war

Charles I and Sir Edward Walker Sir Edward Walker was one of Charles's secretaries. He was proud of his war service, and when the fighting was over, he had the picture below painted to show how he had served the King. Charles is dictating a dispatch; in all but the most desperate situations written orders were less likely to become muddled or altered than verbal ones. In the background you can just see a battle going on. What portable writing equipment has Sir Edward brought with him? In many portraits of Charles he is wearing elaborate armour which covered his whole body. This was tournament armour. There were still occasionally such entertainments at court before the war, but no one would wear it in a battle. People often wore it when they had their portraits painted to suggest courage. Here both men are wearing *buff-coats*, made of thick, oiled ox-hide, with a breast and back plate held on with straps. This equipment gave reasonable protection, but was not so heavy as full armour. It was usually worn in Civil War battles, though Lucy Hutchinson worried about her husband:

←140

Sir Edward Walker with Charles I, by an unknown artist

> He put off a very good suit of armour that he had, which, being musket-proof, was so heavy that it heated him, and so could not be persuaded to wear anything but a buff-coat.

The portrait above shows the confident young Rupert just before the war. Below is the prince in 1645, after the surrender of Bristol. It is by a Royalist artist, William Dobson, who worked in Oxford during the war. It is unfinished, probably because Rupert had little time for sittings at this difficult point in the war, and Dobson may even have been running out of paint.

earn your living

aware

Prince Rupert was a son of Charles's sister, Elizabeth of Bohemia. Although only 23 at the beginning of the war, he was one of the King's most experienced soldiers (he had fought in the German wars) and a good commander. He was dashing, courageous and single-minded; he inspired his men, and had the knack of seeing quickly what was the best course of action. A big white poodle called 'Boy' went everywhere with him; many Roundheads feared the 'devil dog poodle' — they believed he bewitched them and ensured their defeat. The dog was killed at Marston Moor — the first time Rupert was defeated. Rupert had two weaknesses. He often did not manage to discipline his cavalry to return to the battlefield after their thundering first charge, so that they could press home their advantage. (This happened at Edgehill.) Also, he was often tactless in the way he dealt with other Royalist commanders, most of them much older than he was. Rupert knew a great deal about war, but not much about the nobles at his uncle's court at Oxford, with whom he had to work. He made many enemies there. In the end, he displeased the King too.

This letter from Charles to Rupert in September 1645 — and the portrait in the same year — shows the difficulties Rupert faced then. He had to surrender Bristol because his forces were heavily outnumbered, and Charles wrote to him as soon as he heard:

Nephew,

Though the loss of Bristol be a great blow to me, yet your surrendering it as you did is of so much affliction to me, that it . . . is the greatest trial . . . that hath yet befallen me; for what is to be done after one that is so near to me as you are . . . submits himself to so mean an action? . . . You assured me . . . you would keep Bristol for four months. Did you keep it four days? Was there anything like a mutiny? . . . My conclusion is to desire you to *seek your subsistence* . . . somewhere beyond the seas; to which end I send you herewith a pass; and I pray God to make you *sensible* of your present condition, and give you means to redeem what you have lost.

The King finishes by saying he hopes there will be a time when he can, without blushing, assure Rupert that he is 'your loving uncle and most faithful friend'.

1 What was happening to the Royalists when this letter was written?

2 Was Rupert the kind of commander who would surrender easily?

3 What is your opinion of Charles's treatment of his nephew at this point in the war? (He was reconciled to him a few months later, but he did not restore Rupert's command.)

Lord Falkland was also a Royalist. In the peaceful days before the war, Clarendon and a group of other well-educated friends used to stay at his house at Great Tew in Oxfordshire, discussing all kinds of subjects which interested them. Like Clarendon, he sat in the Long Parliament; he did not become a Royalist until Pym introduced the Grand Remonstrance, which he felt went too far. When war broke out, both men joined the King in Oxford, and became ministers. But Falkland became more and more unhappy with the war, and the failure of attempts to make peace, and friends noticed how depressed he was. In the battle of Newbury in 1643, he rode ahead of his troops straight into the enemy, and was killed by a musket shot. It looked like suicide. His friend Clarendon was grief-stricken that this 'odious and accursed civil war' should have slain a man of such goodness and learning — 'that incomparable young man'.

Lord Saye and Sele lived in his family home, Broughton Castle, near Banbury. He was a firm Puritan, and paid for preachers to work in Banbury, which was strongly for Parliament when the war broke out. Lord Saye was an experienced politician, nicknamed 'Old Subtlety' because he was so shrewd and practical. He worked closely with Pym and Hampden, who attended secret meetings at Broughton before the war. These were officially to discuss two business ventures: the founding of two colonies, one near New England — Saybrooke — and the other on Providence Island in the Caribbean. They probably also discussed how to deal with the King once Parliament was called. When war broke out, Lord Saye organised his 'Bluejackets', and briefly occupied Oxford before the King arrived. He may have been at Edgehill, not far from his home; his troops certainly were. Royalist troops then besieged and took both Broughton and Banbury. Lord Saye was by then in London, helping to organise the trainbands which stopped Rupert at Turnham Green. He seems to have been less active as the war went on, and after 1645 mysteriously disappeared for several years — he may even have gone to his colony in Saybrooke. He certainly had a difficult war, with his home and the surrounding area in enemy hands for most of it.

Women's lives were changed by the war too. Some followed their menfolk when they went off to fight, and looked after them if they were wounded. Some even seemed to have become soldiers themselves, if the ballads of the time are anything to go by. High-born women were often left to defend their homes if the opposite side was threatening the area where they lived.

Brilliana, Lady Harley was one of these women. She was a gentle, modest character, devoted to her husband, a busy MP remaining in London. The couple were firmly for Parliament, but their home, Brampton Bryan Castle, near Hereford, was surrounded by Royalists, who (Brilliana wrote in December 1642) were 'in a mighty violence against me'.

In those days, when sieges took place, defenders were first given the chance to surrender and offered a safe-conduct. If they did not surrender, it was understood the attackers could use any means they chose to capture the stronghold, and would not spare their enemies. On 26 July 1643, Brampton Bryon Castle was surrounded by 700 foot soldiers and cavalry, and a trumpeter summoned Brilliana to surrender. In spite of her

An illustration to a ballad sheet called 'The Female Warrior', which told the story of a girl who became a drummer boy — until she had a baby!

Brilliana, Lady Harley

163

fears for the lives of her children and her own danger, she bravely refused, saying it would betray her husband's trust in her, for 'I do not know that it is his pleasure that I should entertain soldiers in his house.' Cannon shot caused casualties amongst the household, and the Royalist earthworks were so close to the castle that the troops' 'rotten language' could be heard. Even when the King wrote to her personally, Brilliana did not give in; after more than a month the castle was relieved briefly by Parliamentarian troops sent to raise the siege of Gloucester. The danger was not over, however, and Royalist troops were soon threatening the castle again. At this desperate moment, Brilliana fell ill and died, amidst 'volleys of sighs and tears' of her household, though her own courage never weakened. The castle fell to the enemy; her three small children were looked after by the Royalists, and her husband lost goods worth £13,000. But Brilliana's heroism was not forgotten by her family and friends.

Soldiers' problems

Supplies and pay for armies on both sides were a constant problem. The signatures on the left come from a document dated August 1642, ordering the Treasury to provide a month's pay for a regiment. The sum comes to £1,044 16s, and includes money for weapons and a surgeon's chest. If you remember that 'S' was often written like a long 'F', you should be able to read these signatures; three are those of people mentioned in this chapter. Decide why two are so firmly at the top, and which side the pay was for. Soldiers received less than an ordinary labourer, and most were not paid regularly. Sometimes they went for months without any money. Also, they were expected to find their own food. How does this help to explain the picture of the soldier on the right? (How many objects on him can you identify?) As the war went on, Parliament usually paid their troops more regularly than the Royalists (though they did not always manage it). Can you work out why they were able to do so?

←35 **The wounded** were usually lucky to survive. Surgeons accompanied the armies, but were not always skilled or knowledgeable. There were of course no anaesthetics. Captain Henry Bellingham was found after Edgehill:

unnoticed

> amongst the dead, and brought off by his friends with twenty wounds, who after ten days died at Oxford by the negligence of his surgeons, who left a wound in his thigh, not dangerous in itself, *undiscerned*, and so by festering destroyed a body very hopefully recovered.

Oliver Cromwell wrote to Colonel Walton about his son, after the battle of Marston Moor:

> Sir, God hath taken away your eldest son by a cannon shot. It brake his leg. We were necessitated to have it cut off, whereof he died . . . . There is your precious child, full of glory, never to know sin or sorrow any more. He was a gallant young man, exceeding gracious.

These two men were officers. Ordinary soldiers who were wounded were more likely to be left on the battlefield without help. However, sometimes there was a better kind of care. The women who went with their menfolk to war were often experienced nurses; that was one of their normal household tasks in peacetime. Lucy Hutchinson describes how:

> she having some *excellent plasters* in her closet . . . dressed all their wounds with such good success that they were all cured in convenient time.

healing ointments

She also insisted on caring for wounded Royalists too, in spite of the disapproval of one of her husband's officers. She said 'she had done nothing but what she thought her duty, in humanity to them, as fellow-creatures, not enemies'.

Disease was also a constant problem, especially in garrison towns like Oxford (which suffered serious epidemics, probably of typhus, in 1644 and 1645), and during sieges. The following note, signed by Pym, was written at the bottom of an order to send £30 to the garrison in Windsor in May 1643:

> We desire this money for the physician may be paid that he may be dispatched to the garrison where many sick men are in much need of him.

1 In all wars before the twentieth century, more soldiers died of disease than from battle wounds. Think of reasons for this fact.

2 Write a letter home from a soldier in the last months of 1642. Decide which side you are on, and why; and what events and problems you experience.

Village life

If ordinary people lived in an area where there was no fighting, their lives were scarcely affected by the war. But the map and table on page 159 and pages 160-1, which tell only part of a complicated story, show also that most areas of England and Wales would have had armies passing through, if not actual fighting.

Once an army was nearby, everyone was affected. Soldiers had a bad reputation anyway, as the pictures here and on the next page show. They were usually billeted (lodged) on the local people, sometimes three or four in an ordinary villager's house; and though the householder was supposed to be paid, the money arrived very late, or, more often, not at all. Horses were always needed, and were valuable property, just like a car today. One village in Cheshire lost 50 horses — probably all they had. A ploughing team could be taken at seed-sowing time. Cattle and other livestock were also taken: this was constantly happening in villages near the King's headquarters in Oxford.

This picture of a soldier festooned with his loot shows what most people thought of seventeenth-century armies. Make a list of the things he has stolen.

A Parliamentary cartoon showing looting Cavaliers

In fact there was usually little to choose between the two sides, though commanders usually did their best to prevent such behaviour.

This is what the small village of Charlescombe near Bath claimed at the end of the war from Parliament, for the time in 1643 when Sir William Waller's army was in the area:

> Sustained loss by Sir William Waller's army at the fight at Lansdowne in hay, grass, and wood to the value of £10

> William Maynard's bill for bread, beer, hay and grass, which was taken from him for the use of Sir William Waller when he fought at Lansdowne
>
> £5 5s 6d

> For bread, beer, barley, malt and other necessaries taken for the use of Sir William Waller, and for *quartering* five *troops* £9 9s 6d

billeting, cavalry

Money values: 20 shillings in £1; 12 pennies (d) in one shilling (s). A shilling was an average daily wage for a labourer by this time.

■ From this list of expenses, think of the ways in which villagers' lives would have been affected by Waller's army in the area, and by the delay in payment.

In areas like the one around Bath, and in Wiltshire, where armies crossed and re-crossed, ordinary people had had enough by 1645. They began to do something about it, as this document shows:

agreement

long-handled cutting tools

> The Desires and Resolutions of the Clubmen of the Counties of Dorset and Wiltshire: with articles of their *Covenant* and Certain Directions for present behaviour, made and agreed at a meeting at Corehedge Corner on 25 May, 1645, and read at Bradbury in Dorset by Mr Thomas Young, a lawyer; when there were present near 4000 armed with clubs, swords, *bills*, pitchforks and other several weapons . . . They will demand both sides to make peace; they will keep constant watch for any army, from either side, and defend themselves from them.

■ Why do you think the leaders of both sides were worried by these 'Clubmen'? Remind yourself from Chapters 1 and 2 what village life was like in normal times. Then, using the facts in this section, describe the experiences of a villager who lived in a Wiltshire village where troops were billeted, and who attended the Clubmen's meeting at Bradbury.

God made them as 'stubble to our swords'

The New Model Army

Corn stubble has little chance of standing up to the sweep of a sharp sword: 'stubble to our swords' is Oliver Cromwell's description of Parliament's first decisive victory against the King at Marston Moor in 1644. He had no doubt that God gave the Roundheads the victory, and that God was always on his side. Other Roundheads believed the same, but this unknown Puritan gentleman from Huntingdonshire had other qualities as well that made him one of the most important men in England by the end of the war.

Oliver Cromwell was a member of the Long Parliament; he strongly supported Pym, and Hampden (he was Hampden's cousin). He even threatened to emigrate to the New World if the Grand Remonstrance was not passed. Cromwell was 42 when the war broke out, with no experience of fighting. Yet straightaway, he saw what was needed. He was at the battle of Edgehill and told John Hampden afterwards that Parliament's troops were just not good enough compared to the Royalists. He went back to Huntingdonshire, determined to train a new kind of cavalry soldier: what he called 'men of spirit'.

First, he picked his men carefully, especially the officers. He said:

> I had rather have a plain *russet-coated* captain that knows what he fights for, and loves what he knows, than what you call a gentleman and is nothing else . . . If you choose godly honest men as captains of horse, honest men will follow them.

a coat made of rough home-spun material

In fact, Cromwell had nothing against gentlemen — he was one himself — and also said they made good officers, as long as they believed in what they were fighting for.

Second, he made sure his troops were well-disciplined. A newspaper report said of the new cavalry:

> No man swears, but he pays twelve pence; if he be drunk, he is set in the stocks or worse . . . How happy it would be if all the forces were thus disciplined!

Needless to say, orders had to be obeyed; for instance, two deserters were publicly whipped in the marketplace in Huntingdon in April 1643.

1 Why did Cromwell have deserters and drunks so harshly punished in public?

2 A trooper was paid 24 pence a day and had to find his food, equipment, and forage for his horse. Do you think the fine for swearing is harsh?

Third, Oliver trained these disciplined troops to avoid Rupert's mistake at Edgehill. They learned to charge at a 'round trot' — fast enough to make an effective charge, but not so fast that they would get out of control. In this way, they could be sent where they were needed in the thick of battle. It was this, and Cromwell's sense of timing, that made his cavalry so difficult to defeat. He could always choose exactly the right moment, and the right place, to use his troops.

Finally, Cromwell cared for his troops. 'I have a lovely company,' he said proudly of them. He also did all he could to see they were paid regularly, though he did not always succeed in this.

This new cavalry first fought as part of an army raised in East Anglia, called the Eastern Association. It quickly gained an impressive reputation. The Eastern Association joined Parliament's northern army (commanded by Sir Thomas Fairfax) and the Scots at Marston Moor. 'Is Cromwell there?' Rupert asked just before the battle. When Rupert had been defeated, he called Cromwell 'Old Ironsides' because his ranks of cavalry were solid as iron. The nickname was soon used of all his troops.

By the summer of 1645, the New Model Army had been formed from all Parliament's armies — the first really national army. Fairfax was made Captain General, and Cromwell his second-in-command. As at Marston Moor, the Ironsides played an important part in the victory at Naseby in June 1645.

Oliver Cromwell's well-used Bible, and his signature on the first page

Cromwell had no doubts about the reason for their success. This is what he wrote after the battle, describing his feelings just before it started:

> I could not (riding about my business) but smile out to God in praises in assurance of victory . . . and God did it.

When a commander and his soldiers felt like that, it was not going to be easy to push them aside after victory was finally won.

1 Write a letter to Cromwell from a local Huntingdonshire man (perhaps a cloth worker or a carpenter) asking to join the Ironsides, and saying why you want to be considered. Date the letter July 1644, just after Marston Moor.

2 Find out what happened in your area in the Civil War. Your local library will help you. Make a timeline of the main events of the war and add a column showing what happened where you live.

←160-1

3 If this is difficult, find out about a place like Oxford, or York, which have particularly interesting stories. You could also do some research on people such as: Charles I, Henrietta Maria, Prince Rupert, Thomas Fairfax, Oliver Cromwell, Lady Bankes (who defended Corfe Castle).

The end of the war

The last fighting in this Civil War was a small skirmish in 1646 near the little Cotswold town of Stow-on-the-Wold. As the King's troops fled, an old Cavalier soldier, Sir Jacob Astley, was found sitting on a drum alone in a field. He said to his captors:

> You have now done your work and may go play, unless you fall out amongst yourselves.

This was the problem. The supporters of Parliament had won the war, but there were deep disagreements about what to do with their victory.

The Army was excited by victory. Many soldiers, ordinary folk who had left home for the first time and found a new independence, were determined to have their voice heard. They wanted to worship as they wished, and they wanted to be paid. Cromwell and the other officers backed them — for the moment. They were, as they said 'no mere mercenary army.' What did they mean? As well as their swords, they had another trump card; a small group of soldiers had removed the King from Parliament's custody, and he was in the Army's hands — first kept at Hampton Court, and then in the Isle of Wight.

Parliament feared the Army. It was becoming too powerful and they could not see how to find the money to go on paying it. They also distrusted the Scots.

The Scots wanted their reward for the help they had given to Parliament in the war, and were determined to be a neglected kingdom no longer. They wanted a say in English affairs. They also wanted a Presbyterian Church in England in which they would have influence.

169

The King was defeated, and he had no army. However, as far as he was concerned, that made no difference. He was still a king, and he believed God would restore his rightful power to him. All he had to do was to wait until his enemies quarrelled. There was no need to keep promises to such wicked men.

The King let both Parliament and the Army think he would make an agreement with them. In the end, however, behind their backs, he made a deal with the Scots, who decided they would get more from the defeated King than their old ally, Parliament. Fighting broke out again.

The second Civil War was brief and bloody. Fairfax defeated the King's forces at Colchester; Cromwell won victories in Wales and Lancashire. Throughout the fighting, the King himself remained a prisoner of the Army. Now they had to decide what to do with him.

Britain without a king

Trial and execution

The Army leaders had no doubt what they should do. Charles Stuart, 'that man of blood', should be put on trial, publicly condemned, and publicly executed. There was to be no hole-and-corner murder; everything was to be open and legal, so that the world could see the rightness of their cause.

First, Parliament must agree. But many MPs were horrified at such a plan. One morning in December 1648, as they entered Parliament, they found the building surrounded by soldiers. The commander of the troops, Colonel Pride, was waiting with a list of MPs expected to disagree. 'Pride's Purge', as it was called, took place: those on the list were not allowed to enter. Only MPs who could be relied upon to support a trial of the King remained; from now on they were called 'The Rump'. It consisted of only 80 of the original 507 who were in the Long Parliament.

Then judges had to be found. 153 'commissioners' were appointed; about a third of them actually attended the trial. The President of the court, John Bradshaw, was an unknown London lawyer; he wore a bullet-proof hat throughout.

Charles was accused of being 'a tyrant, traitor, and murderer, and a public and implacable enemy of the people of England'. He was expected to defend himself — there were never any defence lawyers in treason trials in Early Modern England, and this *was* a treason trial. When the King was brought into the court and heard the charge, 'he laughed in the face of the court'. He refused to recognise it as a court of law at all. The King was the law. No one could appoint a special court like this without his permission, and it had no power to try him.

Many who had fought against him now agreed with him. Fairfax was one of these. When his name was called as a commissioner at the beginning of

The bullet-proof hat worn by John Bradshaw at the trial of the King

the trial, his wife, masked and hooded, called out from the public gallery, 'He has more wit [sense] than to be here'. Fairfax took little further part in public affairs after that; Cromwell was the man of the hour. 'We will cut off his head with the crown upon it,' he said.

We know what Charles looked like at his trial from this portrait by Edward Bower, an artist who was present. The King is older than in the Van Dyck portraits, and his beard is almost white. To show his contempt of the court, he kept his hat on throughout the trial, and refused to answer the charge. He did however expect to be allowed to speak after he had been found guilty and condemned to death; this was a right given to all condemned prisoners. But the judges were afraid to let him do so. 'I am not suffered for to speak: expect what justice other people will have,' he cried. As he left the court, soldiers cried 'Execution! Justice!' The watching crowd was quiet.

Charles I at his trial

The Death Warrant of Charles I

1 How many signatures are on the death warrant? How many should there be? Find Cromwell and Bradshaw.

2 How do we know that some people who took part in the trial were frightened? Why would they be so worried?

3 The people who signed the warrant were called *regicides*. Find the meaning in the dictionary. Also check on *treason* (which you have met many times already) and *tyrant*.

4 Make a list of reasons why even some of the King's enemies opposed the trial, and why Cromwell and the army leaders were so determined to hold it.

5 You could also stage your own class trial, with prosecution and defence, both interrogating the King. Since this will not be like the real trial, you can then have a free vote to decide whether he should die.

An engraving produced at the time of the execution of Charles I

Can you find a clue that the artist is not English? Why would a foreign artist think it worthwhile to produce a picture like this?

Although Charles was very isolated as he faced death, he did not flinch. When he woke early on the morning of 30 January 1649, he told his servant that it was his second marriage day. It was bitterly cold, so he put on two shirts, for he did not want to shiver, and appear afraid. 'I fear not death. Death is not terrible to me.'

The frontispiece of a book called 'Eikon Basilike', published in London immediately after the execution, and said to be a book of prayers and thoughts written by Charles himself

He is shown casting away his earthly crown, and grasping a crown of thorns like Christ. Above, in Heaven, a martyr's crown awaits him.

The King was taken to his beautiful Banqueting House in the Palace of Whitehall, which he had not seen for seven years. Outside, a huge, silent crowd waited. The picture above was made to be printed and sold straight after the event. It shows how many viewing points people found and how many soldiers there were everywhere. When Charles was taken out to the scaffold, he was allowed to make a short speech. He spoke of his people:

> Truly I desire their liberty and freedom as much as anybody . . . but I must tell you their liberty and freedom consists in (being) governed . . . it is not for having a share in government . . . a subject and a sovereign are *clear* [completely] different things . . . it was for this that I came here . . . and therefore I tell you (and I pray God it be not laid to your charge) that I am a Martyr of the people.

He finished by saying he died a Christian of the Church of England: 'I have a good cause and I have a gracious God; I will say no more.'

A few moments later, the axe fell. The block was so low that few could see it (though the artist has changed that); but a boy standing in the crowd said he would remember all his life 'such a groan as I never heard before, and desire I may never hear again' which went up from all around him. How does the picture show the crowd's reactions?

The picture on the left shows how soon many people forgot that they had disliked the way Charles had ruled, and saw him, as he said they would, as a martyr. His death did more for his cause than any of his other actions.

■ Write your own eyewitness account of the execution for a popular newspaper of the time. You must decide whether you see Charles as a martyr, or a 'Traitor to the People of England'.

The world turned upside down

A popular ballad the pedlars were selling in London at the time of the King's execution went like this:

> The Mitre is down and so is the Crown,
> And with them the Coronet too . . .
> There is no such thing as Bishop or King,
> Or Peer but in name or show.
> Come clowns and come boys, come hobbledehoys,
> Come females of each degree,
> Stretch out your throats, bringing in your votes,
> And make good the anarchy [complete disorder]
> . . .
> Then let's have King Charles, says George,
> Nay, we'll have his son, says Hugh,
> Nay, then let's have none, says jabbering Joan,
> Nay, we'll all be Kings, says Prue.

A picture on the front of a pamphlet called 'The World Turned Upside Down'

At the bottom a mouse chases a cat, and a rabbit chases a dog. Decide what is 'upside down' about everything else in the picture.

1 This needs to be chanted out loud, making the rhymes and rhythm very obvious, in order to realise what it sounded like in the streets of London. The clowns, boys, hobbledehoys, and females of each degree (rank) were of course the kind of people who did *not* have a vote, nor any power at all, in Early Modern England. George, Hugh, Joan and Prue are just imaginary ordinary people — are their voices being listened to for the first time? Or is this ballad making fun of them?

2 Make your own cartoon based on the ballad and picture, showing how people felt that their world was being turned upside down.

For many, the fact that England was no longer a monarchy meant that the world was turned upside down. It was a republic, without King, bishops or House of Lords — a *'Commonwealth'*, as it was called. And for a time, some new voices were heard.

The Levellers

The Levellers were people with some very modern ideas: they believed the country should be ruled by a Parliament; Parliament should be elected every two years; everyone over 21 was to have a vote, except servants and women (both these groups, they thought, would be too easily influenced); all the different kinds of Puritans should be able to worship freely; law courts should work more fairly and cheaply.

There were Levellers in London amongst small shopkeepers and apprentices, but their strongest support came from the ordinary soldiers and a few officers in Cromwell's victorious army.

John Lilburne, whose writings influenced Leveller ideas. He was a fiery, independent character who seemed to thrive on trouble. Although he was only in the army a short time, and, as this picture shows, spent most of his time in prison, he was really the most important Leveller leader.

1 Make a list of the methods Levellers used to win support. Do present-day organisations use similar methods?

2 How far do you think Leveller ideas and methods were 'modern'?

The Levellers spread their ideas in best-selling pamphlets; the most famous was called *The Agreement of the People*. Although Levellers did not think women should vote, women *were* active in the movement, and in 1649 marched to Parliament with a petition to release their imprisoned leaders. They were sent away with the words: 'we shall have things brought to a fine pass if women come to teach Parliament to make laws', but that seemed to make them more determined. They were soon back again. Later, when a Leveller soldier had been shot for mutiny, his funeral became a great demonstration in the streets of London, with all the mourners wearing sea-green ribbons (the Leveller colour).

For a time, their ideas were sympathetically considered by Cromwell and the other Army officers. In 1648, before the fate of the King was decided, a debate took place in Putney Church to decide whether Leveller ideas should be adopted by the whole army. The Leveller Colonel Rainsborough said: 'Really I think that the poorest he that is in England hath a life to live, as the greatest he; every man that is to live under a government ought first by his own consent to put himself under that government.'

This is what we do now in Britain and other democracies, when we vote in an election; only now, the poorest 'she' is included as well. These are remarkable words from anyone living in seventeenth-century Britain, and things might have been very different if the Army leaders had agreed with the Levellers in 1648. But they did not. They firmly said that only people with property (who were therefore quite rich) had enough experience and education to vote. That is an argument which has been used often by powerful people who do not believe that those they rule are ready to share their power. It is an argument they usually lose in the end (you could find examples of when this has happened). Britain had to wait another 200 years and more, before ordinary people won the argument there.

Once the Army leaders had turned against the Levellers, they had no chance of success — for soldiers are always trained to obey their officers. In May 1649, 1,200 Levellers made a last desperate attempt at revolt. Cromwell and Fairfax, with loyal troops, caught up with them at the little town of Burford, in Oxfordshire. Most fled or surrendered; 340 prisoners were shut up in Burford church for three days. Then, three were shot; the rest were forced to watch from the church roof. Army discipline had triumphed, and the Army was united once more. That was what Cromwell really cared about, for he believed the peace and security of the new Commonwealth depended on it.

One of the Leveller prisoners carved his name on the font in Burford Church during his three-day imprisonment. It can still be seen today.

174

Diggers and Quakers

Diggers too had unusual ideas for their time. They believed poverty could be cured if the land was shared. In 1649, a group of about 30 men and women took over common land on St George's Hill near Walton-on-Thames. They dug the land, and grew corn, parsnips, carrots and beans. They built huts for shelter, and shared their work and produce. The experiment barely lasted a year, for local landowners saw them as a threat; they were driven out, and their huts and crops destroyed. But interest in their ideas remained, and they have not been forgotten.

The Quakers were founded by George Fox, the son of a Leicester weaver. He had a vision of brotherly love where the spirit of God would inspire people, and there would be no need for organised churches with set services. His followers were called 'The Society of Friends': they met together as friends, to wait for the spirit of the Lord. He travelled all over England spreading his ideas; most of his supporters were ordinary working people in town and country. At their meetings, the Friends waited for inspiration, and once they felt they were receiving it, they often went into trances, quaking and shaking with emotion — people were always more ready to show their emotions then. So they soon earned the nickname of 'Quaker' — another name that was not kindly meant, for Quakers were soon seen as dangerous people who might undermine authority. For instance, they refused to take oaths; they treated everyone as equals, calling them 'thou', and keeping their hats on in the presence of their social superiors. (This was seen as very familiar.) So they were often persecuted.

Unlike Levellers and Diggers, the Society of Friends survived. The Quakers became peaceful people, who dressed simply and lived thriftily. They cared for the unfortunate, and continued to treat each other as equals. They also became great travellers. One of the most famous was William Penn, who founded the colony of Pennsylvania later in the century.

■ Find out more about famous Quakers: William Penn or Elizabeth Fry, who helped to improve terrible conditions for women prisoners nearly a hundred years later. You could also find out about the kind of work Quakers do now, to help suffering and discourage violence.

The Lord Protector

The new Commonwealth was in a very shaky position in 1649. Shock waves of horror spread through Europe at the news of the public execution of the King, and it looked as if the young Charles II, in exile in Holland, might have plenty of help from abroad to reclaim his father's throne. At home, the Army held the power; and the most important man in the Army was their successful general, Oliver Cromwell. Two problems faced him: the military threat of a Royalist invasion through England's 'back doors' of Ireland or Scotland; and the problem of power, and how it was to be used in the Commonwealth.

A

DECLARATION

FROM THE

Poor oppressed People

OF

ENGLAND

DIRECTED
To all that call themselves,
or are called

Lords of Manors,

through this NATION;
That have begun to cut, or that through fear and covetousness, do intend to. cut down the Woods and Trees that grow upon the Commons and Waste Land.

The front page of a Digger pamphlet

A Quaker meeting

Quakers allowed women to preach, which was unheard of, except in groups like the Society of Friends, which had new and unusual ideas.

The Military Threat The most immediate threat seemed to lie in Catholic Ireland. Throughout the civil wars, Parliament's propaganda had made much of the horrors that would result if 'Papist' Irish troops were used by the King; and the general fear of Catholics seemed to focus above all on the Irish. Since some of the Irish chieftains were ready to support the Royalists, and there was already a Royalist army in Ireland, Cromwell took a strong force over there. From 1649 to 1650, he undertook a ruthless campaign to bring Ireland under the Commonwealth's control. This is part of a report he wrote on the capture of one Royalist stronghold, Drogheda, in 1649. After stubborn resistance, the defenders had been driven into a church tower, where they still refused to surrender:

> Whereupon I ordered the steeple . . . to be fired, when one of them was heard to say in the midst of the flames: 'God damn me, God confound me; I burn, I burn.' The next day . . . when (the other) troops submitted, their officers were knocked on the head; and every tenth man of the soldiers killed; and the rest *shipped to Barbados* . . . I am persuaded this is the righteous judgement of God upon these barbarous wretches, who have *imbrued* their hands in innocent blood; and that it will tend to prevent *effusion* of blood in the future.

the punishment of transportation
drenched
shedding

←163

1 Cromwell did not usually behave like this towards the enemy soldiers he captured in England. Why do you think he did here? Does the accepted way of dealing with those who refused to surrender in a siege explain his action?

2 How does he show he believes he is right?

When Cromwell's conquest of Ireland was completed, the land was once more used as a way of imposing English control. All landowners had to prove their loyalty to the Commonwealth; as a result, about 8,000 Catholic landowners were replaced by Cromwell's soldiers, who received land instead of pay; or by English businessmen who lent money for the Irish campaign. (The government could not repay them in any other way.) So, by the mid-seventeenth century, the Tudors, James I and Cromwell had turned Catholic Ireland into a country dominated by English Protestant landlords.

Scotland While the Lowland Presbyterian Scots had fought for Parliament, many in the Highlands supported the King. Under the brilliant leadership of the Marquis of Montrose, the Highlanders had kept fighting longer than the English Royalists. We have already seen that the Lowland Scots decided by 1648 they were more likely to get what they wanted from the King, than from an English Parliament dominated by Cromwell's army. After Charles I's execution, the Lowlanders offered a deal to the young man the Royalists called Charles II: he must accept the Presbyterian Church, and no longer support Montrose (whom they loathed, and quickly executed); they would provide an army. Charles felt he had no choice but to agree — these were the only allies who offered practical help, though he had little sympathy for them or their religion.

The seal of the new Commonwealth, which was used on all important documents. It shows the House of Commons, which now governed the country. On the back is a map of England, Wales and Ireland. In 1649, Scotland was still independent.

In 1650, Cromwell marched north, and on 3 September, won a skilful victory against a much larger Scots army at Dunbar, just outside Edinburgh. The following summer, Charles II, with a mainly Scots army, invaded England in a desperate attempt to claim his throne. At Worcester, once again on 3 September, Cromwell won his last great victory of the civil wars — his 'crowning mercy' as he called it. Amongst the few defeated Royalists who escaped was the young King. For six weeks he was on the run, with a £1,000 reward offered for 'a tall young man two yards high, with hair a deep brown near to black'. Though few English people had been ready to fight for him, they were not prepared to betray him either, and he finally escaped to France in a fishing vessel from the tiny village of 'Brighthemston' — now Brighton. Nine years of frustrating exile lay before him.

Scotland meanwhile became an occupied land, with an army to ensure that the union with the Commonwealth of England was accepted. The Presbyterians were allowed to worship as they wished — but they had to accept (very unwillingly) that other kinds of Protestants should have the same freedom.

The Problem of Power Oliver Cromwell did not want to rely on 'sword rule'. His aim was the 'healing and settling' of the divided country. There must be reform, for instance, of the slow and cumbersome law courts which so often seemed to favour the rich. His army must be paid for its services. His soldiers must be able to worship freely if they wished: there was now no Church of England to insist on a Prayer Book service, but they must not be forced into a Presbyterian church either. Wales must

The young Charles II

His enemies put out a description of him which shows he was a tall man, unlike his slightly-built parents.

A Dutch picture showing Cromwell dissolving the Rump

One of Cromwell's last signatures in 1658

Compare it with the one on page 168. What does 'P' stand for?

not be forgotten; Puritan preachers had already been sent to Wales (and were not popular either among ordinary people or the mainly Royalist gentry), and more must go. All this was expected of the Rump Parliament while the Army was campaigning in Ireland and Scotland.

It soon became obvious that the Rump was not going to achieve much and was probably becoming more interested in clinging to power. Cromwell decided he must act. The next four years saw several experiments in which Cromwell tried to persuade the ruling classes to accept reform, and to provide money for the Army on which he believed peace depended.

By 1658, Cromwell was a sad and sick man. His favourite daughter Elizabeth died of cancer. His beloved Army was divided, especially since he had been offered the Crown. Even though he had refused it, he was too much a king for some of his old soldiers. He was weary of the search to find an acceptable way to govern England.

Experiments in Government	
1653 The Rule of the Saints 'I never looked to see such a day as this' — Cromwell in his speech when the Saints' rule began	Churches all over the country chose 'godly' people to attend Parliament in Westminster. Some of them were landowners; some were zealous Puritans, and more ordinary people. The two groups could not agree, so although there were good ideas for reform, nothing was achieved, and the experiment ended in six months.
1653 The Lord Protector	Cromwell was now given an official title: Protector. He had to rule with a new Parliament, which was little different from Parliament in Charles I's time. Old problems arose; not enough money was voted to pay the Army so Parliament was dissolved. There was a Royalist revolt, and Cromwell had to fall back on the Army once more.
1655 The Major-Generals — 'sword rule'	The country was divided into eleven districts; each was run by a Major-General. He had to collect taxes, keep law and order, and carry out the tasks the local landowners usually did. They much resented this; and ordinary people were not happy when, for instance, their local inn was closed for security reasons.
1657 King Oliver? Two of Cromwell's remarks in 1657: To some officers he said that 'he loved the title, a feather in a hat, as little as they did'; and he was just 'a good constable set to keep the peace of the parish'.	Another Parliament was called. The House of Lords — called the Other House — was restored. Cromwell was offered the Crown, which after much thought he refused. Money problems were not solved.

But to outsiders he still looked strong and effective, and the Royalist cause as good as dead. He was especially strong abroad. England had waged a successful naval war against the Dutch, and then gained their grudging alliance. Sweden, Portugal and finally France all became allies. A naval war against Spain gained Jamaica in the Caribbean, and the Army won its last victory on land near Dunkirk, which became British. Even Clarendon, Cromwell's sworn enemy, who called him a 'brave bad man', said that 'his greatness at home was but a shadow of his greatness abroad'.

In Britain, Cromwell also achieved a good deal, in spite of his difficulties. The British Isles were united, and outwardly peaceful. There was no religious persecution, and Jews were allowed to live freely in Britain for the first time since the thirteenth century. Trade flourished, and for many ordinary people life was a little easier.

As the year wore on, Cromwell's health failed. He died on the anniversary of two of his greatest battles — 3 September. 'There is not a dog wags his tongue, so great a calm we are in,' wrote his secretary.

Oliver's son, Richard, was made Protector, but it soon became obvious that neither he nor anyone else could rule effectively. The country gradually slipped into chaos. Finally, at the beginning of 1660, General Monck, who commanded the Army occupying Scotland, marched south. There was, as he saw it, only one solution. Charles II was invited to return to his kingdom, and claim his crown.

■ Write a newspaper article by one of Cromwell's old soldiers, reporting his death, and how you feel about him as a soldier, and as Lord Protector.

One of the best likenesses we have of Oliver Cromwell, by Samuel Cooper

It shows clearly Cromwell's strong, heavy features, and dislike of elaborate dress.

It was the custom for a dead monarch to be embalmed, and lie in state for all to see, and pay their respects. Although Cromwell had refused the Crown, how much evidence can you find here that he was treated as a King when he died?

9 The King comes to his own again

This Dutch painting shows the 'suit with great skirts' which was fashionable in London in 1660. Pepys told a story of a man who walked around all day without realising he had both legs in one side of these extraordinary wide-cut breeches.

On 1 January 1660, a young Londoner called Samuel Pepys began to keep a diary. He wrote it late at night, and used a kind of shorthand, because he wanted to be free to write what he pleased. He hoped to go up in the world, and might write about important people he met or worked with; he might also write things he did not wish his wife Elizabeth to see. The first entry on that Sunday went like this:

> This morning (we lying lately in the garret) I rose, put on my suit with great skirts, having not lately worn any other clothes but them. Went to Mr Gunning's church . . . where he made a very good sermon. Dined at home in the garret, where my wife dressed the remains of a turkey, and in the doing of it she burned her hand.

We are lucky that Samuel Pepys kept a diary. He was methodical, and did not give up a few days after 1 January, as so many people do; he kept it up for nine years. He was inquisitive and active, and he described both the everyday events of his own life, and the great events he witnessed. 1660 proved to be an exciting year, both for him and the whole country:

> *18 January:* All the world is at a loss to think what Monck will do . . .
> *6 March:* My Lord (Edward Montagu, Pepys's employer) asked me whether I could . . . go to sea as his Secretary and bade me think of it. He also began to talk of things of state and told me that he should now want one . . . that he might trust in . . . Everybody now drink the King's health without any fear, whereas before it was very private that a man dare do it.

Pepys did go to sea, in the great fleet of ships which sailed across to Holland to bring home the exiled Charles II to 'his own' again:

> *23 May:* The King . . . came on board . . . we weighed anchor, and with a fresh gale and most happy weather we set sail for England — all the afternoon the King walking up and down (quite contrary to what I thought him to have been), very active and stirring . . . he fell in discourse of his escape from Worcester. Where it made me weep to hear the stories he told of his difficulties he passed through.

> *25 May:* and so on shore when the King did, who was received with all imaginable love . . . infinite crowd of people and the gallantry of the horsemen, citizens.

Another diarist, John Evelyn described Charles's entry into London on 29 May:

> With a triumph of above 20,000 horse and foot, brandishing their swords and shouting with inexpressible joy; the ways strewed with flowers, the bells

ringing, the streets hung with tapestry, the fountains running wine . . . I stood in the Strand and blessed God. All this was done without one drop of blood shed, and by that very army which rebelled against him.

The Coronation procession of Charles II

Pepys managed to get a seat in Westminster Abbey, and 'never thought to see the like again in this world'.

The 30-year-old King who returned to such a welcome in May 1660 was not an easy man to get to know. Eleven difficult and poverty-stricken years of exile had made him cynical. Bishop Burnet, a Scots observer who disapproved of him, said:

> He thought that nobody did serve him out of love: and so he was quits with the world, and loved others as little as he thought they loved him. He hated business . . . the ruin of his reign was . . . his giving himself up to a mad range of pleasure.

Underneath his easy-going exterior there was a ruthless streak, but he knew how to be witty and charming, and unlike his father and grandfather could get on with ordinary people. He was intelligent, and interested in science, though it was noticed that he was never 'capable of much application or study'.

Charles II was quite clear about one thing. He was never going 'on his travels' again. He knew that, to keep his throne, he was going to have to rule with Parliament, and co-operate with the ruling classes who sat in it. There were many problems, and it was going to be difficult to please all.

A courtier once wrote a joke memorial to the King:
Here lies a great and mighty King Whose promise none relies on; He never said a foolish thing, Nor ever did a wise one. When Charles heard this, he said: 'My words are my own, but my actions are my ministers'.

The new beginning

Charles had no wish for revenge against his enemies, but it was agreed that the *regicides* (see page 171) should be punished. The most important were dead. The body of Cromwell was dug up, and the head stuck on a pole outside Westminster Hall. Those still living were executed. Pepys described the death of one of Cromwell's Major-Generals, Thomas Harrison, 'looking as cheerfully as a man could do in that condition'. Everyone else was pardoned.

Royalists who had suffered through the war now expected their reward; and Charles's court was full of such people, not all of them genuine. There is a story that Charles listened politely to a group who told lengthy tales of all that the King owed them. Then he called for a bottle of wine; he drank their healths, and told them that he had now done as much for them as they had ever done for him. Historians today think that in spite of all the complaints, most Royalists got back what they lost in the war.

Charles II at the time of his restoration

Once, when he saw a portrait of himself, he said: 'Odds fish, I'm an ugly fellow!'

The court of Charles II reflected the King's liking for a 'mad range of pleasure'. It was a worldly, extravagant place. Charles enjoyed the theatre, gambling and horse-racing. His mistresses played a prominent part, especially the cheerful actress Nell Gwynn, and the beautiful but grasping Barbara Castlemaine. Charles had 14 illegitimate children. His favourite was the Duke of Monmouth, who was growing up into a charming, ambitious and rather unreliable young man.

Charles's marriage in 1662 to Catherine of Braganza, a shy Portuguese princess, was of course arranged for political reasons. A Portuguese alliance already existed, and Catherine brought a handsome dowry of £360,000, as well as the ports of Tangier on the North African coast, and Bombay in India. (Tangier proved too expensive and was soon given up.)

Catherine of Braganza had a sheltered and strictly religious upbringing. This is how she looked when she arrived at the worldly English court in 1662. Compare the hairstyle and clothes with those of the fashionable Nell Gwynn.

Nell Gwynn, by the fashionable court painter, Peter Lely

Pepys called her 'pretty, witty Nell'.

For all her shyness, Catherine learned to hold her own. She began to dress fashionably, as this miniature, by Samuel Cooper, shows. This hairstyle was all the rage in the early 1660s. Pepys remarked in 1663 that she 'began to be brisk and play like other ladies'.

Catherine did not have an easy life as Charles II's Queen. When she arrived she was upset to find the King's favourite mistress, Barbara Castlemaine, was her chief lady-in-waiting. She soon learned that tears and hysterics had no effect on her husband; he politely ignored them. Her greatest humiliation was her failure to produce any children — her first duty as Queen. This meant that the heir remained the King's younger brother, then known as James, Duke of York. Charles, however, learned to respect his wife, and so did his subjects, in spite of the fact she was a pious Catholic.

1 Write a conversation between a group of courtiers, gossiping about the King and the Queen in 1663, when they have been married about a year.

2 Using the portraits in this section, make a series of sketches of the fashions of the early 1660s. Try to find out about the beginning of the men's fashion of wearing wigs (mid-1660s).

'Our good old stars govern us again'

This is what the Earl of Clarendon said when he came back with Charles II in 1660, as his chief adviser and Chancellor. Conscientious and fussy, he had served the King faithfully through all the difficult years of exile. Charles knew he could not do without him, though he found his good advice and moral lectures very annoying at times.

The Parliament which was summoned at the beginning of the reign was so loyal that it was called the Cavalier Parliament. But all those loyal members did not solve the Crown's money problems. Even without Charles's extravagant spending on his pleasures, they still did not vote him enough money to run the country.

The ruling classes in Parliament were quite clear about two things. First, there was to be no permanent 'standing army'; they had had enough of soldiers. Charles was allowed to keep only a small part of the New Model Army as his Coldstream Guards, who still guard the sovereign today.

Second, they had also had enough of the more extreme kinds of Puritans, the sects like the Quakers. These sects seemed to undermine the law and ←175 order, which Parliament believed, must be imposed to bring peace and stability. So they brought back the Church of England with its bishops in full force. It had never really disappeared. Under Cromwell, some of its clergy had co-operated, and stayed in their parishes. Many had gone into hiding in Royalist houses where they could quietly and safely use the Prayer Book services. They had also often acted as tutors to the children in these households, and some of the same children were now grown men in this Parliament. The Church had a new martyr too: a service was added to the Prayer Book in memory of Charles I, to be held annually on the anniversary of his death.

A harsh series of Acts of Parliament were passed to make sure the Church of England was the church that all attended.

1661 Act of Uniformity	The Prayer Book had to be used at all services. As a result, nearly 2,000 Puritan clergy gave up their livings.
1664 Conventicle Act	Any kind of Puritan service or meeting with more than five people was forbidden.
1665 Five Mile Act	No Puritan minister was to come within five miles of a town important enough to send an MP to Parliament. So they often went to newer towns or villages which were beginning to grow, like Birmingham, and had a strong following there.

Charles knew he must agree with his powerful subjects, though he was probably much more tolerant himself. What he actually believed is a

John Bunyan, a tinker from Bedford, suffered imprisonment under the Conventicle Act because he refused to stop preaching. In prison, he wrote one of the most famous books in the English language. Here, on the first page, he is beginning to dream of his vision of 'The Pilgrim's Progress'.

Samuel Pepys, by John Hales

mystery. He was certainly sympathetic to the Catholic Church, as we shall see, but he probably always realised that he could never come into the open about this, *and* keep his throne.

The name 'Puritan' began to die out, but Puritan enthusiasm and faith did not. Former Puritans became known as 'Dissenters', because they dissented from (or disagreed with) the Church of England; they were the forerunners of the United Reformed Churches today. It was the Church of England that really suffered in the long run. Because it was the Church of the ruling classes, many of its clergy became cut off from ordinary people. It was a long time before its leaders realised the harm this did, and that it might fail to provide a 'middle way'.

Disappointments

Many people did well at the Restoration. Pepys's employer became the Earl of Sandwich, and helped the Duke of York to run the Navy. Pepys himself was Clerk to the Navy Board, and was responsible for organising all the supplies needed: this was a good job, which he worked hard at for many years.

But by 1666, most people were deeply disappointed. For one thing, London had suffered two terrible disasters: the Plague of 1665, and the Great Fire of 1666. Of course, Pepys tells us what it was like to live in such times in these extracts from his diary for 1665 and 1666:

30 April 1665: Great fears of the sickness here in the City, it being said that two or three houses are already shut up. God preserve us all.

7 June: . . . the hottest day that ever I felt . . . This day, much against my will, I did in Drury Lane see two or three houses marked with a red cross upon the doors, and 'Lord have mercy on us' writ there — which was a sad sight . . . I was forced to buy some roll tobacco to roll and chew.

17 June: . . . going with a hackney coach . . . , the coachman I found to drive *easily and easily* [slower and slower]; at last stood still . . . and told me he was suddenly struck very sick and almost blind . . . so with a sad heart for the poor man and trouble for myself, lest he should be struck with the plague . . . God have mercy on us all.

12 July: A solemn fast day for the plague growing upon us.

12 August: The people die so, that now it seems they are *fain* [forced] to carry the dead to be buried by daylight, the nights not sufficing to do it in.

20 September: No boats upon the river; grass grows all up and down Whitehall Court; . . . nobody but poor wretches in the streets.

16 October: But Lord how empty the streets are, and melancholy, so many poor sick people in the streets, full of sores . . . in Westminster there is never a physician, and but one apothecary left, all being dead.

22 November: I heard this day the plague is come very low; that is 600 and odd, and great hopes of a further decrease because of . . . exceeding hard frost.

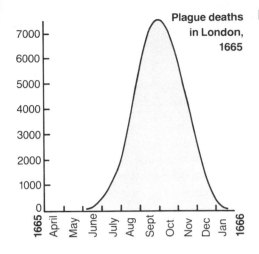

Plague deaths in London, 1665

Graph y-axis: 7000, 6000, 5000, 4000, 3000, 2000, 1000, 0

x-axis: **1665** April, May, June, July, Aug, Sept, Oct, Nov, Dec, Jan **1666**

■ Look back to pages 31–2. Use this graph of London plague deaths each month, and Pepys's diary extracts on the previous page. Write your own account of the plague of 1665. You can do this either as a historian would write it for someone who knows nothing about it — or as an eye-witness.

2 September 1666. Lords Day. [Pepys first saw the fire at 3 a.m. but did not realise its full extent till he took a boat near London Bridge.] Everybody endeavouring to remove their goods, and flinging into the river, or bringing *lighters* . . . Poor people staying in their houses as long as till the fire touched them . . . poor pigeons . . . loath to leave . . . but hovered about the windows and balconies till they were some of them burned . . . the wind mighty high and driving it into the city, and everything after so long a drought, proving *combustible*, even the very stones of churches. I to Whitehall . . . and did tell the King and Duke of York what I saw . . . They seemed much troubled, and the King commanded me to go to my Lord Mayor and command him to spare no houses but to pull down before the fire every way . . . [Pepys eventually found the Lord Mayor] like a man spent, with a handkercher round his neck. To the King's message, he cried like a fainting woman, 'Lord, what can I do? I am spent! People will not obey me. I have been pulling down houses. But the fire overtakes us faster than we can do it.' . . . [In the evening, Pepys describes the scene again.] So near the fire as we could for smoke; and all over the Thames you were almost burned with a shower of fire drops . . . a most horrible malicious bloody flame . . . We stayed till, it being darkish, we saw the fire as

boats

inflammable

The Fire started by accident in a baker's house in Pudding Lane. Afterwards, a memorial was erected nearby (see page 213). This picture shows the city on fire.

Southwark

one entire arch of fire from this to the other side of the bridge . . . It made me weep to see it. The churches, houses, and all on fire and flaming at once, and a horrid noise the flames made, and the cracking of houses at their ruin. So home with a sad heart.

The fire continued for three more days. Cheapside, Old St Paul's, churches, and about 13,000 homes were destroyed. Four-fifths of the area within the old walls was in ruins. London would never be the same again.

Also during these two difficult years, a second Dutch war broke out as a result of continuing trade rivalry. This time it ended not only in defeat, but with the humiliating destruction of the English fleet in its home base in the Medway. Clarendon, the old Chancellor, bore the brunt of everyone's disappointments. He was dismissed and exiled. 'Bid the Chancellor be gone,' was all Charles said, when the old man sent a message pleading for support. At least he was not sent to the Tower; and during his last exiled years, he wrote his *History of the Great Rebellion.* Charles now looked for a powerful ally abroad.

Louis XIV of France (1638–1714) — the Sun King

Louis XIV came to the French throne as a child; he took power himself in 1661. He soon began to build the great palace of Versailles, which became the grandest and most splendid royal palace in Europe. All the nobility of France were sucked into the elaborate ceremonial of court life, with the Sun King at its centre.

France was a country with many resources. Luxury manufactured goods such as tapestry, lace, china and glass brought wealth into the country; she also had the strongest army in Europe.

The rising power of France altered the power structure of Europe. Louis aimed to extend French frontiers northwards towards Dutch territory, and eastwards into Germany. The ruler of the United (Dutch) Povinces, William of Orange, and the Austrian Emperor (who still officially 'ruled' some 300 independent states in Germany) were determined to stop him. As Europe became involved in a series of wars, Louis looked south. Spain had been in decline since the days of Philip II, and by 1700 the French King claimed the Spanish throne for his grandson. The delicate balance of power in Europe was shattered, and English attitudes to France were bound to be involved.

Louis XIV, aged 63, by Rigaud
What has the artist done to emphasise his royal power? Louis once said, 'L'état, c'est moi' — I am the State. His power was absolute; he made all important decisions, and never had to consult a Parliament.

Almost certainly, if Charles II had had a free hand, he would have liked to rule like his Catholic cousin, the King of France. He may well have wanted to adopt his religion too. In 1670, he seems to have tried to do so. A treaty of alliance was made at Dover, in which Charles promised to help to attack Holland; it included a secret clause in which Charles promised to declare himself a Catholic in return for a large sum of money.

Charles must have known he was taking a great risk. Most of his subjects feared the French King as they had once feared Spain. Now Louis was the wicked Catholic bogeyman ready to back any 'Papist' at home who might cause trouble. When the secret deal leaked out, Parliament was outraged. Charles had to consent to a harsh Test Act (1673) which insisted that all members of the armed forces, and those in government service, had to take communion according to the Church of England. Of course no conscientious Catholic could do this. The Act was directly aimed at the King's brother, James, Duke of York, who had become a Catholic, and was Lord High Admiral of the Navy. Soon this harsh rule was extended to MPs. Worse trouble lay ahead.

Whigs and Tories

The heir to the throne

James, Duke of York, was a sincere man, who had made a good job of running the Navy — though that was partly because of Pepys's efficiency in the background. He was, however, much more like his father than Charles was. He could not understand how people could hold opposite views to his own. Above all, he was convinced that the English people, once they were given the chance, would see, as he had done, that the Catholic faith was the only true belief. He was certainly courageous, but it was disastrous for the heir to the throne to take that view in seventeenth-century England. As it became obvious that Charles and Catherine would have no children, the feeling against James grew stronger.

Exclusion

Now, when people in Britain feel strongly about the way the country is governed, they usually join a political party. In the seventeenth century, there were no organisations like that. Members of Parliament had to rely on powerful friends or relations if they wanted something done, and there was no organisation outside Parliament ready to help with publicity and support. However, as opposition to James as the next king built up, something like a modern political party began to develop. Its followers were called Whigs.

■ Before you go on to the next page, make a list of anything that comes into your mind connected with the main political parties in Britain today: Labour, Conservative, SDP, and Liberal. Pool your list with the rest of the class. If you had to explain these parties to someone who had never heard of them, would your list help? Now study the table overleaf.

This portrait of James, Duke of York, was painted by Godfrey Kneller when James was Admiral. Soon after he became King James II in 1685, some additions were made to it. What were they?

187

The Earl of Shaftesbury was a wealthy Dorset landowner, and a shrewd and ambitious politician. He served in Cromwell's Parliaments, and was one of Charles II's ministers, until his distrust of royal policies became so great that he began to organise the campaign to exclude James from the throne.

The great Pope-burning procession organised on the anniversary of the accession of Elizabeth I

'Old Bess in her ruff' was seen as a ruler who had really understood the danger from Catholics — unlike the Stuarts.

A modern political party	The Whigs in 1678
A Programme: All the things the party intends to do if it gains power, by pushing Acts through Parliament	One clear aim: To exclude James from the throne. They would do this by pushing an 'Exclusion Bill' through Parliament.
A Leader: Who is chosen by the party	The Earl of Shaftesbury was the master mind behind the whole campaign.
Organisation: Local groups all over the country who spread the party's ideas, find good candidates for Parliament, and work hard to win votes for them in an election.	A London coffee house called the Green Ribbon Club was the centre of Shaftesbury's organisation.
Publicity: Parties spread their ideas through newspapers, TV and radio, as well as their own pamphlets and newspapers.	Pamphlets and ballads were published and sold especially in London, condemning Catholics in general, and James in particular. Demonstrations were organised, for instance the great Pope-burning procession at the bottom of this page, on the anniversary of Elizabeth I's accession.
A Name: Parties have a well-known name, which everyone uses.	'Whig' was originally a rude nickname for a sour-faced Scots Presbyterian, and only used by their opponents. The Whigs had a nickname for their opponents too — 'Tory', which meant an Irish robber. Both names stuck, though neither accurately described the people who actually made up these two groups.
Support: To survive, a modern political party must have plenty of support, and money to back it — though anyone can start a political party in a free country.	Whig support included: Adventurous courtiers who wanted power. Disgruntled country gentlemen who disapproved of Charles's immoral court. Some were old enough to have fought in the Civil War. Dissenters, including preachers. The London mob: the poor, apprentices and wage-earners who could do little to improve their lot, and were ready to make trouble.

The Whigs' Exclusion Bill had one great advantage. It was clear, easy to understand and was bound to be popular because of the common attitude to Catholics. It is always fairly easy to win support for what should *not* happen: skilfully, Shaftesbury managed to concentrate on getting rid of James, and left the problem of who should be the next monarch for as long as he could. Luck also helped him.

The Popish Plot

In 1678–9, the Whigs were lucky, because a rumour spread that there was a Catholic plot to kill the King, with a silver bullet — or a Jesuit's dagger — or poison. It was all very vague, but it caused wild panic, especially in London. All sorts of wild accusations were flying about that James, and even the blameless Queen, were involved.

TITUS OATES.

Titus Oates (1649–1705) was the man who said he had discovered the wicked Popish Plot. He was an energetic, loud-voiced, squat man with a huge jaw. He looked an obvious villain, and it shows the atmosphere of the time that people were ready to believe him. He had been both a Dissenter, and a Catholic, but for the moment was loyal Church of England. His 'plot' was encouraged by a mystery murder: the London magistrate, Sir Edmund Godfrey, to whom Oates made his statement giving details of the plot, was found strangled a week later. Catholics, desperate to suppress incriminating evidence, were blamed, and panic increased; but the murder was so convenient for Oates and his supporters, that they might well have been guilty themselves.

Four innocent people were hung for Godfrey's murder; five Catholic peers were also executed, and Charles, who had originally scoffed at the plot, had to agree to their deaths, though he managed to protect his Queen. Probably about 30,000 Catholics fled from London. In the end — much too late for the victims — Oates's lies were discovered, and he was imprisoned, and punished in the pillory, as this picture shows.

1 Why do you think Oates managed to make people believe him in 1678?

2 Write a defence by a loyal Catholic Londoner against Oates's accusations.

At the height of all this panic, Charles was in a very weak position, because he was desperately short of money, and people suspected he was sympathetic to the Catholics. His brother's open 'Popery' did not help. Twice, in 1679 and 1680, Shaftesbury introduced his Exclusion Bill into Parliament, and the King only just managed to dissolve Parliament to prevent it becoming law. London was in an uproar. Many feared that another civil war was about to break out. Moderate people were becoming more and more worried; they began to disbelieve all the wild tales of the Popish plot, and to feel that the violent Whig mobs, with their fiery preachers, were more of a danger. Many were also worried because

←155

The Plot first hatcht at Rome by the Pope and Cordaralls

Pictures on playing cards provided a good way of spreading news and propaganda. These two scenes show the Pope planning 'The Popish Plot', and the murder of Sir Edward Godfrey by Catholics, as if they were proved facts.

Sr E.B.Godfree Strangled Girald going to stab him.

←155

Shaftesbury had at last come into the open, and suggested the Duke of Monmouth as the next heir. They did not consider him suitable because he was illegitimate. Charles took advantage of this, for he (like his opponents, the Whigs) had a clear aim: the Crown must not be weakened, and that meant that the succession (the heir to the throne) must not be altered.

Tories agreed with the King. They were like many of the old Royalists; they did not want an all-powerful, absolute king like Louis XIV, but they did not want things turned upside down again either. They were also loyal to the Church of England. So, rather reluctantly, because James was Catholic, Tories felt they must support him as the rightful heir. In all the uproar, more people began to sympathise with the Tories — even some of the moderate Whigs.

In 1681, Charles decided on a showdown. He held a Parliament in loyal Oxford, away from the threatening Whig mobs in London. He also had another trump card. His cousin Louis XIV had so far done nothing to help him, for it had suited him to have a weak and divided England, who could not help his enemies, the Dutch. But Louis now decided that things might go too far; he gave Charles enough money to free him from Parliament's control for a while. When the Exclusion Bill was once more introduced, Charles unexpectedly appeared, made a speech stating his loyalty to the Church of England, and dissolved Parliament. The Whigs were defeated, and Shaftesbury later went into exile; the unsuccessful Whig 'Rye House Plot' in 1683 to kill the King on the way to Newmarket Races was discovered, and lost them even more support from the moderates.

Charles lived four more years. There were no more Parliaments, and no more talk of Exclusion. In February 1685, he had a severe stroke. As he lay stricken (he apologised 'for being such an unconscionable time a-dying'), an old Catholic priest who had helped him to escape after the battle of Worcester was secretly brought to give him the last rites of the Catholic Church. Do you think that is an indication of Charles's real religious beliefs?

1 Make Whig and Tory posters about 'Exclusion'.

2 Make a list of Charles II's successes and failures. What do you think of him?

Catholic King

James II became King peacefully in 1685. He summoned Parliament, which was co-operative, and voted him more money than was usual. He promised he would respect the Church of England: he could sincerely do this, since he was certain that once the Catholic faith was openly practised, everyone would see its truth.

Most of his subjects felt they had time on their side. James was 54, and had two Protestant daughters. Mary, the heir, was married to William of Orange, ruler of the Dutch United Provinces. William was the Protestant champion of Europe against Louis XIV. It was true that James's second wife, Mary of Modena, was much younger than he was, and a fervent Catholic as well; but they had been married since 1673, and had no children. It seemed unlikely there would be any now. It was only a question of waiting for James to die, and the future would be secure. They soon changed their minds: James's actions one by one destroyed their hopes.

Monmouth's Rebellion, 1685

The ambitious young Duke of Monmouth (Charles II's illegitimate son) had been backed by some Whigs: they thought he would be a better future king than James. Monmouth chose this moment to try to win the crown. He landed at Lyme in Dorset, where he hoped for support; those who joined him were farm labourers, and cloth-workers from nearby towns and villages, armed with pitchforks and scythes, and little else. James had already used some of the money voted by Parliament to build up an army, which decisively defeated the rebels at Sedgemoor in Somerset. Monmouth showed little ability as a leader; he fled, was soon captured, and pleaded abjectly for mercy. But James showed no mercy, either to him, or to those who followed him. The harsh Judge Jeffreys held the 'Bloody Assize' in Dorchester. More than 300 were executed, including a sturdy elderly widow, Alice Lisle, who sheltered some of Monmouth's supporters in her house. Also, 800 were transported to the West Indies.

1 What weapons did a well-equipped seventeenth-century army need? (Refer back to page 159.)

2 What kind of people did *not* support Monmouth? What reasons can you find for the failure of the rebellion?

3 Do you think the severity shown to the rebels was justified?

Freedom for Catholics

James set out to give the freedom to Catholics which he believed would soon bring all his subjects to the true faith. But to achieve this he had to set aside important laws made by Parliament:

The laws passed in Elizabeth I's reign on church attendance (see pages 103 and 109).
The laws passed in Charles II's reign, excluding Catholics from important jobs (see page 187).

James believed that, as a King appointed by God, he had the power to do this. Most of his subjects disagreed.

The army used to crush Monmouth's rebellion was stationed on Hounslow Heath, on the outskirts of London. This made people feel uneasy anyway, but James now openly appointed Catholic officers. To make matters worse, from many of his English subjects' viewpoint, many of these new officers were Irish.

The late D. of M. & other Rebells taking shipping for England

The Defeat of the Rebells 2000 Slayn & their Canon taken

The Late Duke of M: taken near the Ld Grey

Playing cards tell the story of Monmouth's Rebellion.

Soon, he appointed a Catholic to be President of Magdalen College, Oxford. The university was strongly Tory, but that meant that as well as supporting the King, they were firmly Church of England. It was unwise to upset such powerful allies.

To make matters worse, the Catholic Mass was celebrated openly, not just at court, but in London churches and elsewhere in great cathedrals like Durham. Catholic priests walked openly in the streets, which had not happened since Mary I's reign. What is more, in 1685, Louis XIV had withdrawn all freedom of worship from French Huguenots (Protestants), and refugees were arriving in England with tales of horrors and persecutions. None of this made the majority of James's subjects change their traditional view of Catholics.

John Evelyn, a typical upper-class Englishman, wrote in his diary:

special cloak worn in a church service

> I went to hear the music of the Italians in the new chapel, now first opened publicly in Whitehall for the Popish service . . . Here we saw the bishop in his mitre and rich *copes*, with six or seven Jesuits and others in rich copes, sumptuously habited . . . I could not have believed I should ever have seen such things in the King of England's palace, after it hath pleased God to enlighten this nation.

■ How does Evelyn feel about 'the Popish service'?

Even James began to realise he must win some more support. He appealed to the Dissenters, who had been so unfairly treated since 1660. He found a willing helper in the Quaker William Penn, who genuinely hoped that there would be justice for all Dissenters at last; and was ahead of his time in thinking that not all Catholics were wicked persecutors.

Twice, the King issued a Declaration of Indulgence which set aside all the laws made in Parliament against Catholics and Dissenters. The second time, in April 1688, he ordered all Church of England clergy to read it from their pulpits. It is not difficult to imagine what the clergy felt about that; and seven leading bishops, including the Archbishop of Canterbury, protested. These bishops also at last had the sense to say that they appreciated the support of the Dissenters — for most of them disagreed with William Penn, and were opposed to the King's action in setting aside laws made by Parliament. They distrusted James, and thought he would force 'Popery' on everyone, once he had the chance.

Once again, playing cards helped to spread the news of the events of the crisis of 1688.

the law court

The bishops were sent to the Tower, and put on trial. Even the judges now disobeyed James, for all seven were acquitted. This is how John Evelyn describes the scene as excited Londoners heard the news on 29 June:

> There was a lane of people from the *King's Bench* to the waterside, on their knees, as the bishops passed and repassed, to beg their blessing. Bonfires were made that night, and bells rung, which was taken very ill at court.

A Catholic heir

Just a fortnight before, when the crisis over the bishops was reaching its peak, Evelyn recorded another momentous event:

> 10th June, 1688. A YOUNG PRINCE born, which will cause disputes. About two o'clock we heard the Tower ordnance discharged, and the bells ring for the birth of a Prince of Wales. This is very surprising.

If you look back to page 190, you will see why this was very surprising, and might 'cause disputes'. It was so surprising, and worrying too, that tales began to spread that the Queen did not have a living child, and a baby boy had been smuggled into the palace in a warming pan (a covered pan, usually filled with hot coals, to warm a bed). No one has ever found evidence to support this story, and the young prince, James Edward, certainly looked like his father.

If you had seen this playing card in 1688, might you have believed the warming pan story?

1 Why was it convenient for people to believe the warming pan story in 1688?

2 Why did the birth of James Edward harden the opposition to James II?

3 On what side were ordinary people in London in the 1640s (see pages 154 and 159) and during the Exclusion crisis? (see page 189) What did they feel about bishops then? How much had their feelings in 1688 changed, and why?

4 Write a conversation between two London apprentices on the evening of 29 June 1688, in which they discuss their feelings about bishops and the King. Use the information Evelyn gives to capture the atmosphere.

5 Make a list of reasons why a Tory country gentleman might have supported James in 1685, and another list to show why he might have changed his mind by 1688.

Choosing another ruler

Almost all the powerful people in England — Whig or Tory — now wanted to be rid of James and they did not want his baby (Catholic) son either. As far as we can tell, ordinary people felt the same way, at least in London and the bigger towns. It was not difficult to find an alternative, for James had made that easier by executing Monmouth, who, if he had lived, might still have had some support. Most people looked to James's daughter Mary, and her husband, William of Orange. There was an added advantage: William was an experienced general with a good army which would be very useful if James sought help from his powerful cousin, Louis XIV. Seven leading Whigs and Tories wrote secretly to William, saying they would support him if he brought an army to England against James.

William's problem, autumn 1688

William wanted English help against Louis XIV, and was more likely to get it if he and his wife ruled England. But as he considered the invasion of England in the autumn of 1688, he faced several problems. If the invasion

William of Orange was a shy, reserved man, and a devout Calvinist (see page 58). He was never popular in England, preferring the company of his Dutch advisers. Mary, however, was charming and outgoing. She had been brought up as a Protestant, but apart from that, her education was very different from the well-taught Tudor

Queens; she learned a little French, and to sing, sew, draw and dance. In 1688 she had to face a terrible conflict of loyalties between her father and her husband. Having made her choice, she seems to have been content to be a submissive wife.

was successful just because of the support of the powerful English ruling classes, he might not be free to make the decisions he wanted. Also, Europe was poised on the brink of war and Louis XIV was preparing to attack. It was not clear where he would move first, but his most likely objective was Holland. Could William risk taking his best troops to England at this moment? Finally, as it was late autumn, an invasion fleet might have to face storms and gales in the Channel. The prevailing wind anyway blew the wrong way for a fleet sailing from Holland.

Two pieces of luck solved William's problem. Louis XIV decided to attack the Protestant Prince of the Palatinate in Germany. He wanted to leave William free to invade England, because he thought it would lead to a long war in England, which would leave her weak and divided, and also keep William's army tied down. This turned out to be a major mistake on Louis' part.

Then, unusually for November, the wind changed, to blow from the north-east and speed William's fleet down the Channel. As he reached Torbay in Devon, a safe landing place, and far from any opposition, it changed again, bringing his ships safely to shore. Later it was nicknamed 'the Protestant wind'. As William began to march slowly towards London, John Evelyn described the situation there:

William

5th November: I went to London; heard the news of the *Prince* having landed at Torbay, coming with a fleet of near 700 sail, passing through the Channel with so favourable a wind, that our navy could not intercept, or molest them. This put the King and Court into great consternation.

14th November: The Prince increases every day in force. Several Lords go to him. (He also mentions regiments joining William.) The city of London in disorder . . .

2nd December: The great favourites at Court, Priests and Jesuits, fly . . . The Papists in office lay down their commissions, and fly. Universal consternation amongst them; it looks like a revolution . . .

13th December: The King flies to sea, puts in at Faversham for ballast; is rudely treated by the people; comes back to Whitehall . . .

18th December: I saw the King take barge to Gravesend at 12 o'clock — a sad sight! The Prince comes to St James's, and fills Whitehall with Dutch guards . . . All the world go to see the Prince . . . he is stately, serious and reserved.

24th December: The King passes into France, whither the Queen and child were gone a few days before.

1 Explain what Evelyn meant when he said 'it looks like revolution'.

2 Is there any evidence in this account that William's troops had to fight?

3 What did James's supporters do?

4 Work out how James escaped. Why do you think he was allowed to do so? He lived in France for the rest of his life, and died in 1701.

This was 'The Glorious Revolution': James II was forced to give up his throne without bloodshed. There were no executions and no battles. But all revolutions which force a change of government have to solve two important questions: *Who* is to rule? With *how much power?*

Who is to rule?	
Suggestion 1 James should keep the title of King. William and Mary should rule for him as regents. **BUT**	1. James might return to claim his title, with a French army. 2. William refused to be regent.
Suggestion 2 Mary, the legal heir if James's son was ignored, should be Queen **BUT**	William said he would not be 'his wife's gentleman lackey (servant)'. Many MPs agreed. One said: 'Does anyone think that the Prince of Orange will come in to be a subject to his own wife in England? This is not possible, nor ought to be . . .'. (The old view that women were not capable of being reigning queens had not changed.)
The agreed solution William and Mary should reign as joint and equal sovereigns **BECAUSE**	1. Both William and Mary were happy to accept this. 2. The ruling classes in Parliament were pleased, because Parliament had made this unusual arrangement, so Parliament could decide how much power the new sovereigns should have.

How much power?	
Some of these limits on royal power were set down in a famous Act of Parliament called the Bill of Rights (1689). Others were worked out soon afterwards.	
Religion	The monarch should not be a Catholic, and should not marry a Catholic. For the British people, there were the small beginnings of toleration. Dissenters were allowed to worship freely (for William himself was really one of them). But a university education, the best jobs, and the right to vote and be an MP, were reserved for members of the Church of England. Another century would pass before Dissenters and Catholics began to win equal rights.
The laws of the land	The Crown had no right to set aside the laws made by Parliament, as James II had done.
Parliament	There must be new elections for Parliament every three years. In 1716, this was changed to seven years.
Money	Britain now became involved in a long and costly war with Louis XIV. This vast expense meant a solution had to be found to the Crown's money problems. The armed forces were paid for separately, and a 'Civil List' was voted regularly to the Crown for other expenses. The present Queen's income voted by Parliament is still called the Civil List.
The army	Although the monarch still commanded the Army, Parliament also had some control, because a Mutiny Act had to be passed each year to enforce army discipline.

All this was worked out in London, mainly by Englishmen. The Welsh gentry, since some of them sat in Parliament, could also feel they had a hand in it. But the Irish and the Scots still had to decide whether they would accept this Glorious Revolution, and the change of ruler which went along with it. The next chapter will tell what happened there.

In some ways, monarchs have always had to win the support and co-operation of their subjects, as we have seen in this book. The story of the Stuart kings in Britain in the seventeenth century shows what could happen when they failed to do so. Until 1689, there was no way that they could be checked, except by violence. In 1689, a set of rules — or a constitution — was made. Subjects had always had to obey rules; now monarchs had to do so as well. Britain became a 'constitutional monarchy'; there could be no 'absolute' all-powerful ruler as there was in France.

These rules were made by the powerful landowners who were represented in the English Parliament — the ruling classes who have also played an important part in the events in this book. The next big step lay more than a hundred years in the future, when the rest of the peoples of Britain began gradually to take a real share in power.

10 The widening world

During the Early Modern Age, the people of Britain were living in a world of change. By the end of the seventeenth century, it is possible to see how important some of these changes were. It is also possible to see what had *not* changed. History is always a mixture of strands of change weaving amongst continuous threads which remain very much the same.

Wider horizons: Trade and colonies

The fashionable people in the pictures on this page are all making use of a wide variety of goods. As well as coffee, they could also now drink chocolate or tea, out of delicate china bowls (which were so called because they came from China). It was easy to sweeten these drinks, or make elaborate sweetmeats, for sugar was no longer a rare luxury. By the end of the seventeenth century, there had been a huge increase in Britain's trade in all kinds of different goods. Even the Duchess of Portsmouth's servant (or slave) is almost certainly there because of a profitable trade. Only a few of these goods would have been available, at great cost, to families like the Pastons at the beginning of the Early Modern Age.

1. What was the single trade on which England's prosperity depended in the Pastons' time? (pages 17–19) What was the usual drink for most people then? (page 29)

2. Make a list of the goods in the pictures, and those mentioned in this paragraph, which are probably imports. You will use this list later.

Coffee houses became very fashionable in the late seventeenth century: there were over 2,000 in London by 1700. Friends, business men, Whigs and Tories all had their special ones where they met to gossip and read the newspapers (which were now beginning to be published regularly). In this lively scene, a great deal of talking, joking and pipe-smoking is going on. A servant in the foreground pours out a cup of coffee; there are more cups on the table, but saucers were not yet used.

The Duchess of Portsmouth was a mistress of Charles II, and is dressed in the height of fashion in 1682. Her dress is a beautiful blue silk, and under it she wears a 'shift' or underdress of fine muslin cotton. Her servant is dressed in similar materials.

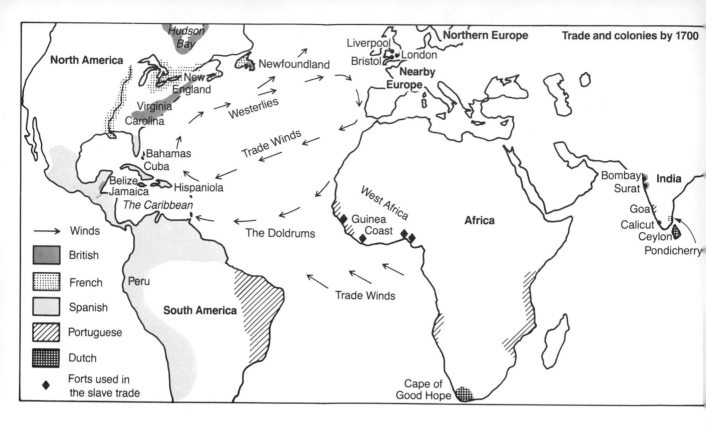

The map shows: Hudson Bay, North America, New England, Virginia, Carolina, Bahamas, Cuba, Belize, Jamaica, Hispaniola, The Caribbean, Peru, South America, Newfoundland, Westerlies, Trade Winds, The Doldrums, Liverpool, London, Bristol, Nearby Europe, West Africa, Guinea Coast, Africa, Trade Winds, Cape of Good Hope, Bombay, Surat, Goa, Calicut, Ceylon, Pondicherry, India.

Key:
- Winds
- British
- French
- Spanish
- Portuguese
- Dutch
- Forts used in the slave trade

The beginning of colonies

←133

Sir Francis Drake was one of the most famous and successful privateers. Try to find out about his adventure with Sir John Hawkins in 1568, and his journey around the world (1577–80) in the 'Golden Hind'. On his return the Queen knighted him and received five packhorses load of treasure herself. This miniature was painted in the same year.

In the reign of Elizabeth I, English merchants and nobles (not forgetting the Welshman, John Dee) began to see the advantage of Britain's island position, and to look westwards across the Atlantic, for adventure and profit. 'Privateering' became a profitable occupation. Privateers were ships owned by trading companies and by courtiers such as Sir Walter Raleigh. They had plenty of cargo space, and were well armed with cannon. Their aim was to seize valuable cargoes from other ships. The only difference between them and real pirates was that they operated under a set of rules, and had to give some of their profits to the Queen, and some to their owners. Since Spanish treasure ships were their main target, Elizabeth unofficially encouraged them, as the conflict with Spain developed. It was often difficult to make a successful attack on the heavily armed Spanish galleons, but privateers won enough booty to make the risks worthwhile. In the 1580s and 1590s, there were about 100 privateering voyages each year, and useful cargoes were unloaded at the docks in London, Bristol and Southampton. A particularly lucky 'catch' from a Spanish ship captured in the West Indies, 1595: cochineal, hides, sugar, taffeta, China, silk, pearls, emeralds, gold rings and chains, sapphires, topazes — £777 17s in Spanish *rials* (silver coins).

1 Which trades would make use of cochineal (not used to colour food as it is now) and hides?

2 Why was it easy for Elizabethan ships to sail to and from the West Indies?

The booty which Elizabethan sailors captured was the least important result of their voyages, though they would no doubt have been surprised to be told that. What became far more important was that they realised the rich gains to be made in the Caribbean. The best way to attack the Spaniards there, and to make one's fortune, was to find a base nearby, on the American mainland. This was how English settlements, or 'colonies', began in the New World. Other reasons helped them to increase, as this map and table show. By 1700, 12 of the 'Thirteen Colonies' were established; some 70 years later, these would break free to become the United States of America.

English settlements in North America

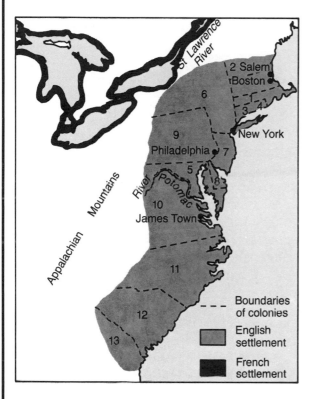

Key

1 Massachusetts	1620:	Pilgrim Fathers settled at New Plymouth.
	1629:	Massachusetts Bay Company set up. The first 400 settlers were mainly strict Puritans who disliked the King's religious policies. They enforced their own views very harshly.
2 New Hampshire **3 Connecticut** **4 Rhode Island** }		By 1644 these had broken away from Massachusetts, where they did not have enough freedom. They remained Puritan. New Englanders made their living by farming and trading.

(1, 2, 3 and 4 are still known as New England.)

5 Maryland	1632:	The Catholic Lord Baltimore founded a settlement where Catholics could worship freely, and he could profit from selling land to settlers
6 New York **7 New Jersey** **8 Delaware** }	1614:	The area settled by Swedes and Dutch — who called it New Netherlands, and the main town, New Amsterdam.
	1664:	Charles II granted New Amsterdam to James, Duke of York, who re-named the town after his own title: New York, although he never went there. The whole area became 'English'.
9 Pennsylvania	1681:	Founded by William Penn as a Quaker settlement, though he offered settlers practical profits as well. Scots-Irish and Germans joined English settlers there.
10 Virginia	1608:	The Virginia Company was set up — to find gold, believed to be inland, and grow crops like tobacco. (Sir Walter Raleigh failed to found a much larger settlement in 1585). It also provided a base to attack Spanish shipping.
11 & 12 **North and South Carolina**	1663:	Eight English noblemen founded a settlement to produce sugar, tobacco and indigo (a dark blue dye).
13 Georgia		Georgia was set up a little later, from 1733, as a defence against the Spaniards and French who were settling to the south (Florida) and west (Louisianna).

Atlantic and Caribbean Islands (not shown on the map)	1609:	**Bermuda** a useful mid-Atlantic base
	1624:	**St Kitts**
	1625:	**Barbados** } bases for trade in tobacco, sugar
	1654:	**Jamaica** } and slaves — and, later, cotton

1 Make your own copy of the map, and a list of settlements in the order in which they were founded. List the main motives for settlement, and the European races who settled there. Look up the word 'colony' and write its meaning under your lists.

2 The map and key completely leaves out a very important group of people affected by this story — the native Americans. Why did the settlers call them 'Red Indians'? There is a great deal to find out about their culture and way of life, and what happened when they came in contact with Europeans (especially in Virginia, Massachusetts, and Pennsylvania).

Great profits were made in England from the trade with these colonies in the New World (and the East as well). London became a gigantic warehouse, receiving silks, cottons, tobacco, tea, coffee, sugar, chocolate and dyestuffs; some goods were sold profitably in Britain, others exported equally profitably to Europe and beyond — the colonies also provided a convenient market, mainly for goods manufactured in England.

Coffee, tea and cocoa first arrived in quantity when Oliver Cromwell was Protector, and imports then increased steadily. In 1678, the brewers produced a pamphlet which they said was *The Women's Petition Against Coffee . . . that Drying, Enfeebling Liquor*, in which men were urged not to:

> trifle away their time, scald their *chops* [mouths], and spend their money, all for a little base, black, thick, nasty, bitter, stinking, nauseous Puddle Water.

1 Why did brewers object to coffee drinking?

2 Does it seem to have been common to have milk or sugar with coffee at this time?

3 Can we take this as evidence that women did not like coffee? What might some wives object to about the new habit?

Sugar imports too increased steadily from the 1650s, from Barbados and Jamaica (particularly as people began to sweeten the 'Puddle Water'). By the 1680s, the price had halved, and about two-thirds of imports were re-exported, with a good deal of the boiling and refining done in British ports. (Before this great increase, at the beginning of the Early Modern Age, the average sugar consumption per head was probably one teaspoonful *a year*.)

Tobacco is usually said to have been introduced into England by Sir Walter Raleigh's ill-fated expedition to settle Virginia in 1585. (Sir Walter did not actually go on the expedition himself.) His Elizabethan sailors may have learned the habit from the native Americans. Although at first it was a luxury, a foreign observer as early as 1590 said he saw Londoners 'constantly smoking'. Puritans soon became worried about the habit. The trade from Virginia grew so profitable that it was made a government monopoly, though the little Cotswold town of Winchcombe was one place that kept an illegal home industry going quite successfully for a time —

The Royal Exchange in 1644

Here merchants from many countries met to make business deals, many of them in goods imported from the New World and the East. This building was burned down in the Great Fire of 1666, and rebuilt by 1671. Why do you think such a large and elaborate building was replaced quite quickly?

there is still a field on the edge of the town called Tobacco Close. In the year 1700 alone, 17 million kilos of tobacco arrived in British ports. About 6½ million kilos were consumed at home; the rest was exported mainly to Europe to make further profits. Tobacco by then cost about a shilling a pound in England — cheap enough for quite poor people to buy it.

1 How was tobacco smoked at this time? (See page 197.)

2 Which British monarch disapproved of smoking? Why do you think his disapproval had little effect?

The slave trade

When Europeans arrived in the New World, they were looking for resources to exploit. There were goldmines in Peru; and later sugar, tobacco and cotton plantations in the Caribbean and North America. Since they had guns, they could force the local people to work for them; but the wars they fought, and the diseases they brought with them, almost destroyed these populations both in the Caribbean and in southern America. From this tragic situation, the slave trade grew.

At the same time, Europeans were exploring the West African coastline. There, they found many different African peoples. Though some lived in small, simple villages, well-organised kingdoms like Benin were producing works of art which are still admired today. First the Portuguese sailors (see page 46), then the English sailors who came in Elizabeth's reign, found these cultures strange and difficult to understand. Though we find it horrifying now, the Europeans saw little wrong in buying and selling people as slaves, as if they were hardly human. They were able to build on an existing trade in slaves (usually prisoners taken in local wars); and they soon saw the chance to profit from the need for labour in the New World.

So, by the mid-seventeenth century, there was a profitable slave trade, organised mainly by the English, Portuguese and French. English ships sailed from London and Bristol (the first Liverpool slave ship sailed in 1700), carrying cheap textiles, muskets, and brass and iron goods. On the Guinea coast, a string of 'forts' grew up, where slaves could be bartered for these goods. They were packed into the lower decks of the waiting ships in appallingly crowded conditions. The crews suffered considerably, but the slaves far more. They could not speak the language of their captors; they had little idea where they were going; and there was no attempt to keep families together.

In the West Indies, the cargoes of these ships changed again. The slaves who had survived the journey were sold to sugar plantation owners. The men worked cutting the tough sugar cane, and in the hot sugar-boiling sheds; the women and children mainly as house servants. Some made another journey, to the tobacco plantations on the North American mainland; some went as far as Britain. The ships returning to England

A Dutch visitor to the city of Benin in 1602 was very impressed with its size and splendour, and the beauty of its carved decorations. He may have seen bronze heads like this one of a Queen Mother, which are still famous today. Her majestic air is a reminder that women played an important part in the affairs of the kingdom.

201

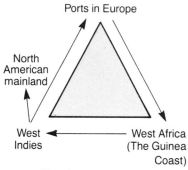

The slave trade triangle

loaded their holds with sugar, rum and molasses (both sugar products) — and tobacco.

The whole operation was a triangle, with chances of fat profits for slave ship owners at each of its three points. Draw your own diagram of the triangle, filling in the cargoes on each of the three sides. Make a block graph to represent the figures below.

Numbers of slaves shipped across the Atlantic, 1701–10 by European powers:

Portugal	83,700
France	27,000
England	119,600

The East

food

> Agra and Fatehpur are two very great cities, either of them much greater than London, and very populous. Between Agra and Fatehpur are twelve miles and all the way is a market of *victuals* and other things.

This description of two great Indian cities was written by an Elizabethan traveller, Ralph Fitch. He visited — amongst many other places in the East — the court of the great Mughal Emperor, Akbar, who ruled from 1562 to 1605, and extended his power over most of the great sub-continent of India. Akbar built the beautiful red sandstone palace of Fatehpur Sikri, which Fitch describes, to celebrate the birth of his son. When Fitch returned home, he set London talking with the wonders he had seen in the East. Not long after, in 1600, Elizabeth I granted a charter to the East India Company, giving it the right to trade in the profitable luxuries of the East. The English were certainly not the only European power trading there; ←46 Portugal found the sea route to India, and she built forts and trading posts along its east coast. The Dutch too were active, and competitive; their main bases were in the 'Spice Islands', mostly the area now known as Indonesia. The visit of Thomas Roe, James I's ambassador, to the court of Akbar's son, Jahangir, in 1615 to 1618 was the next important step forward for the East India Company:

less important lower

> I went to the Court at four in the evening, to the Durbar, which is the Place where the Mughal sits out daily, to entertain strangers, to receive petitions and presents, to give commands, to see, and to be seen . . . The King sits in a little gallery overhead; Ambassadors, the great men and strangers of quality within the inmost rail under him, raised from the ground, covered with canopies of velvet and silk, underfoot laid with good carpets, the *meaner* men representing gentry within the first rail, the people without in a *base* court, but all so they may see the King . . . I delivered his Majesty's letter translated and after . . . my presents were well received . . . He dismissed me with more favour and grace . . . than was ever shown to any ambassador.

■ How does Thomas Roe show that he is impressed by Jahangir's court, and is pleased with his visit?

In this portrait of the Mughal Emperor, Jahangir, his power is shown by the radiant double halo of the sun and moon; it is so bright that the little cherubs shield their eyes. But he is seated on an hour glass, with the sands running out, and offering a book to a holy Muslim teacher. He ignores the two important rulers in the picture — the Sultan of Turkey, and James I of England. What do you think he wants his picture to say?

The artist Bichitr has put himself in the bottom left-hand corner, holding a tiny picture in which he bows down to the Emperor. In it are two horses and an elephant which were probably presents which show the picture pleased Jahangir. Bichitr is very skilled, and makes use of western pictures he has seen. The likeness of James is very good, and probably copied from one of the presents Thomas Roe gave the Emperor. The cherubs have a western look to them too, but the artist is not interested in western ideas of creating distance and space (see page 41). Instead, the beautiful patterned carpet, which looks almost vertical, makes a wonderful background to the picture. You could copy some patterns from the carpet or the border, in rich colours.

Jahangir gave permission for English merchants to have a base at Surat, on the east coast, which they used to trade in calico and muslin (both cotton materials), luxury silks, saltpetre (used for gunpowder) and indigo. Later, other bases were set up, and forts and guns were needed to defend them. As the seventeenth century wore on, the power of the Mughal Emperors declined; the French arrived on the scene (their East India Company was set up in 1664), and both England and France wanted riches and prestige from their bases in the Indian sub-continent. The stage was set for a power struggle that ignored the ancient civilisation of this 'brightest jewel' in the East.

By 1700, Britain was laying the foundations of an overseas Empire in North America, the Caribbean and India. She faced two problems: rivalry with other European powers with the same ambitions, and the fact that the lands she controlled were already occupied by peoples with their own culture and traditions. When the Europeans first came to India, for a time they respected the civilisation they found there. But it would be a long time before they gave the same respect generally to lands and peoples with cultures different from their own.

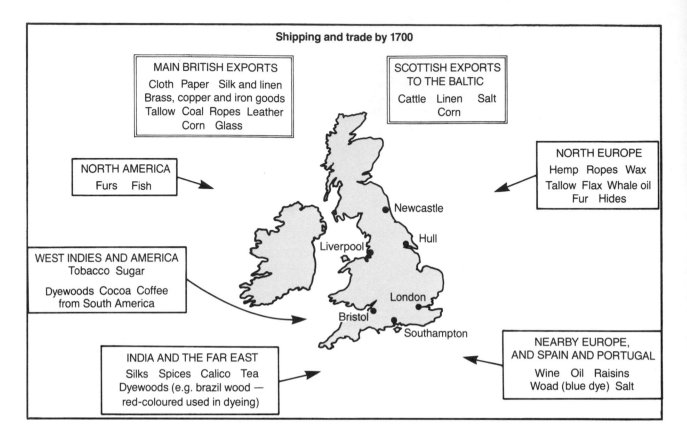

Shipping and trade by 1700

MAIN BRITISH EXPORTS
Cloth Paper Silk and linen
Brass, copper and iron goods
Tallow Coal Ropes Leather
Corn Glass

**SCOTTISH EXPORTS
TO THE BALTIC**
Cattle Linen Salt
Corn

NORTH EUROPE
Hemp Ropes Wax
Tallow Flax Whale oil
Fur Hides

NORTH AMERICA
Furs Fish

WEST INDIES AND AMERICA
Tobacco Sugar

Dyewoods Cocoa Coffee
from South America

INDIA AND THE FAR EAST
Silks Spices Calico Tea
Dyewoods (e.g. brazil wood —
red-coloured used in dyeing)

**NEARBY EUROPE,
AND SPAIN AND PORTUGAL**
Wine Oil Raisins
Woad (blue dye) Salt

Newcastle
Hull
Liverpool
London
Bristol
Southampton

1 Was the English cloth industry still important by 1700?

2 Using your list of items used by the people in the pictures on page 197, add the places which produced the goods, and find out as much as you can about the goods themselves. (A dictionary may help.)

3 Trade rivalry with the Dutch has been mentioned, and there is more to find out about that. What reasons did Britain have to be *friendly* with the Dutch in the late seventeenth century? (See especially Chapter 9.)

The great ocean of truth

People in the Early Modern Age were beginning to find out more about the world in which they lived. By the end of the seventeenth century, there were some important advances in scientific knowledge.

←184 Progress in medical knowledge was slow. The causes of disease were still not really understood, though some of the killers were beginning to disappear. There was no further epidemic of bubonic plague after 1665. The black rat, on which the plague-carrying fleas lived, was ousted by the brown rat; but the reason is not clear, although the stone and brick houses built in London after the Fire must have helped. Sweating sickness disappeared, but smallpox remained a scourge till vaccination became general more than 100 years later.

William Harvey (1578–1657) first discovered the circulation of the blood. This was an important step forward in the understanding of how the human body worked, but it did Harvey little good. His friend John Aubrey wrote:

> I have heard him say, that after his book of the Circulation of the Blood came out, he *fell mightily in his practice* [he lost a great many patients] and 'twas believed . . . he was crack-brained.

It also did not lead directly to an improvement in medical care. The bleeding and purging which must have contributed to so many deaths continued well into the nineteenth century.

Disease and death still surrounded people living in 1700 — especially young children — in a way that it does not in our modern age. Nevertheless, the population continued to creep up; more stone houses, more washable cotton clothes, and a more varied diet for at least some of the population, probably brought this about.

In late seventeenth-century Britain however, many people wanted to find out more about science. This curiosity helped to lay the foundations of modern scientific knowledge.

Charles II, who was himself genuinely interested in science, founded the Royal Society in 1660. The aim of the Society was to encourage investigation into all scientific matters.

Robert Hooke's microscope, which he designed himself

He used it to make this detailed drawing of a flea — an accurate scientific observation.

Some inquiries of the Royal Society in 1666

These inquiries were sent to different places, and to several people 'because it is altogether necessary to have confirmation of the truth from several hands, before they be relied on':

To the East: If diamonds were buried, did they grow again after several years? Whether the iron in Japan be better than ours? Whether Japan be truly an island?

To Virginia and Bermuda: How did the tides work there? Whether a 'large and beautiful spider ensnared birds'?

To Guinea: Whether 'the negroes have such sharp sights that they can discover a ship at sea much further off than Europeans can'?

To Egypt: To discover if it ever rained.

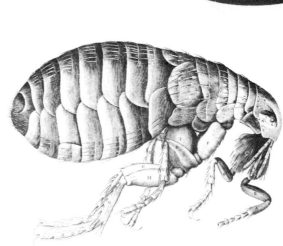

The steeple of St Mary-le-Bow, one of Christopher Wren's many and varied designs for the City churches he rebuilt after the Fire of 1666

They observed the stars; they experimented to see whether blood could be transfused from one sheep to another — it could: the bled sheep died, and the receiver of the blood was 'strong and lusty'. Unfortunately, no one saw that this could also benefit humans. They even tested the old belief that a spider would not climb out of a circle of unicorn's horns — it did, and they still believed in unicorn's horns!

Some members were interested amateurs like the King, Prince Rupert (who lived in England after 1660), and Samuel Pepys, who was President in 1684. There were also the great scientific minds of the day: Robert Boyle (1627–91) the chemist; Robert Hooke (1635 1703), a professor of geometry, astronomer, and designer of a microscope and marine barometer.

Christopher Wren (1632–1723) was another famous President. Like the other scientists of his day, he did not have one specialist skill. He was Professor of Astronomy at Oxford University when he designed his first building — the D-shaped Sheldonian Theatre, designed as a setting for university ceremonies. There was no training for architects then, but Wren worked out the mathematical principles that ensured that the structure of his elegant buildings was absolutely sound. His greatest triumph was St Paul's Cathedral — the great dome has stood solidly for nearly three centuries, and withstood the air-raids of the Second World War.

The most distinguished scientist of all was Isaac Newton (1642–1727). He studied at Cambridge, but left in 1665 because of the Plague, and spent the next two years at home, when his mathematical studies began in earnest. Modern studies of his notebooks show he was not well taught — he worked it all out for himself. Optics fascinated him. He worked painstakingly on experiments on light and concluded that:

> the most surprising and wonderful composition was WHITENESS . . . I have often with admiration beheld that all the colours of the prism being made to converge . . . reproduced light, entirely and perfectly white.

For years he worked on his theory of gravity; from this theory he was able to calculate the orbits of the planets. Newton was a reserved, rather difficult man, and did not publish his work partly because of troubles with Robert Hooke, with whom he worked. It was the astronomer Edmund Halley, discoverer of the comet's orbit, who smoothed things over, and paid for the printing of Newton's famous book *Principia*.

Newton then became famous and successful, but right to the end of his life, he never lost his sense of wonder at what could still be discovered:

> I do not know what I may appear to the world: but to myself I seem to have been only like a boy playing on the sea-shore, and diverting myself in now and then finding a smoother pebble or a prettier shell than ordinary, while the great ocean of truth lay before me.

In our modern world, Newton's discoveries in the 'great ocean of truth' have formed the basis of our understanding of what a modern scientist has called 'the majestic clockwork of the universe'.

Superstition did not die overnight. Many scientists, including Newton, were still interested in alchemy. This aimed to turn cheap metals into gold; to discover the 'panacea', a medicine which would cure all diseases; and to discover the 'elixir of life' which would preserve youth for ever. Since success in alchemy might solve most of the world's problems, it is not surprising that scholars were still fascinated by it, even as the 'scientific age' dawned. However, as education spread, superstition declined. The decreasing number of witchcraft prosecutions shows that.

1 Make a list of the 'school subjects' which the inquiries and experiments of the Royal Society covered. Which of the inquiries would we now regard as scientific?

2 Make up a 'superstitious' experiment that might have been conducted in the 1660s (perhaps in alchemy).

A united kingdom?

We have seen in this book some of the problems which arose between the different peoples of England, Wales, Ireland and Scotland. By the end of the Early Modern Age, England had gone some way to securing her 'back doors' and achieving a United Kingdom in the British Isles. Wales had now been part of the English government system for more than a century, though her language and traditions survived. In both Ireland and Scotland, there were important developments at the end of the seventeenth century. We must now find out how far their peoples were becoming part of the widening world.

Ireland: A problem unsolved

An English view of the Irish: The Irish live like beasts . . . are more uncivil, more uncleanly, more barbarous in their customs . . . than in any part of the world.

An Irish view of the English: The greatest murderers and the proudest people in all Europe and I am surprised that God tolerates them so long in power . . . I shall say no more, because I should use all my ink and paper on this subject.

Both these statements were written in the sixteenth century and, sadly, later events did nothing to change either side's view of the other.

When James II lost his English throne in 1688, he tried, with French troops to help, to win back his crown by capturing Ireland. He attacked Ulster (where its strongly Protestant settlers lived alongside Catholic Irish) and laid siege to Londonderry. Even the name of this town shows the divisions of Ireland. It was originally Derry, and was colonised by the City of London under James I; it then became Londonderry. To this day few Catholics like to use the longer name. James's army laid a boom across the narrow river estuary, so that none of William III's ships could bring in supplies. The city's Protestant defenders were reduced to eating rats, mice, dogs and candles, but refused to surrender. Finally William's ships

←152

Pictures and slogans like this are used in 'Orange' marches in Ulster today. What does it tell people in Ulster not to forget? How is loyalty to the British Crown shown?

lurking outside the harbour broke through the boom, and tied up at the city's quay with the desperately needed food and ammunition, and the siege came to an end.

William III (or William of Orange, as he is still remembered in Ireland) then arrived in person, and defeated James and his Irish-French forces at the Battle of the Boyne in 1690. The 'Orange Order' is an organisation of Northern Ireland Protestants, who still march today to celebrate that siege and battle, when, as they see it, 'King Billy' prevented a 'Papist' take-over. And Catholics in Ulster march to protest against the injustices which followed.

Rebellion was over for the time being. The grievances over religion and the land remained. No Catholic could be a lawyer, soldier or MP, and Catholics were not allowed to send their children abroad to be educated, though schools and universities in Ireland were — officially — Protestant. As for the land, the figures in the margin tell the story clearly. A terrible legacy of tragedy was left in Ireland, and most of the Irish people felt left out of the widening world. To understand what is happening in Ireland in our modern times, begin in the Early Modern Age.

Scotland: An unwilling bargain

In 1707, the two Parliaments of England and Scotland struck a bargain, and agreed to become one united kingdom. It was an unwilling bargain, especially on the Scots side, and there was little rejoicing as the final decision was taken. It happened — as most bargains do — because each side needed the other.

The Scots were still two peoples: the clansmen and the Highlands, and the Lowlanders, mostly farmers and traders in the south. The whole country

---

Percentage of the land owned by the Irish Catholics

1640 : 59%
1658 : 22%
1714 : 7%

Draw three circles (pie charts), each representing 100%, for the three dates given. Colour in the correct sized sector of each circle to represent land owned by the Irish Catholics.

was still poor compared with England. The climate and soil had always made farming difficult; trade in cattle, linen and coal (mainly in the Baltic) had been disrupted by the wars with Louis XIV (look at the map on page 204 to work out why England's trade was less affected). Also, times were particularly hard in the 1690s because of a series of cold, wet summers which affected the crops and caused some deaths from starvation.

The Highlands	The Lowlands
The clansmen were loyal above all to their chiefs, and unwilling to submit to anyone else. Feuds and cattle-raiding were still a way of life. Many were Catholic, some Church of England. They mostly supported James II, and his son, James Edward.	Mostly Presbyterian; farmers and traders. They supported William III and Mary mainly for religious reasons. They resented English trading prosperity, and the fact that they had no share in it, or in her colonies.

Two reasons why William III was unpopular in Scotland

1692: The Massacre of Glencoe
All the Clan chiefs had to swear an oath of loyalty to William and Mary by 1 January 1692. The Macdonald chief was late in doing this, and when he was entertaining government troops, they suddenly turned on him and his clan. Thirty-six were killed, including four women and children. The rest escaped, but most of them died on the hills in the bitter Scots winter. William probably did not know of the official orders given to the troops by his minister on the spot, but he was held responsible.

1698–1700: The failure of 'Caledonia' — a Scots colony
The Scots tried to set up a colony in Darien, near Panama. They hoped it would become a base from which to trade profitably in silks and spices. But it was a rain-soaked, fever-ridden swamp. It was also in an area controlled by Spain, so England, who had first backed the scheme, pulled out, because Spain was an ally in the war against Louis XIV. Many ordinary Scots put money into the scheme; it was all lost, for the scheme was a total failure. Most of the colonists who tried to settle there died in shipwrecks or of fever. The Scots blamed the English for failing to support them.

The English were not interested in helping the Scots to share in their trade and colonies. However, most English were quite clear that they did not want the Catholic James II, or his son, on the throne. In 1702, on the death of William, Mary's younger sister Anne became Queen of England. Although she had many children, none of them lived, so it was arranged that a descendant of Elizabeth of Bohemia, George, Elector of Hanover in Germany, should succeed, to ensure that the next ruler was Protestant. ←155

The Scots saw their chance to get good terms out of England, and at first threatened to choose their own ruler when Queen Anne died — even James Edward. It also seemed possible that they might revive the 'Auld Alliance' with Louis XIV's France. Reluctantly, England offered favourable terms. Reluctantly, the Scots accepted them. And because it really suited both sides, the 'union' stuck.

The flag of union between England and Scotland

How does it differ from the modern Union Jack?

The bargain struck

The Scots Parliament disappeared. In the English House of Commons there were 513 members, of which 45 were now Scots. There were 16 Scots peers in the House of Lords. The Scots kept their own Presbyterian Kirk, their own law courts, and their own system of education. England paid off Scots debts, including the money lost in the Darien scheme. The Scots now had the chance to benefit from English trade, and to settle in her colonies.

1 Design an anti-union pamphlet produced in Scotland around 1700.

2 Write a letter to an English newspaper from a country gentleman, arguing against the union from the English point of view. Use the same date.

Strangers in Britain

There have always been some 'strangers' who have come from foreign lands to live in Britain. In the Early Modern Age, three particular groups of strangers arrived, who each in their way gave a wider view of the world. Some were brought here with little choice, and some came of their own free will.

Black people

Look back at the picture of the Duchess of Portsmouth on page 197 and its date. It was quite common for fashionable people to have black slaves then. Think of reasons why the Duchess chose to have her young slave girl in her portrait. Look carefully at the girl's dress, and at what she is holding.

Almost all the black people in Britain in the second half of the seventeenth century came as slaves (there were a few sailors and students). It became a fashionable craze from the 1650s for rich people to have a black slave in their household. A modern historian, Peter Fryer, points out that what began it all was the everyday act of putting a teaspoon of sugar in the new drinks, tea, coffee and chocolate. Do you see why?

Here is some more evidence on black people in Britain in the second half of the seventeenth century.

A Part of a letter written to a slave trader in 1651 as he set out on the 'Triangle':

> We pray you buy for us 15 or 20 young lusty Negroes of about 15 years of age, bringing them home with you for London . . . (There will be needed) 30 pairs of shackles and bolts for such of your negroes as are rebellious and we pray you to be very careful to keep them under and let them have their food . . . that they rise not against you, as they have done in other ships.

B Two advertisements for runaway slaves (there were plenty in the newspapers of the time):

> 1686: A 15-year-old boy called John White has run away from Colonel Kirke: he has a Silver Collar round his neck, upon which is the Colonel's Coat of Arms.

Sir John Hawkins' crest

There were black people in Britain long before the 1650s. Sir John Hawkins first sailed the 'slave triangle' in 1562. He was pleased with his success, and saw nothing wrong in designing himself this new crest. It may have been his ships which brought some of the black people we know were in London in Elizabeth I's reign.

1690: A negro Boy called Toney is lost ... He has a brass collar on with directions where he lives.

C Names of slaves

We have sometimes seen that the way people use names tells us about their attitudes. Slaves never seem to have kept their real names (see B). Sometimes they were given rather grand Roman names like Pompey. One family always called any slave they owned 'John Morocco'.

1 Explain in your own words why there were more slaves in Britain from the 1650s.

2 Write your own conclusions from this evidence on how black people were treated in Britain in the late seventeenth century. Try to be fair; for instance, what evidence can you use from the Duchess's portrait, which may differ from A, B and C?

The Huguenots

The divisions in the Christian churches in the Early Modern Age led to many conflicts between Catholics and Protestants in Britain and Europe. England was often a Protestant refuge; in Elizabeth I's reign, refugees from the Netherlands fled there to escape the war with Catholic Spain. In 1685, Louis XIV cancelled the right of the French Huguenots to worship freely, and many Huguenot refugees flooded into England. Some had foreseen trouble, and come earlier. They received generous help; for instance, in James II's reign £40,000 was collected in London and arrival ports, and given to 15,500 refugees.

In the margin you can see two examples of skills the Huguenots brought to England. They were also silversmiths, makers of navigation instruments, and doctors; one became a Governor of the Bank of England.

Some Huguenot names still common in Britain (some you should recognise): Cazenove, Chenevix, Courtauld, De La Mare, Bosanquet, Faber, Garrick, Jarman, Dollond, Millais, Mercier, Massy, Lefroy, Olivier, Tessier, Savage, Vanner.

1 What was happening in England from about 1680, which would make most powerful people in England ready to welcome the Huguenots? (Clue: attitudes to France, and to the King of England, see Chapter 9.)

2 Why did the Huguenots find it fairly easy to earn their living, and become part of the British nation?

The Jews

Long ago, in 1320, Jews were officially expelled from England. In fact, some seemed to have managed to stay: there was a small group of Jews in London in the sixteenth century, mostly money-lenders, and Elizabeth I had a Jewish doctor. But in 1656, Oliver Cromwell gave them official permission to live and work in England, and to practise their religion. From that date, the Jewish community grew, especially in London. By 1695 there were about 800 there.

Huguenot silkweavers settled in Spitalfields, in the East End of London. Designs like this one for patterned silk fabrics became very fashionable. Skilled Huguenot clockmakers made beautiful time pieces like the watch below, and taught English craftsmen a good deal. Because so many Huguenots fled to England, there was a shortage of good cloakmakers in France, and in the early eighteenth century English clockmakers had to be employed at Versailles.

They made their living as doctors, merchants and 'brokers' who put up money for colonial and business ventures. In 1697, 12 Jews were admitted to the Royal Exchange, though they felt it necessary to arrange to give the Lord Mayor of London an annual present of 50 guineas and a valuable piece of silver. William III employed Jewish businessmen to organise his war supplies in the long struggle against Louis XIV.

←200

Jews were allowed to have their own synagogue, and its Quaker builder in 1701 charged only for its basic costs, saying he would 'take no profit from building a House of God'. This beautiful building at Bevis Marks in the City of London still stands today. Not everyone was so tolerant. In James II's reign, 37 Jews were arrested for not obeying the old Elizabethan laws insisting on attendance at Church of England services, though James prevented any further punishment — why did he not like the laws either?

1 Find out about the character of Shylock in Shakespeare's play *The Merchant of Venice*. What does this show about attitudes to Jews in Elizabethan England? Would most Englishmen have been able to meet any Jews or know much about them?

2 What facts show that English attitudes to Jews in the late seventeenth century were rather mixed? Think of reasons for this.

3 What kind of things might native populations anywhere find difficult to accept in immigrant groups? What do immigrants find difficult?

A country like Britain, which is an island, is bound to be involved in seafaring, trade, and travel. In the Early Modern Age, her horizons began to widen. Strangers had always come to trade; and some to settle. Now, for differing reasons, more were beginning to come to live in Britain, to add a greater variety and richness to her population.

London by 1700

London continued to grow, and there was by 1700 a solid built-up area between the two old cities of London and Westminster; its population was over 600,000.

←185

After the Fire of 1666, rebuilding created many problems, mainly because property owners wished to rebuild in the same place. Charles II, who had done his best to help during the Fire, issued this proclamation soon afterwards:

important

> We . . . declare our express will and pleasure, that no man whatsoever shall presume to erect any house or building, great or small, but of brick or stone . . . We do declare that Fleet Street, Cheapside, Cornhill and all other *eminent* . . . streets shall be of such breadth as may, with God's blessing, prevent the mischief that one side may suffer if the other be on fire . . . In the meantime we resolve, though all streets cannot be of equal breadth, yet none shall be so narrow as to make the passage uneasy or inconvenient.

If you know the City of London, you will be able to judge how far the last suggestion was carried out. Fire remained a problem. Small water carts were the main fire-fighting equipment, usually provided by fire insurance companies. These companies put their badges on the buildings of those who insured with them and were therefore allowed to use their equipment.

1 Why was it difficult to carry out Charles II's two main orders?

2 What problems can you see in London's fire-fighting arrangements?

3 What advantages were gained by the sort of rebuilding you can see in the picture? (Compare this building with the house on page 11.)

4 Write a protest letter against the King's proclamation by a small shopkeeper in Pudding Lane, where the Fire started, and where everything was destroyed.

Living in 1700

In this chapter we have looked at some of the many changes which took place in the Early Modern Age in Britain:

The growth of trade all over the world.
The growth of colonies.
The increase of scientific knowledge.
The beginning of a 'United Kingdom' of Britain, with a population of more varied origins.
The growth of a better-built London.

London rebuilt: Fish Street, with the 61.5 metre high Monument designed by Wren to mark the place where the Fire of 1666 (page 185) broke out (the inscription blamed the Catholics)

The four-storey houses with chimneys are built of brick or stone: in main streets like this one, the Royal Proclamation was obeyed. One of Wren's new City churches is further up the street.

All this affected different people in Britain in all kinds of ways, but it is impossible for us to know how much they realised the importance of these changes at the time. Like us, their first concern was to get on with the ordinary, everyday business of living.

Squire and villagers

At the beginning of this book, a picture gave us clues to ordinary lives around 1450. A late seventeenth-century picture, which you can see on pages 216-7, provides us with evidence about living around 1700.

The Tichborne Dole shows a ceremony which took place annually in front of the big house in the village of Tichborne in Hampshire, when the squire gave out food to the very poor.

The great house dominates everyone in the picture as they stand outside it taking part in the ceremony. It is a rather old-fashioned Elizabethan building; a prosperous landowner at this time might well be rebuilding in a more up-to-date way — a square well-proportioned house, probably made of stone, and some way from the village, in its own carefully laid out grounds. Inside, his family would use a separate drawing room and dining room, away from the servants; there would be no great hall where everyone might eat and sit together. The social classes were continuing to become more separate.

The gentry stand in the place of honour in the centre foreground. The squire, in a dark loose tunic, and big lace collar, is in the centre. Behind him stand his wife and another possibly unmarried female relation. His four children are there — the smallest girl is old enough to be fashionably dressed like an adult, but the little boy is still in skirts. Two village children of about the same age stare at them — in wonder? Compare the squire with his fashionable visitor from London on his left, who wears a wig, a lace cravat at his neck, a buttoned coat and a sash. A country squire did not always want to spend much time in London, where he could keep up with the latest fashions; in what ways is his costume rather out of date?

Upper-class women still wore heavy, elaborate clothing, though the materials were more varied. Their bodices were stiffened with a board or strips of wood, which ensured they stood or sat in an upright, stiff position. Their waists were sharply pulled in, and they wore at least three layers under their outer skirts. It was hardly the dress for an active life. The women in the picture were probably less well-educated than high-born Tudor girls — remember the contrast between the way Elizabeth I and Mary II were educated. Some schools in London and other larger towns offered girls a wider education; but women still had to show a great deal of drive and determination to become independent in any way.

The house servants are on the left and in the centre background, with baskets of provisions ready to distribute. They have rather more status and security than the ordinary villagers, though their lives are completely controlled by their employers. The steward, in his dark tunic and plain white linen collar (only gentlemen wore lace), is a man of importance. He is responsible for the day-to-day running of the house and all the lands belonging to it. He collects the rents, pays out the wages, and deals with problems when they arise; he controls the lives of the villagers as well as the servants, though of course, in the end, the final decision is the squire's. Next to him is the housekeeper in a white cap and collar and holding a cloth. The daily running of the house, and the happiness and efficiency of the female servants, depend on her.

The villagers wait on the right to receive their 'dole'. An old man shuffles forward to be given his share. It is difficult to tell just how poor these villagers are. The artist may have tidied them up for a rather grand picture like this. Who was the most likely person to have arranged for this picture to be painted?

Although about 16 per cent of the population now lived in the growing towns and cities, the great majority still lived and worked in the country like these villagers; and they depended for housing and employment on the gentry in the big house. Villagers rented houses from the landowner, and worked for him for wages. The squire was likely to be the local MP, and probably helped to pass laws in Parliament which directly affected the villagers. These included Corn Laws to protect the corn produced on his land from cheap foreign imports, and so keep up the price of bread in times of shortage; and Game Laws, which imposed harsh punishments for poaching a rabbit or a pigeon from the squire's land. If these laws were disobeyed, then the squire was also the Justice of the Peace (or magistrate), who tried offenders. If the villagers did not attend their parish church, the squire as well as the parson was likely to be displeased with them. The characters of both these men and their families affected them; concerned and caring people in the big house and the parsonage would help them in difficult times, and be involved in their lives, and interests. But the gentry's power could be used harshly too.

Probably most villagers were grateful for any help they could get, and accepted their 'dole', and their position in life, without question. There is little to tell us whether more independent-minded people resented their low wages and lack of freedom — though this would certainly come later.

For ordinary people, in fact, it might not have seemed 'A World of Change'. They used the same farming tools as those on pages 9 and 10. They continued to wear heavy woollen cloth made locally or at home, and obviously did not keep up with fashion. (It is worth thinking why it is easier now for everyone to wear reasonably fashionable clothes.) They were unlikely to be able to afford much tobacco, or the fashionable new drinks of tea, coffee and chocolate which the rich enjoyed from the growth in trade; they might be able to afford some sugar occasionally. Their longest journey was almost certainly to the local market town and they were very unlikely to have seen London. If one of the old women was accused of witchcraft, they still might believe she was guilty, though the gentry would be much less interested in bringing her to trial. Their houses were still

'The Tichborne Dole', by Gilles von Tillborch, 1670

mostly of thatch and plaster, and damp and cold in winter; they were still victims of many diseases (so were the rich), and their children often died young. A bad harvest could still bring them close to starvation. If they could have walked back into Bruegel's picture at the beginning of this book, everything would have been very familiar to them.

Links: Topic books and A *World of Change*

A World of Change is complete in itself, but has also been designed to provide a number of stepping-off points for 'patch studies'. Opportunities for this kind of work are provided by the eight topic books which are clearly linked to the themes of the main book. However, the topic books can be used on their own if desired.

The relevant chapters of *A World of Change* are listed below for each topic book:

Children in Tudor England

Chapter 1   Apprentices; pp 15, 16
Chapter 2   Parents, children and schools; pp 27–9
  Edward VI; p 97
Chapter 5   Tudor princesses; pp 98, 99
Chapter 6   Poverty; pp 134–6

Scolding Tongues

Chapter 2   Attitudes and beliefs; p 36
Chapter 3   Changes in the Church; pp 50–3
Chapter 5   The parish church; pp 114–16
Chapter 6   The problem of poverty; pp 134–6
Chapter 7   James I; pp 137–9
Chapter 8   provides background to Matthew
  Hopkins; especially pp 173–5
Chapters 5, 7 and 8   provide information on
  Puritans; (*See* Index)
Chapter 10   The great ocean of truth (advances
  in science); pp 204–7
  Living in 1700; pp 214–17

Bare Ruined Choirs

Chapter 3   Problems in the Church; pp 51–3
Chapter 5   The King's Great Matter; pp 83–96
  especially The end of the monasteries pp 88–91

Elizabeth and Akbar

Chapter 4   The Renaissance Prince; p 60
Chapter 5   The King's 'Great Matter' (Anne
  Boleyn); pp 83–8
  The daughters of Henry VIII; pp 98–100
  The middle way; pp 103–14
Chapter 6   The Court of Elizabeth I; pp 125–7
  The marriage game; pp 127–8
  Money Problems; Elizabeth and her Parliaments;

pp 130–2
The End of an Era; p 136
(*See also* Index for references to women)
Chapter 3   Europe discovers the world; pp 42–7
Chapter 10   Trade and the colonies; pp 197–204
  especially pp 202, 203 on European contact with
the Mughal Empire

Exploring Other Civilisations

Chapter 3   Europe discovers the world; pp 42–7
Chapter 10   Trade and colonies; pp 197–204

The Cromwell Family

Chapter 1   Surnames; p 13
Chapter 2   The Four Sorts; p 23
  Going up in the world; p 24
  Marriage and the family; pp 25–8
Chapter 5   New men and a new plan; pp 86–96
Chapter 6   Royal favour; pp 117–22
  Money problems, pp 122–5
Chapter 8   *Especially* God made them as 'stubble
  to our swords'; pp 167–70
  Britain without a king; pp 170–79

A City at War

Chapter 7   Archbishop Laud; pp 148–51
  especially Steps to war; pp 151–4
Chapter 8 pp 156–72

To The New World: The Founding of Pennsylvania

Chapter 8   The world turned upside down;
  pp 173–5
(*See also* Quakers in the Index)
Chapter 9   William Penn and James II; p 192
Chapter 10   Trade and colonies; pp 197–204

Index

Akbar, Mughal Emperor 202
Anne, Queen (1702–14) 209
Anne of Cleves 95
apprentices 14–16
Armada 111–13, 126
Arthur, Prince 74, 84, 119
Aske, Robert 94
Astley, Sir Jacob 169

Babington Plot 109
Bess of Hardwicke (Elizabeth, Countess of Shrewsbury) 134
Bible, The 52, 55–6, 91–3, 96–7, 102–3, 146
Bill of Rights (1689) 196
Black people 210–11 (see also Slaves)
Boleyn, Anne 83–6, 94–5
Bosworth, Battle of 71
Bothwell, Lord 106–7
Boyle, Robert 206
Buckingham, Duke of 139, 141–4
Bunyan, John 184

Cabot 47
Calvin, John 57–9
followers of 59
Campion, Edmund 109, 116
Castlemaine, Barbara 182
Catesby, Robert 146
Catherine of Aragon 74, 76, 83–5, 93, 95
Catherine of Braganza 182, 187, 189
Caxton, William 49, 65, 68
Cecil, William 127–8
Robert 128, 138, 144
Cely family 18–19, 63
Chancellor, Richard 47
Charles I 138–41, 142–61, 170–2
II 176–7, 180–90
V, Emperor 84–5, 95, 99
Charterhouse, monks of 93–4
Clarence, Duke of 67
Clarendon, Earl of (Edward Hyde) 140, 156, 163, 183, 186
cloth trade 19
Clubmen 166
Columbus, Christopher 46
Commonwealth, The 173, 175
Cranmer, Thomas 86–7, 91, 94, 96, 97, 101, 116
Cromwell, Oliver 160, 164, 167–79, 181, 200, 211
Thomas 86–91, 95, 119, 123–4

Darnley, Lord 106–7
Dee, John 133

Diaz, Bartholomew 46
Diggers 175
disease 12, 29–35, 165, 184–5, 204
Dissenters 184, 189, 192, 196
Drake, Francis 108, 111, 112, 198
Drogheda, capture of 176
Duccio 41
Dunbar, Battle of 177

Edgehill, Battle of 160, 162, 167
Edward IV 63–8, 71
V 69–70
VI 95, 97–9, 105, 116
Elizabeth I 32, 88, 94, 98–100, 103–115, 125–8, 130–2, 136, 198, 201–2
of Bohemia 138, 142, 162, 209
of York 71, 74
enclosures 10
Erasmus 53–4, 58
Essex, Earls of (1567–1601) 128, 131 (1591–1646) 158, 160
Evelyn, John 180, 192–3, 194–5
Exclusion Crisis 187–90
exploration 42–8

Fairfax, Sir Thomas 161, 168–71, 174
Falkland, Lord 162
farming 9, 10, 215
Fawkes, Guy 147
Fire of London (1666) 186–7, 211–12
Fisher, Bishop John 93
Fitch, Ralph 202
Flodden, Battle of 77, 105
Florence 40, 49
Foxe, John 102, 114

Gama, Vasco da 46
George I, Elector of Hanover 209
Glencoe, massacre of 209
Grand Remonstrance 153, 156, 162, 167
Grey, Lady Jane 99
Guilds 14, 17
Gunpowder Plot 147
Gutenberg 49
Gwynn, Nell 182

Hampden, John 145, 151, 153, 156–7, 159–60, 167
Harley, Lady Brilliana 163–4
Harvey, William 205
Hatton, Christopher 128
Hawkins, John 210
Henrietta Maria 143, 148, 151, 153–4, 157

Henry VI 61–4, 67–8
VII 68–74
VIII 74–7, 83–6, 88, 93–6, 117–24
Prince of Wales 138–9, 141
Hilliard, Nicholas 126
Holbein, Hans 120
Hopton, Sir Ralph 160
houses 6, 12, 134, 212
Howard, John, 1st Duke of Norfolk 71
Catherine 95–6
Thomas, 3rd Duke 83, 86, 94–6
Thomas, 4th Duke 109
Hudson, Henry 47
Huguenots 59, 211
Hutchinson, Lucy 157, 165
Hyde (see Clarendon)

Inquisition 59
Ireland 1–2, 72, 131, 152, 160, 176, 207–8
Italy 38–40

Jahangir, Mughal Emperor 202–3
James I of England 107, 137–9, 141–2, 144–5
II of England 182, 187–95, 207–9
IV of Scotland 75, 77
V of Scotland 105
James Edward 193, 209
Jesuits 58, 108, 192
Jews 211–12
Jones, Inigo 140
jousting 76, 121

Knox, John 105–6

Lancastrians 63, 67, 63
Latimer, Bishop Hugh 101
Laud, Archbishop William 148–9, 151
Leicester, Earl of 108, 128
Leonardo da Vinci 38, 41
Levellers 173–4
Lilburne, John 174
London 20–22, 212–13
Fire of 187
Louis XIV of France 186–7, 190–4, 196, 209, 211, 212
Loyola, Ignatius 58
Luther, Martin 55–9, 85

Machiavelli 60
Magellan, Ferdinand 47
Margaret of Anjou 61–4, 67
Beaufort 68
of Burgundy 71–2
Tudor 75, 77

Mary I 83, 85, 88, 94, 98–102, 109
    II 190, 194, 195, 209
    of Guise 105
        Queen of Scots 105–10, 131
    of Modena 191, 195
Marston Moor, Battle of 160, 167–8
medicine 33–5, 164, 205
Merchant Adventurers 19
monasteries 88–91, 95, 100, 124
Monck, General 179
Monmouth, Duke of 182, 190–1
Monopolies 131, 145, 152
More, Sir Thomas 54, 59, 93–4, 136

Naseby, Battle of 161, 168
Newbury, Battle of 160, 163
Newcastle, Earl of 159, 160
New Model Army 161, 167–8
Newton, Isaac 206
Northumberland, Duke of 97, 99

Oates, Titus 189

Parliament, Short 151
    Long 151–4
    Rump 170, 178
    Cromwell's parliaments 178
    Cavalier parliament 183

Parma, Duke of 111–12
Parr, Catherine 96, 98
Paston family 24–6
Penn, William 175, 192, 199
Pepys, Samuel 180, 184–6, 206
Petition of Right 144
Philip of Spain 99–100, 103, 108, 110–11, 116, 127
Pilgrimage of Grace 94, 118
Pilgrim Fathers 148, 199
plague 31–2
    (1665) 184–5
Pole, Cardinal 101, 103

Popish Plot (1678) 189
population 10, 205
poverty 5, 134–6, 215
Prayer Book 96, 97, 103, 115, 149–50, 183
Presbyterians 59, 138, 146, 150, 152, 169, 176, 209
Price rise 10, 124, 130, 136
Pride's Purge 170
printing 48–9
Privateers 198
Prynne, William 149
Puritans 104, 130, 146, 149, 167, 184

Quakers 175, 183, 212

Raleigh, Sir Walter 128, 198–200
Reformation 55–7, 59, 88, 114
Renaissance 38
Riccio, David 106
Richard III 65, 69–71, 81
Ridley, Nicholas 101
Roe, Thomas 202
Roses, Wars of 63
Rupert, Prince 158, 160, 162, 167–8, 206
Rye House Plot 190

Saye and Sele, Lord 159, 163
schools 28, 214
Scotland 1–2, 71–2, 75, 106, 149–51, 169, 176–7, 179, 208–10
Sedgemoor, Battle of 191
Seymour, Jane 94–5
Shaftesbury, Earl of 188–90
Shakespeare, William 129, 138
Ship Money 145
ships 44–6, 111, 112, 123, 198
Shrewsbury, town 11–12
    Countess of (Bess of Hardwicke) 134
Simnel, Lambert 72

slaves 201–2, 210
Solway Moss, Battle of 105
Somerset, Duke of 97–8, 105
Strafford, Earl of 150–1
Supremacy, Act of 88
Surrey, Earl of 71, 77

Test Act 187
Tetzel, John 53, 55
theatre 129
Tichborne Dole 214
Tories 187–93, 197
towns 11–16, 20
trade 11–18, 46, 197–204, 209

Van Dyck, Anthony 140
Verney family 156–7, 160

Wales 1–2, 74, 133, 207
Walker, Sir Edward 161
Waller, Sir William 166
Walsingham, Sir Francis 109, 128
Warbeck, Perkin 72, 74
Warham, William 87
Warwick, Earl of 64, 66–7
weapons 159
Whigs 187–90, 191–3, 197
William of Orange 191, 193–6, 207–8, 209
Willoughby, Hugh 47
witchcraft 37, 57, 115, 138, 216
Wolsey, Thomas 77–80, 85–6, 93
women 17, 25–7, 33, 163–4, 173–4, 195, 214
Woodville, Elizabeth 66, 69
wool 17–19
Worcester, Battle of 177
Wren, Christopher 206
Wyatt, Sir Thomas 99

Yorkists 62–3, 71–2